**THE LORD
BLESS YOU**

TOUCHSTONE TEXTS

Stephen B. Chapman, Series Editor

The Good Samaritan: Luke 10 for the Life of the Church
 by Emerson B. Powery

The Lord Bless You: Numbers 6 for the Life of the Church
 by Stephen B. Chapman

The Lord Is My Shepherd: Psalm 23 for the Life of the Church
 by Richard S. Briggs

The Lord's Prayer: Matthew 6 and Luke 11 for the Life of the Church by William M. Wright IV

The Suffering Servant: Isaiah 53 for the Life of the Church
 by J. Gordon McConville

THE LORD BLESS YOU

Numbers 6 for the Life of the Church

STEPHEN B. CHAPMAN

Baker Academic
a division of Baker Publishing Group
Grand Rapids, Michigan

© 2025 by Stephen B. Chapman

Published by Baker Academic
a division of Baker Publishing Group
Grand Rapids, Michigan
BakerAcademic.com

Printed in the United States of America

All rights reserved. No part of this publication may be reproduced, stored in a retrieval system, or transmitted in any form or by any means—for example, electronic, photocopy, recording—without the prior written permission of the publisher. The only exception is brief quotations in printed reviews.

Library of Congress Cataloging-in-Publication Data
Names: Chapman, Stephen B., 1962– author.
Title: The Lord bless you : Numbers 6 for the life of the church / Stephen B. Chapman.
Description: Grand Rapids, Michigan : Baker Academic, a division of Baker Publishing Group, [2025] | Series: Touchstone texts | Includes bibliographical references and index.
Identifiers: LCCN 2024059178 | ISBN 9781540960610 (cloth) | ISBN 9781493449910 (ebook) | ISBN 9781493449927 (pdf)
Subjects: LCSH: Bible. Numbers VI, 24–26—Criticism, interpretation, etc. | Priestly blessing.
Classification: LCC BS1265.6.B5 C43 2025 | DDC 222/.1406—dc23/eng/20250114
LC record available at https://lccn.loc.gov/2024059178

Unless indicated otherwise, Scripture quotations are from the New Revised Standard Version Bible, copyright © 1989 National Council of the Churches of Christ in the United States of America. Used by permission. All rights reserved worldwide.

Scripture quotations labeled CEV are from the Contemporary English Version © 1991, 1992, 1995 by American Bible Society. Used by permission.

Scripture quotations labeled MSG are from *The Message*, copyright © 1993, 2002, 2018 by Eugene H. Peterson. Used by permission of NavPress. All rights reserved. Represented by Tyndale House Publishers.

Scripture quotations labeled NIV are from the Holy Bible, New International Version®, NIV®. Copyright © 1973, 1978, 1984, 2011 by Biblica, Inc.® Used by permission of Zondervan. All rights reserved worldwide. www.zondervan.com. The "NIV" and "New International Version" are trademarks registered in the United States Patent and Trademark Office by Biblica, Inc.®

Scripture quotations labeled NLT are taken from the *Holy Bible*, New Living Translation, copyright © 1996, 2004, 2015 by Tyndale House Foundation. Used by permission of Tyndale House Publishers, Carol Stream, Illinois 60188. All rights reserved.

English translation of the *Benedictus* © 1988 English Language Liturgical Consultation (ELLC). www.englishtexts.org. Used by permission.

Jacket art: Stained glass in the Church of Saint-Pierre, Chartres, France / Charles Walker Collection / Alamy Stock Photo

Baker Publishing Group publications use paper produced from sustainable forestry practices and postconsumer waste whenever possible.

25   26   27   28   29   30   31   7   6   5   4   3   2   1

For Will Willimon,
whose life is a blessing to me and many others

Contents

Series Preface ix

Preface xi

Acknowledgments xix

Abbreviations xxi

1. The Blessing in Worship 1
2. The Blessing's Thesis 21
3. Unpacking the Thesis 75
4. Putting the Blessing into Practice 127

Appendix: Translation 173

Selected Bibliography 175

    Commentaries and Exegetical Treatments 175

    Additional Secondary Literature 177

Scripture and Ancient Sources Index 187

Subject Index 193

Series Preface

In writing workshops, "touchstone texts" are high quality writing samples chosen to illustrate teaching points about compositional techniques, genre conventions, and literary style. Touchstone texts are models that continually repay close analysis. The Christian church likewise possesses core scriptural texts to which it returns, again and again, for illumination and guidance.

In this series, leading biblical scholars explore a selection of biblical touchstone texts from both the Old Testament and the New Testament. Individual volumes feature theological *exposition*. To exposit a biblical text means to set forth the sense of the text in an insightful and compelling fashion while remaining sensitive to its interpretive challenges, potential misunderstandings, and practical difficulties. An expository approach interprets the biblical text as a word of God to the church and prioritizes its applicability for preaching, instruction, and the life of faith. It maintains a focus primarily on the biblical text in its received canonical form, rather than engaging in historical reconstruction as an end in itself (whether of the events behind the text or the text's literary formation). It listens to individual texts in concert with the rest of the biblical canon.

Each volume in this series seeks to articulate the plain sense of a well-known biblical text by what Aquinas called "attending to the way the words go" (*salva litterae circumstantia*). Careful exegesis is pursued either phrase by phrase or section by section (depending on the biblical text's length and genre). Authors discuss exegetical, theological, and pastoral concerns in combination rather than as discrete moves or units. They offer constructive interpretations that aim to transcend denominational boundaries. They consider the use of these biblical texts in current church practice (including the lectionary) as well as church history. The goal of the series is to model expositional interpretation and thereby equip Christian pastors and teachers to employ biblical texts knowledgeably and effectively within an ecclesial setting.

Texts were chosen for inclusion partly in consultation with the authors of the series. An effort was made to select texts that are representative of various biblical genres and address different facets of the Christian life (e.g., faith, blessing, morality, worship, prayer, mission, hope). These touchstone texts are all widely used in homiletics and catechesis. They are deserving of fresh expositions that enable them to speak anew to the contemporary church and its leaders.

Stephen B. Chapman
Series Editor

# Preface

I was just about to head out to the beach one summer when Jim Kinney of Baker Academic phoned me with an idea for a new commentary series. Its distinctive feature would be a focus on key biblical passages rather than biblical books—a sort of "greatest hits" of the Bible. I immediately liked the idea. I also knew that I would want the series to aim for a sweet spot where the academy and the church could meet, to produce the kind of theologically oriented exegesis that would be genuinely helpful for Christian pastors, seminarians, and lay leaders. Central to my vocation is a commitment to the ideal of a learned clergy.

As I reflected further, I began to develop an *expositional* framing for the series. One of the main things I had learned from writing a theological commentary on the book of 1 Samuel[1]—and I do not think I would have learned it except by attempting to write such a commentary—was the difference between textual explanation and exposition. Most commentaries explain, or try to explain, a biblical passage. They talk *about* a biblical passage, but somehow without saying what the biblical *passage* is finally about, let alone attempting to recast its "aboutness" in a contemporary mode of expression.[2]

---

1. *1 Samuel as Christian Scripture: A Theological Commentary* (Grand Rapids: Eerdmans, 2016).

2. Also in the field of history, explanation is often touted as a goal but remains resistant to consensus because it relies on a prior understanding of causation and

How should one hear the testimony of Exodus or Isaiah or Mark or Hebrews today? Karl Barth famously tried to do this very thing with his 1919 Romans commentary, and it earned him a lot of disapproval from biblical scholars (and still does).[3]

Biblical studies continues to be largely captive to historicist categories and assumptions, typically wanting to get back to *something* behind the text, although it is not always clear just what or why.[4] One of the resources that I have found helpful for understanding this situation and charting an alternative is the work of Paul Ricoeur, particularly his hermeneutical distinction between "archaeology" and "teleology."[5] Biblical scholars have expended enormous energies on investigating the biblical text's archaeology: how the text came to be. But despite a growing interest in the history of the Bible's reception, biblical scholars still pay far less attention to how these texts have functioned once they became what they are. Biblical scholarship has tended to treat the biblical texts as if they are "dead," as if they are frozen deposits of time-bound messages from the past.[6]

---

causation is a contested concept. See Allan Megill, "Recounting the Past: 'Description,' Explanation, and Narrative in Historiography," *AHR* 94, no. 3 (1989): 627–53.

3. For the ongoing debate, see Christophe Chalamet, Andreas Dettwiler, and Sarah Stewart-Kroeker, eds., *Karl Barth's Epistle to the Romans: Retrospect and Prospect* (Berlin: De Gruyter, 2022).

4. Cf. Angelika Berlejung, "Methods," in *T&T Clark Handbook of the Old Testament: An Introduction to the Literature, Religion and History of the Old Testament*, ed. Jan Christian Gertz, Angelika Berlejung, Konrad Schmid, and Markus Witte (London: T&T Clark, 2012), 31–57 (here 31): "The purpose of exegesis . . . is to come as close as possible to the original historical sense of the text in its original historical setting, always in critical awareness of possible errors stemming from one's own preconceived notions. Exegesis, therefore, paves the way for the text itself." Note how historical reconstruction and exegesis become conflated in this formulation. Yet exegesis does not reconstruct an event; it interprets a text.

5. See Paul Ricoeur, *Freud and Philosophy: An Essay in Interpretation*, trans. Denis Savage (New Haven: Yale University Press, 1970), 459–93, and his "A Philosophical Interpretation of Freud," trans. Willis Domingo, in *The Conflict of Interpretations: Essays in Hermeneutics*, ed. Don Ihde (Evanston, IL: Northwestern University Press, 1974), 160–76.

6. E.g., Robert Morgan with John Barton, *Biblical Interpretation*, Oxford Bible Series (Oxford: Oxford University Press, 1988), 7: "Texts, like dead men and women, have no rights, no aims, no interests." They also insist (269): "A text has no life of its own. It 'lives' only as an electric wire is alive. Its power originates elsewhere: in a human author."

Moreover, the relationship between text and community is usually assumed to be almost laughably direct and one-sided, as if biblical texts are either straightforward transcripts of historical circumstances or reflexive allegories of social existence. Bengt Holmberg has perceptively criticized the underlying "postulate of complete and positive correlation between a text and a social group that carries and receives it," noting that a text can stand "in a negative correlation to the situation of the receivers" as well, to "challenge or try to change it," and that the difference between these two postures often remains indeterminable.[7] He further argues: "This means that one should at least ask oneself if the correlation between the analysed text and its social situation is complete or partial, positive or negative."[8] Moreover, since "the process of correlation very likely is a dialectical one, this increases the impossibility of concluding to the social situation from the end result. . . . It seems inevitable that, once we leave the primitive idea of strong, direct correlation between ideas and social basis of an almost deterministic kind, we are bereft of the possibility to say anything much about correlations at all."[9] The relationship between text and history, just like the correlation between text and community, is neither direct nor immediate.[10]

Texts do not only express; they also address. Texts are not static; they move through time. Even the most hardnosed historical critics, those who imagine that the socio-historical context of a biblical text *determines* what it means, are increasingly compelled to concede that few (if any) biblical texts are the product of a *single* historical context. Most of the biblical texts do not even have a single author. They do have what Ricoeur terms "itineraries of meaning."[11] I am less interested in

---

7. Bengt Holmberg, *Sociology and the New Testament: An Appraisal* (Minneapolis: Fortress, 1990), 124–25.
8. Holmberg, *Sociology and the New Testament*, 125.
9. Holmberg, *Sociology and the New Testament*, 139.
10. Cf. Edgar Krentz, *The Historical-Critical Method*, GBS (Philadelphia: Fortress, 1975), 42: "Sources are not themselves history and do not give immediate access to history. The source survives and is examined in our twentieth-century world; it is no longer in its original context. It is a historicist delusion to think that we can ever actually see it, read it, or use it in its original context."
11. Paul Ricoeur, *Figuring the Sacred: Religion, Narrative, and Imagination*, ed. Mark I. Wallace, trans. David Pellauer (Minneapolis: Fortress, 1995), 145.

how the biblical texts *became* texts—partly because of the real limits on our ability to chart that process in detail or with confidence, and partly because I view the socio-historical origins of biblical texts to be less determinative of their meaning. I am more interested in where these texts have been *as texts* and where, again as texts, they seem to want to go.

The commentary series that Jim and I developed (with the assistance of Bryan Dyer at Baker), which eventually received the name Touchstone Texts, prioritizes an approach in which the effort is made to say anew what well-known biblical passages are fundamentally *about*, and to do so in a manner that will have traction for contemporary Christian communities.[12] From the outset, Jim graciously said he hoped that I would contribute one of the volumes in the series myself. In considering the possibilities, I soon opted for the Priestly Blessing—mostly because of a growing interest on my part in blessing. What was it? I was not sure that I really knew, although it seemed like an important biblical theme. Time spent on such a question, I thought, stood to yield rich biblical and theological insights. It also promised to encourage further conversation between biblical studies and liturgical studies, two areas that have not always talked to each other as much as they should, especially in Protestant scholarship.[13] (After writing this book, I think so even more.) Additionally, a review of the exegetical literature convinced me that a lacuna would be filled by a volume on the Priestly Blessing. I could find many freestanding volumes on the Ten Commandments and the Lord's Prayer, but very few on the Priestly Blessing.[14] All in all, it appeared that a book on

---

12. Accordingly, this undertaking is more ecclesial than the approach described in Matthew C. Baldwin, "The Touchstone Text: A Forensic Rationale for Biblical Studies in American Liberal Education," in *Teaching the Bible in the Liberal Arts Classroom*, ed. Jane S. Webster and Glenn S. Holland (Sheffield: Sheffield Phoenix, 2012), 12–27, although I do think there are similarities. The notion of a "touchstone text" extends beyond religious tradition into the cultural realms of the arts and music, and the Bible is also a "touchstone text" in these areas.

13. For Protestant reflections on liturgy and the Old Testament in particular, see Jürgen Ebach, *Das Alte Testament als Klangraum des evangelischen Gottesdienstes* (Gütersloh: Gütersloher Verlagshaus, 2016); Michael E. W. Thompson, *Greatly to Be Praised: The Old Testament and Worship* (Eugene, OR: Pickwick, 2016).

14. Aside from the mostly all-too-brief discussions in commentaries on Numbers, the two most penetrating stand-alone treatments are also unavailable in English translation: those by Franz Delitzsch and Klaus Seybold.

the Priestly Blessing might helpfully address an ecclesial need. Indeed, one scholar has made the judgment that "few liturgical phenomena in the Church today are as little understood as blessings."[15]

From what I can tell, blessing is either almost entirely forgotten in the contemporary church or remembered but misused. The left wing of the church considers blessing too superstitious and "magical," avoiding it altogether or promoting a watered-down version of blessing that is "spiritual" without having any concrete ethical-theological import or even being identifiably Christian. The right wing harnesses blessing to a conservative political agenda or equates it with personal advancement, turning it into a guaranteed formula for success ("fourteen steps to blessing!").[16] The one thing both sides have in common is their willingness to participate in the commercialization of blessing through the purchase of blessing-oriented religious products.[17] It is difficult not to feel in response that the Christian church in the United States colludes in the diminishment of its own integrity, willingly becoming a pale reflection of the capitalistic marketplace and the American two-party political system.[18] Many North American churches emulate the Democratic Party at prayer, while many others mimic the Republican Party at prayer. America has become our church.[19]

---

15. Daniel G. Van Slyke, "Toward a Theology of Blessings: Agents and Recipients of Benedictions," *Antiphon* 15, no. 1 (2011): 47.

16. E.g., Creflo A. Dollar Jr., *Total Life Prosperity: 14 Practical Steps to Receiving God's Full Blessing* (Nashville: Nelson, 1999).

17. There are hundreds of blessing products for sale online, including not only the usual mugs, t-shirts, and wall hangings, but items more particular to certain blessing practices, such as blessing bracelets, blessing jars, and prayer shawls. For an overview of consumerist Christianity in the contemporary US, see James B. Twitchell, *Shopping for God: How Christianity Went from In Your Heart to In Your Face* (New York: Simon & Schuster, 2007). For a strategy of constructive engagement, see Laura M. Hartman, *The Christian Consumer: Living Faithfully in a Fragile World* (New York: Oxford University Press, 2011).

18. See Tim Alberta, *The Kingdom, the Power, and the Glory: American Evangelicals in an Age of Extremism* (New York: Harper, 2023); Darren E. Grem, *The Blessings of Business: How Corporations Shaped Conservative Christianity* (New York: Oxford University Press, 2016); Patrick Keith Miller and Keith Simon, *Truth Over Tribe: Pledging Allegiance to the Lamb, Not the Donkey or the Elephant* (Colorado Springs: Cook, 2022).

19. Cf. Lesslie Newbigin, *Foolishness to the Greeks: The Gospel and Western Culture* (Grand Rapids: Eerdmans, 1986), 27: "The nation-state replaces the holy church and the holy empire as the centerpiece of the post-Enlightenment ordering

And yet it may be that the biblical tradition of blessing offers a resource that could help the church regain its integrity and distinctive witness to the wider culture. As I move further into my fourth decade of pastoral work and theological education, I find myself hoping more than ever that the followers of Jesus Christ will be people who bless, rather than (as has become all too often the case) those who are quick to condemn. I pray that Christians will be people who bless not only their families and friends but also those who do not "deserve" their blessing, especially those who condemn and curse them. Jesus enjoins Christians not merely to tolerate but to *bless* their enemies (Luke 6:27–28; cf. Rom. 12:14; 1 Cor. 4:12; 1 Pet. 3:9). I long for the day when Christians will again be known (as they sometimes have been known) as *a kind and generous people* whose words and actions appealingly exhibit a spirit of peace, and whose lives and bodies witness eloquently and self-sacrificially to the name of God Most High.

In keeping with the series format, this volume pays close attention to the wording of the Priestly Blessing, its literary form, and its narrative function. I have tried to keep the main discussion broad but then provide indications of the basis for the argument in the notes—along with pointers to where interested readers might pursue various topics further. My goal is not only to unpack the theological riches of this one compact biblical text, but also to pursue an approach to theological exegesis that is unapologetically textual and able to operate successfully without the kind of secure and exhaustive historical information often deemed necessary for the task. I do think historical-critical scholarship has genuine value and can make positive contributions to biblical interpretation (rather than, say, only possessing the negative function of ruling things out). I try to model here how I think that can be done.

The Priestly Blessing does not originate in a single historical situation or reflect a lone set of socio-historical circumstances. However, it does partake fully in an ancient world much different from our own, borrowing its customary words and thought pictures to speak of God and God's way with Israel. Yet over the course of the twentieth century

---

of society. . . . [It] has taken the place of God as the source to which we look for happiness, health and welfare."

a rapid increase in historical and archaeological data did not make it easier to resolve historical questions, only harder. The challenge at present is to develop a chastened, more modest form of historical-critical inquiry,[20] one cognizant of its limitations and just as eager to explore the post-compositional history of the Bible as its pre-compositional and compositional history. In fact, what we need is not less historical work but more.[21] In particular, the historical-critical tradition itself has to be contextualized historically and its own working assumptions more fundamentally questioned. The deeper problem with historical criticism has been its self-deceptive belief that all biblical know-how culminated in the arrival of the modern, and that the modern was somehow uniquely unconditioned by its own contexts and presuppositions.[22]

In the first chapter, I treat the history of the Priestly Blessing's use in Judaism and Christianity in broad strokes to provide a basic framework for what follows. Then in the next two chapters, I work through the blessing word by word, endeavoring to tease out the implications of its idioms and attempting to situate its thought pictures anew within a contemporary context. In the final chapter, I focus on current questions of personal, pastoral, and ecclesial practice: How might the church bless more often and more robustly? What are some pitfalls to a contemporary use of blessings and how might those pitfalls be overcome? My main point throughout is that the Priestly Blessing casts a vision of lived religion as "name bearing," and that such an understanding of the Christian faith is ripe for revival.

20. See Stephen B. Chapman, "Historical Criticism, Moral Judgment, and the Future of the Past," in *A Sage in New Haven: Essays on the Prophets, the Writings, and the Ancient World in Honor of Robert R. Wilson*, ed. Alison Acker Gruseke and Carolyn J. Sharp (Munster: Zaphon, 2023), 297–307. Cf. Robert D. Miller, "Yahweh and His Clio: Critical Theory and the Historical Criticism of the Hebrew Bible," *CurBS* 4, no. 2 (2006): 149–68.

21. Cf. Karl Barth, *Der Römerbrief*, 2nd ed., Karl Barth Gesamtausgabe (Zurich: Theologischer Verlag, 2010), 66: "Kritischer müssten mir die Historisch-Kritischen sein" (To me, the historical critics need to be more critical [my trans.]).

22. A needed remedy is thus what Pope Benedict, in a much-discussed address, terms "a criticism of the criticism." See "Biblical Interpretation in Conflict: On the Foundations and the Itinerary of Exegesis Today," trans. Adrian Walker, in *Opening Up the Scriptures: Joseph Ratzinger and the Foundations of Biblical Interpretation*, ed. José Granados, Carlos Granados, and Luis Sánchez Navarro (Grand Rapids: Eerdmans, 2008), 1–29 (here 8).

I have tried to discuss all this in a mostly nontechnical fashion, which has been both daunting and, well, fun. I enjoy the challenge of venturing to describe the best up-to-date scholarship in my field, while at the same time doing so in a way that does not depend on a lot of prior knowledge or specialized expertise. Accordingly, foreign language terms are transliterated, and translations of biblical texts are taken from the NRSV unless otherwise indicated. The NRSV translation of Num. 6:22–27 is provided for reference at the beginning of the first three chapters. A fresh translation of the Priestly Blessing, in line with my exegesis, appears as an appendix.

I hope that I have succeeded in speaking beyond, as well as to, an academic audience, and that readers will not only gain a better understanding of the Priestly Blessing but also discover new ways of talking about the Bible and theology more generally, especially in church settings. This volume and the Touchstone Texts series are openly geared toward Christian readers, but not in a narrowly confessional manner. It will please me if this book finds Jewish readers as well as readers from other religious faiths, and even post-Christian or secular readers who might think this type of treatment would be too pious for them. I have certainly tried to draw on the profound heritage of blessing within Judaism, and to situate a Christian understanding of blessing in relation to it in a fashion that will honor, and not plunder, Jewish tradition. Indeed, one of my key points in this volume is that fuller awareness of the Priestly Blessing can help Christians become more appreciative of Jewish theology and more respectful of their Jewish neighbors. Perhaps in part because I am a Christian Old Testament scholar, I feel the burden of the Holocaust's legacy keenly. It haunts me, and I do not understand why it often does not seem to have much of an effect on the work of many other contemporary Christian biblical scholars and theologians.

My foremost hope is that this book will not only encourage a better understanding of blessing in contemporary church life and a more frequent practice of blessing by Christians but also remind Christians and Jews of the blessings they share.[23]

---

23. For further reflections in this vein, see Clark M. Williamson, *Way of Blessing, Way of Life: A Christian Theology* (St. Louis: Chalice, 1999).

Acknowledgments

Research on this book was done, and portions of it drafted, during a sabbatical from my teaching at Duke Divinity School. Part of that time was spent at the University of Glasgow, where I had the honor of serving in the fall of 2021 as the William Barclay Distinguished Visiting Fellow in Biblical Studies. I particularly wish to express my thanks and gratitude to Doug Gay, the principal of Trinity College Glasgow, and to Mark W. Elliott, who was instrumental in arranging my stay and a highly gracious host. I also want to thank the good people at the Wellington Church of Scotland, who gave me office space and a warm welcome.

A portion of chapter 2 was presented as "Reflected Glory: The Imposition of the Divine Name as Theophany" for a May 2022 colloquium hosted by Wycliffe College at the University of Toronto. I am grateful to the organizers, to the other participants, and to Stephen Andrews, principal of the college, for their hospitality and our rich discussions.

Gary Anderson and Walter Moberly kindly read an earlier draft of this book, offering encouragement and expert criticisms. The book is better thanks to their generous assistance. Dustyn Keepers at Baker conveyed thoughtful comments as well. Tim West, also at Baker, was very helpful in preparing the manuscript for publication. Cody Hinkle provided expert proofreading.

Treasured friends at Duke have contributed to the book in a variety of ways. I want above all to thank Curtis Freeman, Lester Ruth, Brent Strawn, Laceye Warner, Brittany Wilson, and Lauren Winner for many illuminating conversations. Each of these colleagues posed insightful questions and made instructive observations. Lauren's writing was especially helpful to me as I sought to situate my exegetical work in a contemporary context. As a fellow Baptist, Curtis has helped me more than once to see how my biblical explorations tend to take a characteristically Baptist shape, which is all the more interesting to me because it is not something that I intentionally set out to do. It is more a matter of my Christian formation than any conscious authorial decision. I have no doubt that Curtis will gain another example from this book, which—as I can see clearly only now that it is completed—charts a bright line from the Priestly Blessing to Christian baptism and the Christian life as a lived witness. These are certainly traditional Baptist distinctives. I would hasten to add, however, that I do not believe they are exclusively Baptist concerns.

And then there is Will Willimon, from whom I have gained exceptionally fruitful ideas while working on this book, and whose friendship is a great gift. On one particular road trip together, we hashed out important issues relating to blessing practices in the church. Will also kept encouraging me not to pull my punches. So if that aspect of the book does not sit well with you, it is his fault. Will's boundless energy and intellectual curiosity put him in a category of his own. This book is dedicated to him.

Abbreviations

Biblical

Old Testament

Gen.	Genesis	Song	Song of Songs
Exod.	Exodus	Isa.	Isaiah
Lev.	Leviticus	Jer.	Jeremiah
Num.	Numbers	Lam.	Lamentations
Deut.	Deuteronomy	Ezek.	Ezekiel
Josh.	Joshua	Dan.	Daniel
Judg.	Judges	Hosea	Hosea
Ruth	Ruth	Joel	Joel
1–2 Sam.	1–2 Samuel	Amos	Amos
1–2 Kings	1–2 Kings	Obad.	Obadiah
1–2 Chron.	1–2 Chronicles	Jon.	Jonah
Ezra	Ezra	Mic.	Micah
Neh.	Nehemiah	Nah.	Nahum
Esther	Esther	Hab.	Habakkuk
Job	Job	Zeph.	Zephaniah
Ps(s).	Psalm(s)	Hag.	Haggai
Prov.	Proverbs	Zech.	Zechariah
Eccles.	Ecclesiastes	Mal.	Malachi

New Testament

Matt.	Matthew	Acts	Acts
Mark	Mark	Rom.	Romans
Luke	Luke	1–2 Cor.	1–2 Corinthians
John	John	Gal.	Galatians

Eph.	Ephesians	Heb.	Hebrews
Phil.	Philippians	James	James
Col.	Colossians	1–2 Pet.	1–2 Peter
1–2 Thess.	1–2 Thessalonians	1–3 John	1–3 John
1–2 Tim.	1–2 Timothy	Jude	Jude
Titus	Titus	Rev.	Revelation
Philem.	Philemon		

Apocryphal / Deuterocanonical Books

Sir.	Sirach

Other Ancient Writings

Ant.	Josephus, *Jewish Antiquities*	Herm. Sim.	Shepherd of Hermas, Similitudes
Apol.	Justin, *Apologia*	m.	Mishnah
b.	Babylonian Talmud	t.	Tosefta
1–2 Clem.	1–2 Clement		

General

BCE	before the Common Era	lit.	literally
CE	Common Era	MT	Masoretic Text
cent.	century	pl.	plural
cf.	*confer*, compare	sg.	singular
ed.	edited by	trans.	translation, translated by
H	Hebrew (in biblical references, identifying differing versification between the English and Hebrew)		

Bible Versions

CEV	Contemporary English Version	NJPS	*Tanakh: The Holy Scriptures: The New JPS Translation according to the Traditional Hebrew Text*
MSG	*The Message: The Bible in Contemporary Language*, by Eugene H. Peterson. Colorado Springs: NavPress, 2002	NLT	New Living Translation
		NRSV	New Revised Standard Version (1989)
NIV	New International Version (2011)		

Contemporary Sources

AB	Anchor Bible
ABS	Archaeology and Biblical Studies
AHR	*American Historical Review*
AJEC	Ancient Judaism and Early Christianity
AnBib	Analecta Biblica
ANESSup	Ancient Near Eastern Studies Supplement Series
ANF	*Ante-Nicene Fathers*
AOAT	Alter Orient und Altes Testament
AThR	*Anglican Theological Review*
AUSS	*Andrews University Seminary Studies*
BASOR	*Bulletin of the American Schools of Oriental Research*
BBB	Bonner biblische Beiträge
BBR	*Bulletin for Biblical Research*
BBRSup	Bulletin for Biblical Research Supplements
BDB	The Brown-Driver-Briggs Hebrew and English Lexicon. Francis Brown, S. R. Driver, and Charles A. Briggs. Peabody, MA: Hendrickson, 2003 (reprint of the 1906 edition)
BibAn	*Biblical Annals*
BibOr	Biblica et Orientalia
BIS	Biblical Interpretation Series
BJS	Brown Judaic Studies
BN	*Biblische Notizen*
BSac	*Bibliotheca Sacra*
BT	The Bible Translator
BTB	Biblical Theology Bulletin
BVB	Beiträge zum Verstehen der Bibel
BZAW	Beihefte zur Zeitschrift für die alttestamentliche Wissenschaft
BZNW	Beihefte zur Zeitschrift für die neutestamentliche Wissenschaft
CBQ	*Catholic Biblical Quarterly*
ChrCent	*Christian Century*
ConBOT	Coniectanea Biblica Old Testament Series
CT	*Christianity Today*
CurBS	*Currents in Research: Biblical Studies*
DDD	Dictionary of Deities and Demons in the Bible. Edited by Karel van der Toorn, Bob Becking, and Pieter W. van der Horst. Leiden: Brill, 1995; 2nd rev. ed., Grand Rapids: Eerdmans, 1999
EstBib	*Estudios bíblicos*
ETL	Ephemerides Theologicae Lovanienses
ExpTim	*Expository Times*
FAT	Forschungen zum Alten Testament
FOTL	Forms of the Old Testament Literature

FRLANT	Forschungen zur Religion und Literatur des Alten und Neuen Testaments
GBS	Guides to Biblical Scholarship
HALOT	*The Hebrew and Aramaic Lexicon of the Old Testament*. Edited by Ludwig Koehler, Walter Baumgartner, and Johann J. Stamm. 2 vols. Leiden: Brill, 2001
HBT	*Horizons in Biblical Theology*
HSS	Harvard Semitic Studies
Int	*Interpretation*
JAOS	*Journal of the American Oriental Society*
JBL	*Journal of Biblical Literature*
JHS	*Journal of Hellenic Studies*
JNES	*Journal of Near Eastern Studies*
JPS	Jewish Publication Society
JQR	*Jewish Quarterly Review*
JSJ	*Journal for the Study of Judaism in the Persian, Hellenistic, and Roman Periods*
JSJSup	Supplements to the Journal for the Study of Judaism
JSNTSup	Journal for the Study of the New Testament Supplement Series
JSOT	*Journal for the Study of the Old Testament*
JSOTSup	Journal for the Study of the Old Testament Supplement Series
JSQ	*Jewish Studies Quarterly*
JSS	*Journal of Semitic Studies*
JTI	*Journal of Theological Interpretation*
JTISup	Journal of Theological Interpretation, Supplements
JTS	*Journal of Theological Studies*
LCC	Library of Christian Classics
LHBOTS	Library of Hebrew Bible/Old Testament Studies
LSTS	Library of Second Temple Studies
LTJ	*Lutheran Theological Journal*
NCB	New Century Bible
NCBC	New Century Bible Commentary
NIB	*The New Interpreter's Bible*. Edited by Leander E. Keck. 12 vols. Nashville: Abingdon, 1994–2004
NICOT	New International Commentary on the Old Testament
NIDOTTE	*New International Dictionary of Old Testament Theology and Exegesis*. Edited by Willem A. VanGemeren. 5 vols. Grand Rapids: Zondervan, 1997
NIVAC	NIV Application Commentary
NTL	New Testament Library
NTOA	Novum Testamentum et Orbis Antiquus
OBO	Orbis Biblicus et Orientalis
OBT	Overtures to Biblical Theology

OTL	Old Testament Library
OTT	Old Testament Theology
ProEccl	*Pro Ecclesia*
PRSt	*Perspectives in Religious Studies*
RGRW	Religions in the Graeco-Roman World
RPP	*Religion Past and Present: Encyclopedia of Theology and Religion.* Edited by Hans Dieter Betz et al. 4th ed. [English version.] 14 vols. Leiden: Brill, 2007–13
RW	*Reformed Worship*
SBB	Stuttgarter biblische Beiträge
SBLDS	Society of Biblical Literature Dissertation Series
SBT	Studies in Biblical Theology
SJOT	*Scandinavian Journal of the Old Testament*
SNTW	Studies of the New Testament and Its World
STDJ	Studies on the Texts of the Desert of Judah
StPohl	Studia Pohl
SymS	Symposium Series
TBT	*The Bible Today*
TDNT	*Theological Dictionary of the New Testament.* Edited by Gerhard Kittel and Gerhard Friedrich. Translated by Geoffrey W. Bromiley. 10 vols. Grand Rapids: Eerdmans, 1964–76
TDOT	*Theological Dictionary of the Old Testament.* Edited by G. Johannes Botterweck and Helmer Ringgren. Translated by John T. Willis et al. 17 vols. Grand Rapids: Eerdmans, 1974–2021
ThTo	*Theology Today*
TJ	*Trinity Journal*
TLOT	*Theological Lexicon of the Old Testament.* Edited by Ernst Jenni and Claus Westermann. Translated by Mark E. Biddle. 3 vols. Peabody, MA: Hendrickson, 1997
TSAJ	Texts and Studies in Ancient Judaism
TWOT	*Theological Wordbook of the Old Testament.* Edited by R. Laird Harris, Gleason L. Archer Jr., and Bruce K. Waltke. 2 vols. Chicago: Moody Press, 1980
TynBul	*Tyndale Bulletin*
USFSHJ	University of South Florida Studies in the History of Judaism
VC	*Vigiliae Christianae*
VCSup	Supplements to Vigiliae Christianae
VT	*Vetus Testamentum*
VTSup	Supplements to Vetus Testamentum
WA	Martin Luther, *Werke: Kritische Gesamtausgabe.* Weimar: Herman Böhlau, 1883–2009
WTJ	*Westminster Theological Journal*
WUNT	Wissenschaftliche Untersuchungen zum Neuen Testament

WW	*Word and World*
ZABR	*Zeitschrift für altorientalische und biblische Rechtgeschichte*
ZAW	*Zeitschrift für die alttestamentliche Wissenschaft*
ZKWKL	*Zeitschrift für kirchliche Wissenschaft und kirchliches Leben*

For indeed, Jesus Christ himself, who is the Lord and the Creator of the soul, is said to be the clothing of the saints, as the Apostle says, "Put you on the Lord Jesus Christ."

—Origen[1]

Stung into action, I returned to the place where Alypius was sitting, for on leaving it I had put down there the book of the apostle's letters. I snatched it up, opened it and read in silence the passage on which my eyes first alighted: "Not in dissipation and drunkenness, nor in debauchery and lewdness, nor in arguing and jealousy; but put on the Lord Jesus Christ and make no provision for the flesh or the gratification of your desires." I had no wish to read further, nor was there need. No sooner had I reached the end of the verse than the light of certainty flooded my heart and all dark shades of doubt fled away.

—Augustine[2]

"Putting on Christ" . . . is not one among many jobs a Christian has to do, and it is not a sort of special exercise for the top class. It is the whole of Christianity. Christianity offers nothing else at all.

—C. S. Lewis[3]

---

1. Origen, *On First Principles: A Reader's Edition*, trans. John Behr (Oxford: Oxford University Press, 2019), 2.3.2 (80), citing Rom. 13:14.
2. Saint Augustine, *The Confessions*, trans. Maria Boulding, Vintage Spiritual Classics (New York: Random House, 1998), 8.12.29 (168), citing Rom. 13:13–14.
3. C. S. Lewis, *Mere Christianity* (New York: Macmillan, 1960), 166.

1

The Blessing in Worship

Many Christians know the Priestly Blessing almost as well as the Lord's Prayer.[1] The evocative cadences of this blessing are a cherished source of comfort and encouragement for many.

> The LORD bless you and keep you;
> the LORD make his face to shine upon you and be gracious to you;
> the LORD lift up his countenance upon you and give you peace. (Num. 6:24–26)

Yet unlike the Lord's Prayer, the words of the Priestly Blessing are not recited by Christian congregations in worship. They are heard rather than recited. They are typically spoken as a benediction by a clergyperson at the conclusion of the service. The words are familiar because they have been heard so often. Sometimes they are sung by a choir. A much-loved musical setting, with its chant-like vocal lines and stirring sevenfold amen, was composed by Peter C. Lutkin, the first dean of the School of Music at Northwestern University.[2] Another

---

1. Franz Delitzsch, "Der mosaische Priestersegen Num. VI, 22–27," *ZKWKL* 3 (1882): 113.
2. Peter C. Lutkin, "The Lord Bless You and Keep You: Farewell Anthem with Sevenfold Amen," originally published by Clayton F. Summy Co., 1900, and now

setting popular with many congregations is by English composer John Rutter.[3] Numerous contemporary praise choruses also offer settings of the blessing's words.[4]

Other benedictions are used in Christian worship as well. Many of them come from (or are patterned after) benedictions in the New Testament, such as:

> The grace of the Lord Jesus Christ,
> the love of God,
> and the communion of the Holy Spirit be with all of you.
>   (2 Cor. 13:13)

This blessing is sometimes called the Apostolic Benediction and has a trinitarian shape: Christ—God—Spirit. While Christian benedictions are not always trinitarian, a trinitarian framework is often partially present or implied. One example comes from Paul's letter to the Romans:

> May the God of hope fill you with all joy and peace in
>   believing,
> so that you may abound in hope by the power of the Holy
>   Spirit. (Rom. 15:13)

Liturgical benedictions often repurpose language from the introductions or conclusions of the letters contained in the New Testament.[5]

The Priestly Blessing is different. It comes from the Old Testament, from the worship life of ancient Israel. It could have been part of the liturgy of Solomon's temple. It has survived long centuries to hold a recognized place today in both the synagogue and the church.

---

in the public domain. Oddly, this setting transposes the blessing's second and third phrases, although most people never notice it.

3. John Rutter, *The Lord Bless You and Keep You*, Oxford Easy Anthems, ed. David Willcocks (Oxford: Oxford University Press, 1981).

4. I particularly like Ted Pearce's upbeat "Aaronic Benediction," with lyrics in English and Hebrew, https://tedpearce.com/track/649339/aaronic-benediction.

5. These epistolary blessings may in turn have found their way into the letters from prior use in early Christian worship. See Anthonie Van den Doel, "Blessing and Cursing in the New Testament and Related Literature" (PhD diss., Northwestern University, 1968), 167.

Excursus on Terminology

When I use the term "Old Testament" in this book, I mean to designate the first main part of the two-Testament Christian Bible. I do not mean to suggest that other names are illegitimate. The Jewish and Christian Scriptures have always had many names. But from my perspective, it is necessary to be clear about the context in which this body of literature is being read because there is finally no purely neutral way of doing so. When people try to be neutral about it, they invariably smuggle various presuppositions into their supposed neutrality.[6] However, this criticism should not be taken to suggest that there is no value in interpretive fairness, both to the text and other readers. It is precisely by being clear about one's own presuppositions that genuine dialogue can occur, with the text and its many readers, rather than merely a superficial dialogue in which the most important commitments of the dialogue partners are sidestepped and left out of the discussion.[7]

In the modern Jewish synagogue, the Priestly Blessing (known in Hebrew as the *Birkat Kohanim*) preserves a fundamental link with the Jerusalem temple and its rituals. The blessing reminds Christians that, as Karl Barth phrased the point, the church is "a guest in the house of Israel."[8] It is nothing short of miraculous that ancient Israel's words continue to speak so directly to the Christian experience of faith.

---

6. On this crucial point, see Jon D. Levenson, *The Hebrew Bible, the Old Testament and Historical Criticism: Jews and Christians in Biblical Studies* (Louisville: Westminster John Knox, 1993). For a comparison of titles, see Stephen B. Chapman, "Collections, Canons, and Communities," in *The Cambridge Companion to the Hebrew Bible/Old Testament*, ed. Stephen B. Chapman and Marvin A. Sweeney (New York: Cambridge University Press 2016), 28–54.

7. Cf. Slavoy Žižek's description of "today's tolerant multiculturalism as an experience of the Other deprived of its Otherness" in Žižek, *The Puppet and the Dwarf: The Perverse Core of Christianity* (Cambridge, MA: MIT Press, 2003), 96.

8. Karl Barth, *Church Dogmatics* IV/3.2 (Edinburgh: T&T Clark, 1961), 877. In *Church Dogmatics* II/2 (Edinburgh: T&T Clark, 1957), 284, Barth also insists: "The Church can understand its own origin and its own goal only as it understands its unity with Israel."

Christians, Jews, and the Liturgy

Christians have often exhibited a tendency toward spiritual amnesia and a triumphalist appropriation of Israel's prayers. The Jewishness of Israel's prayers is crucial for Christians to sustain because it testifies to God's constancy and grace. The word of God to Israel did not fail (Rom. 9:6).[9] There was genuine faith, prayer, repentance, and forgiveness in ancient Israel. In due time, gentile Christians were grafted into Israel's promises (Rom. 11:17), which is not a cause for boasting because the new branches do not support the root; rather, "[it is] the root that supports you" (Rom. 11:18), Paul avows. In Israel, "all the families of the earth shall be blessed" (Acts 3:25; cf. Gen. 12:3). "Salvation is from the Jews," says Jesus (John 4:22). There was indeed something new in Christianity, but Christians at the outset were a Jewish sect and they exhibited a basic continuity with Jewish tradition even as they developed their own distinctive beliefs and practices.[10]

It should be a deep cause for concern that contemporary Christians have so little awareness of modern Judaism and often disregard or minimize the horror of the Holocaust (or Shoah), the murder of six million European Jews during the Second World War.[11] Even when the Holocaust is remembered, it can sometimes seem like only

---

9. The presumption of Israel's failure in historical reconstructions by Christians is exposed in Rolf Rendtorff, "The Image of Postexilic Israel in German Old Testament Scholarship from Wellhausen to von Rad," in *Canon and Theology: Overtures to an Old Testament Theology*, OBT (Minneapolis: Fortress, 1993), 66–75.

10. For this reason, the essence of Christianity is not best recounted in terms of newness alone. John Webster, *The Culture of Theology*, ed. Ivor J. Davidson and Alden C. McCray (Grand Rapids: Baker Academic, 2019), 60, avoids this danger by describing Christianity as being about "roots and astonishment." In developing this formulation, he acknowledges the influence of Simone Weil, *The Need for Roots: Prelude to a Declaration of Duties towards Mankind* (London: Routledge & Kegan Paul, 1952). A sense of astonishment does lie at the heart of Christianity, as Karl Barth, *Church Dogmatics* IV/3.1 (Edinburgh: T&T Clark, 1961), 287, powerfully describes. But some of that astonishment consists in the fact that what was true in the past is confirmed by and coheres so perfectly with the Christ event. The New Testament is radically new but not wholly new.

11. Cf. Erich Zenger, *Das Erste Testament: Die jüdische Bibel und die Christen* (Dusseldorf: Patmos, 1991), 12: "After Auschwitz the church must read the 'Old Testament' differently" (my trans.).

one terrible chapter in a long world history full of terrible chapters. After all, millions also died under Stalin and Pol Pot in the twentieth century. Other people groups have faced bigotry, persecution, and genocide. Yet from a Christian perspective, the Holocaust has a unique place in this list of terrors because in Christian understanding the Jewish people are special. According to the Bible, God singled them out for a unique role in God's effort to redeem a broken world. Within Christian theology, this conviction is known as the doctrine of election, and it witnesses to the way in which God faithfully and characteristically works.[12]

God works toward the universal through the particular. God is committed to the world that God has made, and God has chosen to redeem it by means of one specific people group and its place vis-à-vis the world. They are the Jews. Jesus was a Jew. The first Christians were all Jews (with a few exceptions). The God that Christians worship is the God of the Jews. In truth, there is no other. So the organized, mass killing of Jews in the Second World War was not only a catastrophic injustice and a tragic loss of life, it represented a concerted, blasphemous effort to annihilate the work of God in the world. In traditional theological language (Jewish as well as Christian), the Holocaust was the work of the Antichrist.[13]

This sense of shared identity and commitment does not mean that Christians should support everything that the modern State of Israel does. It is also deeply Christian to care about Palestinians (whether they are Christian, as many are, or Muslim, or part of another faith tradition) and all people in the Middle East, and to labor steadfastly for peace. Friends sometimes have to say hard things to one another. Christian churches in the US should also be better informed about the Middle East, more aware of the Jewish roots and parallels to their faith, and more appreciative of how contemporary Jews are their

---

12. For a sympathetic presentation of this idea, see Joel S. Kaminsky, *Yet I Loved Jacob: Reclaiming the Biblical Concept of Election* (Nashville: Abingdon, 2007).

13. On the historical conjunction of these ideas, see Robert Weldon Whalen, *Assassinating Hitler: Ethics and Resistance in Nazi Germany* (Selinsgrove, PA: Susquehanna University Press, 1993), 102–21. Antichrist language must be employed carefully, since demonizing perpetrators can either diminish their responsibility or concede too much power to them. Cf. the cautions articulated in Denis de Rougemont, "On the Devil and Politics," *Christianity and Crisis* 1, no. 9 (1941): 2–5.

spiritual sisters and brothers. Indeed, an urgent matter for Christians today is to articulate how the gospel of Jesus Christ can be said to be good news for their Jewish neighbors *as Jews*.[14]

This kind of consciousness is needed not only on the part of individual Christians but within the context of Christian community and Christian worship. Contemporary German Protestant churches have an annual "Israel Sunday" on which they mark God's eternal and unbroken faithfulness to the Jewish people. The Roman Catholic Church recommends that Catholics pray for the Holocaust's victims and their survivors on the Sunday closest to International Holocaust Remembrance Day (*Yom HaShoah* in Hebrew), which occurs on the 27th of Nissan according to the Jewish calendar and was the day of the Warsaw Ghetto uprising in 1944.[15] An annual observance of this sort in North American Protestant churches would do much to counter antisemitism, correct Christian misperceptions of Judaism, and encourage theological recognition of the common ground shared between the two faiths. Of course, the most important feature of such an observance would need to be its biblical-theological character, lest it be co-opted by a contemporary political agenda.

Much urgent work needs to be done in the church to educate Christians theologically about Jews and Judaism. When Christian views of Judaism are formed primarily by the negative portrayal of the Pharisees in the Gospels, a false narrative takes root.[16] Too many Christians still think that God has rejected the Jewish people or that Jews are responsible for killing Jesus, views that are contradicted by a better reading of the biblical witnesses and a fuller understanding of history.[17]

---

14. Paraphrasing Chris Boesel, *Risking Proclamation, Respecting Difference: Christian Faith, Imperialistic Discourse, and Abraham* (Eugene, OR; Cascade Books, 2008), 5.

15. See the document, published by the National Conference of Catholic Bishops, titled "God's Mercy Endures Forever: Guidelines on the Presentation of Jews and Judaism in Catholic Preaching" (September 1988), section 29, http://usccb.org/resources/god-s-mercy-endures-forever-guidelines-presentation-jews-and-judaism-catholic-preaching.

16. See instead Joseph Sievers and Amy-Jill Levine, eds., *The Pharisees* (Grand Rapids: Eerdmans, 2021).

17. See Ron Simkins, *Truth, Tears, Turning, and Trusting: A Pastor's Plea to End Our Ongoing Anti-Semitism and Anti-Judaism* (Eugene, OR: Resource Publications, 2020).

Modern Christians are often unaware of just how anti-Jewish the Christian tradition has been. Supersessionism in the form of "replacement theology" was historically a central feature of official Christian teaching. For Catholics, it was only officially disavowed at Vatican II in the document *Nostra Aetate*.[18] A key component of the traditional teaching was the notion that God had rejected the Jews and "turned" to (gentile) Christians—often invoking passages like Matt. 21:43; Acts 13:46; 18:6; 28:28—so that Judaism as an ongoing religious tradition was either without any genuine theological purpose or, worse, lay under a curse. Even the German "Israel Sunday" can be traced back to the Protestant tradition of "Jew Sunday," observed from the time of the Reformation onward, which featured antisemitic teachings. In medieval Catholic Europe, Lent, Holy Week, and Good Friday were often characterized by waves of animosity toward Jews, becoming conventional times for Jewish persecution.[19] It was so common to throw stones at Jews during Holy Week that multiple popes felt compelled to outlaw the practice.[20] Forced conversions and massacres occurred regularly during this liturgical season. Even today, Holy Week can make Christians' Jewish neighbors nervous.[21] The medieval church's "teaching of contempt" about Judaism selectively combined certain biblical passages (such as the "blood curse" in Matt. 27:25 and criticisms of "the Jews" in John's Gospel) with ingrained cultural prejudices, forming a toxic, murderous disdain.[22]

---

18. There are other definitions of "supersessionism." A clear, concise overview of the tradition that I am opposing is sketched in Richard C. Lux, "Supersessionism/Replacement Theology," in *Jesus Wasn't Killed by the Jews: Reflections for Christians in Lent*, ed. Jon M. Sweeney (Maryknoll, NY: Orbis Books, 2020), 52–57. See also Charlotte Klein, *Anti-Judaism in Christian Theology*, trans. Edward Quinn (Philadelphia: Fortress, 1978).

19. Rita Ferrone, "Anti-Jewish Elements in the Extraordinary Form," *Worship* 84, no. 6 (2010): 498–513.

20. Cecil Roth, "The Eastertide Stoning of the Jews and Its Liturgical Echoes," *JQR* 35, no. 4 (1945): 361–70.

21. See Theresa Sanders, *Tenebrae: Holy Week after the Holocaust* (Maryknoll, NY: Orbis Books, 2006).

22. Jules Isaac, *The Teaching of Contempt: Christian Roots of Anti-Semitism*, trans. Helen Weaver (New York: Rinehart and Winston, 1964). See also Jeremy Cohen, *Christ Killers: The Jews and the Passion from the Bible to the Big Screen* (Oxford: Oxford University Press, 2007); Robert Michael, *Holy Hatred: Christianity, Antisemitism, and the Holocaust* (New York: Palgrave Macmillan, 2006).

The Good Friday service traditionally featured sung antiphons "on behalf of" unbelieving Jews—"perfidious" Jews in the language of the medieval liturgy—and included a string of rhetorical "reproaches" (known in Latin as the *Improperia*), in which the speaking voice of God arraigns the Jewish people for being faithless.[23] A couple of examples will give an idea of their form and tone:

> I opened the sea before you, but you opened my side with a spear. My people, what have I done to you? How have I offended you? Answer me!

> I led you on your way in a pillar of cloud, but you led me to Pilate's court. My people, what have I done to you? How have I offended you? Answer me![24]

These elements of the Good Friday liturgy were rightly called into question at Vatican II and have gone increasingly unused, but they remain in the Roman Missal (the official Catholic worship service book). Varied forms of the reproaches also appear in the Good Friday services of some Anglican, Lutheran, Methodist, and Presbyterian churches.

In the Catholic guidelines for Holocaust commemoration, by contrast, sample petitions like these are proposed:

> For the victims of the Holocaust, their families, and all our Jewish brothers and sisters, that the violence and hatred they experienced may never again be repeated, we pray to the Lord.

> For the Church, that the Holocaust may be a reminder to us that we can never be indifferent to the sufferings of others, we pray to the Lord.[25]

---

23. Martin Dudley, "The Jews in the Good Friday Liturgy," *AThR* 76, no. 1 (1994): 61–70; Richard L. Miesel, "The Good Friday Liturgy and Anti-Semitism," *Lutheran Forum* 34, no. 3 (2000): 19–24.

24. For this translation and the reproaches in their entirety, see https://www.catholicculture.org/culture/liturgicalyear/activities/view.cfm?id=1040&repos=3&subrepos=1&searchid=2512038.

25. "God's Mercy Endures Forever," section 29. These sentiments are a good start, but they stop short of confessing any responsibility or guilt for the Holocaust. On the

Protestant groups could learn from this example and develop their own Holocaust remembrance liturgies. Some have already done so, but such liturgies do not appear to be in widespread use.[26] The Pontifical Biblical Commission statement "The Jewish People and Their Sacred Scriptures in the Christian Bible" (2001) also contains a number of important insights and valuable theological formulations for biblical interpretation, theology, and liturgy.[27] Finally, every Christian Bible study group would be well served to use *The Jewish Study Bible* as one of its standard resources,[28] and all Christian preachers should work carefully through Amy-Jill Levine's *The Misunderstood Jew: The Church and the Scandal of the Jewish Jesus*.

At its best, Christian liturgy has preserved and witnessed to the shared heritage of Christians and Jews. While liturgical scholars today acknowledge that Christian worship grew out of Greco-Roman as well as Jewish practices,[29] the links to early Jewish worship are real and substantial—although there are also apparent differences as well as many historical unknowns.[30] Indeed, the book of Acts tells of how the apostles visited the Jerusalem temple daily *after*

---

need to take responsibility, see Robert Michael, *A History of Catholic Antisemitism: The Dark Side of the Church* (New York: Palgrave Macmillan, 2008).

26. Many Protestant denominations have issued important public statements and developed study guides on Judaism. They could do a much better job of making their members aware of these materials. For an overview, see Helga Croner, ed., *Stepping Stones to Further Jewish-Christian Relations: An Unabridged Collection of Christian Documents* (New York: Stimulus Books, 1977), and *More Stepping Stones to Jewish-Christian Relations: An Unabridged Collection of Christian Documents, 1975–1983* (New York: Paulist Press, 1985); Carol Rittner, Stephen D. Smith, and Irena Steinfeldt, eds., *The Holocaust and the Christian World: Reflections on the Past, Challenges for the Future* (New York: Paulist Press, 2019).

27. See https://www.vatican.va/roman_curia/congregations/cfaith/pcb_documents/rc_con_cfaith_doc_20020212_popolo-ebraico_en.html.

28. Edited by Adele Berlin and Marc Zvi Brettler, 2nd ed. (New York: Oxford University Press, 2014). See also *The Jewish Annotated New Testament*, ed. Amy-Jill Levine and Mark Zvi Brettler, 2nd ed. (Oxford: Oxford University Press, 2017).

29. See the broad summary by John F. Baldovin, "Christian Worship to the Eve of the Reformation," in *The Making of Jewish and Christian Worship*, ed. Paul F. Bradshaw and Lawrence A. Hoffman (Notre Dame, IN: University of Notre Dame Press, 1991), 156–83.

30. There is now much more information about early Christian worship than was available in the previous generation of liturgical scholarship (and so older works should be used with caution), but far less certainty. See Paul Bradshaw, *The Search*

Pentecost (2:46; cf. 3:1), of how the temple was a key site for early Christian teaching (5:17–26, 42), and of Paul's willingness to undergo a purification ritual to show that even he, the great apostle to the gentiles, remained a Torah-observant Jew (21:17–26).

Most striking of all is the *hermeneutical* shape and character of Christian worship, which is fundamentally organized around and devoted to the interpretation of Scripture. The familiarity of this aspect of Christian worship can obscure its distinctiveness.[31] There is no particular reason why religious worship should be focused on expounding a religious text. Worship has a different character in many religions. But in Christian worship, reading and expositing the biblical text lies at the heart of the service. Even in the Catholic mass, which privileges the Eucharist, the reading and preaching of Scripture occurs—and the Eucharist itself is set within the scriptural account of the Lord's Supper and Christ's passion, thereby functioning as the core hermeneutical act.[32] This basic interpretive dimension of Christian worship derives from first-century Judaism, in which the reading of the Torah was a central feature of the synagogue service (Acts 15:21), and it ultimately extends back to the distinctive nature of worship in ancient Israel.[33]

The Ketef Hinnom Amulets

The Priestly Blessing is the oldest biblical text ever discovered in an archaeological context. In 1979 two amulet texts containing the blessing were discovered in a substantial burial complex at Ketef Hinnom, just

---

for the Origins of Christian Worship: Sources and Methods for the Study of Early Liturgy, 2nd ed. (Oxford: Oxford University Press, 2002), x.

31. See Ronald P. Byars, *What Language Shall I Borrow? The Bible and Christian Worship* (Grand Rapids: Eerdmans 2008); Gordon W. Lathrop, *Saving Images: The Presence of the Bible in Christian Liturgy* (Minneapolis: Fortress, 2017).

32. Note the close connection between sharing a meal and the interpretation of Scripture already in Luke 24.

33. Ruth Langer, "From Study of Scripture to a Reenactment of Sinai: The Emergence of the Synagogue Torah Service," *Worship* 72, no. 1 (1998): 43–67; Johanna von Siemens, "The Functions of the Judaean Synagogue in the First Century and the Torah as Its Unifying Element," *EstBib* 80, no. 2 (2022): 225–56. As Langer details, the earlier pedagogical character of Torah study in the synagogue evolved over time into a liturgical event understood as a reenactment of the Sinai theophany.

to the southwest of the Old City of Jerusalem.[34] They are tiny, fragile scrolls of silver foil, which took considerable time and care to unroll and read.[35] Their size and character are important, because they underscore that these texts were not written to be read but to be used symbolically.[36] Silver was both costly and shiny.[37] It could be used to cover statues of deities, enhancing perceptions of their radiant beauty and power (Isa. 30:22).[38] Its use in the tabernacle account (Exod. 25–31; 35–40) illustrates its importance within Israel's worship tradition and might suggest that the wearers of the Ketef Hinnom amulets sought to retain a connection with the Jerusalem temple outside its precincts.[39] In this sense, the amulets might have been a way to "miniaturize and personalize the temple ritual for the body."[40] They could have even reminded individuals of YHWH's "shining face" (Num. 6:25).[41] In the Bible, silver is also associated with YHWH's precious, pure words (Ps. 12:6 [7H]).[42]

Although the amulet texts differ from each other in some of their details, as well as from the biblical text of Num. 6:24–26, they are unmistakably versions of the Priestly Blessing. The crucial portion of Amulet 1 reads "May Yahweh bles[s] you and [may he] guard you. [May] Yahweh make [his face] shine." Amulet 2 yields a fuller form of the blessing: "May Yahweh bless you, guard you. May Yahweh

---

34. See Erik Waaler, "A Reconstruction of Ketef Hinnom 1," *Maarav* 16, no. 2 (2009): 225–63, 277–79.

35. Gabriel Barkay, Marilyn J. Vaughn, Andrew G. Vaughn, and Bruce Zuckerman, "The Amulets from Ketef Hinnom: A New Edition and Evaluation," *BASOR* 334 (2004): 41–71.

36. Jeremy D. Smoak, *The Priestly Blessing in Inscription and Scripture: The Early History of Numbers 6:24–26* (New York: Oxford University Press, 2016), 17.

37. Jeremy D. Smoak, "'You Have Refined Us Like Silver Is Refined' (Ps 66:10): Yahweh's Metallurgical Powers in Ancient Judah," *Advances in Ancient, Biblical, and Near Eastern Research* 1, no. 3 (2021): 100–101.

38. Jeremy D. Smoak, "Wearing Divine Words: In Life and Death," *Material Religion* 15, no. 4 (2019): 438.

39. Smoak, "Wearing Divine Words," 439–40.

40. Smoak, "Wearing Divine Words," 440.

41. Smoak, "'You Have Refined Us,'" 106.

42. Jeremy D. Smoak, "Silver Scripts: The Ritual Function of Purified Metal in Ancient Judah," in *New Perspectives on Ritual in the Biblical World*, ed. Laura Quick and Melissa Ramos, LHBOTS 701 (London: T&T Clark, 2022), 237–53 (here 248). The number designated as "H," here and below, refers to the Hebrew text when it varies from the English translation.

make his face shine upon you and give you peace."[43] The remainders of both inscriptions further make clear that these amulets had an "apotropaic" function: to protect their wearers from evil.[44] While some scholars have disagreed, most now accept a late seventh-century or early sixth-century BCE date for these texts.[45]

The texts would probably have been placed in a pouch or container that was attached to a cord around the wrist or the neck (cf. Prov. 3:1–4; 7:1–3). Such amulets seem to have been commonly worn, and the practice persisted into later periods of Jewish and Christian history. Ephraim Urbach details how amulets are mentioned both incidentally and substantially in Mishnaic rabbinic traditions.[46] In December 2024, the translation of a silver amulet scroll discovered in a Roman gravesite near Frankfurt, Germany, was announced. Dating to 230–70 CE, the inscription's eighteen lines of text provide the earliest evidence of Christianity in northern Europe. It begins with the words "Holy, holy, holy! In the name of Jesus Christ, Son of God" and goes on to quote Phil. 2:10–11.[47] There is also plentiful medieval evidence for the continued widespread use of amulets in Christian as well as Jewish communities.[48] Amulets were worn for personal protection, healing, and magic. Because of the mortuary context in which the Ketef Hinnom texts were discovered, it is also likely that they were thought to bring honor to the dead as grave goods indicative of wealth and status,[49] and possibly to assist the dead with their journey to the underworld.[50]

---

43. The translations are from Smoak, *Priestly Blessing*, 19, 31. The words in brackets are reconstructed.

44. Smoak, "Wearing Divine Words," 436.

45. Smoak, *Priestly Blessing*, 14–16.

46. Ephraim E. Urbach, *The Sages: Their Concepts and Beliefs*, trans. Israel Abrahams (Cambridge, MA: Harvard University Press, 1979), 129–30.

47. See https://www.archaeologisches-museum-frankfurt.de/index.php/de/.

48. Robert Ousterhout, "Permanent Ephemera: The 'Honourable Stigmatisation' of Jerusalem Pilgrims," in *Between Jerusalem and Europe: Essays in Honour of Bianca Kühnel*, ed. Renana Bartal and Hanna Vorholt (Leiden: Brill, 2015), 94–109; Don C. Skemer, *Binding Words: Textual Amulets in the Middle Ages* (University Park: Pennsylvania State University Press, 2006).

49. Smoak, "'You Have Refined Us,'" 88–90.

50. See Baruch A. Levine, *Numbers 1–20: A New Translation with Introduction and Commentary*, AB 4A (New York: Doubleday, 1993), 242–43. Other scholars are skeptical of this idea.

In today's fast-paced world, where people struggle to keep up with constant change and there is little regard for the wisdom of tradition (only its deficiencies), the Priestly Blessing represents an uncanny survival from the past, a living link to a storied heritage of faith. Its words echo to contemporary Christians over the expanse of millennia. In the Priestly Blessing, Christians hear the same words that their ancestors in the faith did, and they are encouraged and enriched by them, even as their forebears were.

History of Reception

According to the Mishnah, the Priestly Blessing was proclaimed at the Jerusalem temple at the conclusion of communal prayers but before the Tamid or main sacrificial offering (m. Tamid 7:2), which took place in the morning and afternoon (cf. Exod. 29:38–42; Num. 28:1–8).[51] However, strong evidence suggests that earlier the Priestly Blessing was recited *after* the sacrifice, at the very end of the service.[52] Either way, the Priestly Blessing was the climactic spoken event of the temple ritual. The high priest, together with the rest of the priests, would recite the Priestly Blessing outside the temple building, on its front steps, with the priests facing the people (cf. m. Tamid 5:1). They raised their hands above their heads and spoke the blessing over the worshipers who were gathered in the temple courtyard. The high priest was to raise his hands only as high as the golden rosette and frontlet on his turban, which read "Holy to YHWH" (Exod. 28:36–38). This physical stance was no doubt meant to draw the worshipers' eyes to

---

51. Cf. Ismar Elbogen, *Jewish Liturgy: A Comprehensive History*, trans. Raymond P. Scheindlin (Philadelphia: Jewish Publication Society, 1993), 62. The Priestly Blessing could also be recited during an additional noontime service or at the "locking of the gates" in the evening, which means that the blessing was not inextricably bound to the sacrifice.

52. The Bible never specifies the precise timing of the blessing in the service, but it comes after the sacrifice in Lev. 9:22–23 and Sir. 50:13–21. The pattern of serving/ministering and (then) blessing in Deut. 10:8; 21:5; 1 Chron. 23:13 is also suggestive. See Robert D. Macina, *The LORD's Service: A Ritual Analysis of the Order, Function, and Purpose of the Daily Divine Service in the Pentateuch* (Eugene, OR: Pickwick, 2019), 53–59; Martin Noth, *Numbers: A Commentary*, trans. James D. Martin, OTL (Philadelphia: Westminster, 1968), 58.

the gleaming headgear, underscoring the blessing's theocentric nature (it was about God), theophanic aspect (it displayed God), and name-oriented or "onomastic" character. The recitation of the Priestly Blessing was treated as a liturgical manifestation of God and God's name.

At the Jerusalem temple, again according to the Mishnah, the blessing was delivered as a single unified affirmation, and God's holy name (YHWH) was pronounced out loud (m. Yoma 6:2; m. Tamid 7:2). The only other time God's name was spoken aloud was by the high priest on the Day of Atonement (m. Tamid 3:8). When recited outside of Jerusalem, however, the three phrases of the blessing were delivered as three separate affirmations, and another word was substituted for God's name (m. Tamid 7:2). Outside Jerusalem, priests were also only supposed to raise their hands as high as their shoulders when giving the blessing. In later rabbinic Judaism, the Priestly Blessing was eventually incorporated into the central morning prayer of the synagogue service, the *Amidah*, ultimately finding a place at the end between the eighteenth and nineteenth benedictions, a spot reminiscent of its concluding position in the temple liturgy.[53] Jews of priestly descent still go to the front of the synagogue today to recite the blessing in Orthodox Judaism, but not in Reform and some Conservative congregations, in which the blessing is read by a lector (or "precentor") instead.[54]

Jewish tradition features many other blessings as well, and they are used extensively in daily life. Rabbinic teaching encouraged faithful Jews to utter one hundred blessings a day (b. Menahot 43b).[55] Indeed, prayer in Judaism gradually became practically synonymous with blessing.[56]

A winsome description of such lived Jewish piety is offered by James Kugel:

> The main idea of Judaism, reaching back into biblical times, may be summarized in the Hebrew phrase *'avodat ha-Shem*, the service of God.

---

53. Elbogen, *Jewish Liturgy*, 65; Ron Isaacs, *Every Person's Guide to Jewish Blessings* (Brooklyn, NY: KTAV, 2021), 56.
54. Elbogen, *Jewish Liturgy*, 66.
55. E. J. Bickerman, *Studies in Jewish and Christian History*, ed. Amram Tropper, 2 vols. (Leiden: Brill, 2007), 2:585.
56. Isaacs, *Every Person's Guide*, 1.

> This is the *raison d'être* of the Jewish religion. One might wonder why this is so. I believe the answer is that Judaism rests on a basic (I might say, universal) construction of the human encounter with God. It is not an encounter of equals. You can't just walk into God's office, put your feet up on the desk, and start chatting. The only way, at least the only Jewish way, to come before God is in the role of His faithful servant, eager to be His full-time employee. But how does someone serve God? The traditional Jewish answer is by performing a lot of little humdrum tasks every day—for example, reciting a fixed blessing as we get out of bed, another as we put on our clothes, our shoes, and so forth. All these everyday acts are to be performed in a certain way and accompanied by these formulaic blessings and they are thereby connected to the divine.[57]

Kugel's description underscores how blessings surround and shape Jewish life, perhaps even more fundamentally outside of synagogue worship than within it. Personal or lived religion within Judaism is not only about continually reciting blessings; it also involves persistently looking for opportunities to offer such blessings. It is a life in which seeking an occasion to bless is a chief expression of faith in God and a fundamental aspect of what it means to be a human being.

Jewish blessings may be recited in response to a wide variety of daily experiences, especially when encountering God's creation. According to the novelist Louis Zangwill:

> In these Blessings we find a very jubilation of life—a spontaneous lyric appreciation of earth: joy in the fruits of the tree, the vine and the field: enchantment in the fragrant odours of barks, plants, fruits and spices; exaltation at the sight of stars, mountain, desert, sea and rainbow. Beautiful trees and animals, spring-blossoms equally with scholars and sages, all evoke their grace of appreciation. For storms and evil tidings, too have their graces—in fortitude! The Hebrew genius could find growth through sorrow; and for the Hebrew, good tidings have their grace, no less than fair sights and experience. Everywhere the infiltration of Earth by Heaven.[58]

---

57. James Kugel, "The Irreconcilability of Judaism and Modern Biblical Scholarship," *Studies in the Bible and Late Antiquity* 8 (2016): 12–31 (here 27–28).
58. As quoted in William W. Simpson, *Jewish Prayer and Worship: An Introduction for Christians* (London: SCM, 1965), 25.

Jewish blessings provide a tangible means of experiencing the created world as a sacred gift from God. Traditional blessings, as they were formulated by the rabbis, all begin with the phrase "Blessed are You, O Lord our God, King of the Universe" (cf. b. Berakhot 40b), which ensures that the gifts of creation are never severed from their Giver.[59] The creational dimension of Jewish blessings is particularly important to recognize because it reveals how the act of blessing is fundamentally an expression of creation theology.[60]

Previous generations of Christians have done something similar with short "sentence prayers," thanking God for the sights and sounds of daily life as they are experienced ("Thank you, God, for making such a beautiful tree"), or asking for God's help when facing a particular challenge ("Help me, O Lord, to reach my home safely"). Regrettably, this kind of Christian prayer seems to have diminished in modern Christianity.[61] The practice of blessing was similarly once commonplace in daily life and Christian families but also appears to have declined.

Somewhat surprisingly, the Priestly Blessing is not cited explicitly in the New Testament. The blessing was certainly known in early Christianity ("Lord, make your face to shine upon us," 1 Clem. 60:3), but Christian use of the blessing today does not reflect a history of unbroken continuity on the part of the church with ancient Jewish worship practice. The situation is more interesting than that. Rather than simply being a historical holdover, use of the Priestly Blessing in Christian worship today is the fruit of constructive reflection on the Old Testament at the time of the Reformation.

In the Apostolic Constitutions (4th cent. CE), a version of the Priestly Blessing is recited by a bishop ("high priest") just *prior* to the celebration of the eucharistic sacrifice (2.57), a position strikingly

---

59. Simpson, *Jewish Prayer and Worship*, 25.
60. On the Priestly Blessing and creation theology, see J. Gerald Janzen, *When Prayer Takes Place: Forays into a Biblical World*, ed. Brent A. Strawn and Patrick D. Miller (Eugene, OR: Cascade Books, 2012), 38–49.
61. For a biblical example, see Gen. 24:48–49. While there are many collections of sentence prayers available online, they are basically just short prayers articulating vague abstractions. The type of practice I have in mind instead operates as an extemporaneous response to specific objects, individuals, challenges, or gifts that a person may encounter.

reminiscent of its position in the Jerusalem temple liturgy (as related in the Mishnah).[62] But the blessing was only seldom used as a liturgical text in medieval Christianity.[63] Nor did it attract significant exegetical attention.[64]

As Nathan MacDonald points out, the prominent place of the blessing in contemporary Christianity began as a liturgical innovation by Martin Luther.[65] The Priestly Blessing was not used as a post-eucharistic benediction in the traditional Roman Catholic mass. Instead, the mass concluded in Luther's time with the "Roman" benediction: "May Almighty God bless you: the Father, and the Son, and the Holy Ghost."[66] In his initial work on revising the mass in 1523, Luther allowed for this Roman blessing still to be used, but he also suggested that Num. 6:24–26 or the similarly worded Ps. 67:6–7 (7–8H) could be substituted instead.[67] His presentation arguably gave a slight edge to the Priestly Blessing by describing it as the blessing that "the Lord himself appointed"[68] and expressing his conviction that Christ had used a blessing like Num. 6:24–26 or Ps. 67:6–7 at his ascension (Luke 24:50–51).

---

62. "Constitutions of the Holy Apostles," ed. James Donaldson, *ANF* 7:385–508 (422).

63. Klaus Seybold, *Der aaronitische Segen: Studien zu Numeri 6,22–27* (Neukirchen-Vluyn: Neukirchener, 1977), 11n6, mentions its use as a papal blessing in the Mozarabic and Gallican liturgies.

64. Ulrich Heckel, *Der Segen im Neuen Testament: Begriff, Formeln, Gesten; mit einem praktisch-theologischen Ausblick*, WUNT 150 (Tübingen: Mohr Siebeck, 2002), 78–79, 357–58. The sole reference listed in *Biblia patristica: Index des citations et allusions bibliques dans la littérature patristique* (Paris: Éditions du Centre national de la recherche scientifique, 1975) is 1 Clem. 60:3.

65. Nathan MacDonald, "A Trinitarian Palimpsest: Luther's Reading of the Priestly Blessing (Numbers 6.24–26)," *ProEccl* 21, no. 3 (2012): 299–313. MacDonald does trace a sporadic pre-Reformation exegetical tradition of interpreting the blessing, as represented primarily by Theodoret of Cyrus, Procopius of Gaza, Rabanus Maurus, and Rupert of Deutz.

66. Earlier, the post-eucharistic Catholic conclusion was even shorter—basically just a dismissal. However, sometimes various benedictions, apparently modeled after the Priestly Blessing, had been used prior to communion. See Josef A. Jungmann, *The Mass: An Historical, Theological, and Pastoral Survey*, ed. Mary Ellen Evans, trans. Julian Fernandes (Collegeville, MN: Liturgical Press, 1976), 207, 213–14.

67. Martin Luther, "An Order of Mass and Communion for the Church at Wittenberg (1523)," in *Luther's Works (American Edition)*, vol. 53, ed. Ulrich S. Leupold (Philadelphia: Fortress, 1965), 15–40.

68. Luther, "Order of Mass," 30.

Luther did not provide additional reasons for the new alternatives, but his other comments suggest that he was attempting to introduce more Scripture into the Sunday service as a means of reforming it. He also stressed the need for a degree of "liberty" in worship practice, noting that neither Scripture nor early church authorities stipulated a set liturgical order.[69] As MacDonald observes, Luther's sightly later "German Mass" of 1526 then included only the Priestly Blessing at the end of the service, without any mention of either the Roman blessing or Ps. 67.[70] It was this format that was to exercise significant influence over time on the Reformation traditions and Protestantism generally.[71]

Use of the Priestly Blessing in Protestant worship eventually expanded, becoming a well-known standard in the twentieth century. This development has not been without controversy. In eighteenth-century Germany, some theologians and liturgists objected to this use of a Jewish blessing, since in their view the Old Testament's ceremonial law had been abolished in Christian worship.[72] In the twentieth century, even Karl Barth appeared to consider the Priestly Blessing unsuitable as a Christian blessing, largely because of its absence from the New Testament.[73] Yet as Richard Briggs counters in response to Barth's judgment, "The specific blessings of grace and peace, in the presence of (or before 'the face' of) God are surely widely taken up in the New Testament, and it is difficult to understand why

---

69. Luther, "Order of Mass," 37.

70. MacDonald, "Trinitarian Palimpsest," 302. See Martin Luther, "The German Mass and Order of Service," in *Luther's Works (American Edition)*, vol. 53, ed. Ulich S. Leupold (Philadelphia: Fortress, 1965), 51–90 (here 84).

71. As MacDonald also notes ("Trinitarian Palimpsest," 302–4), the Anglican tradition represented a noteworthy exception by retaining the Roman benediction. However, MacDonald argues that Luther's influence was initially evident in the inclusion of biblical language containing the words "peace" and "keep" in the 1549 Prayer Book ("The peace of God which passeth all understanding, keep your hearts and minds in the knowledge and love of God, and of his Son Jesus Christ our Lord"), which were spoken immediately prior to the Roman benediction.

72. Heckel, *Der Segen im Neuen Testament*, 358.

73. Karl Barth, *Church Dogmatics* III/2 (Edinburgh: T&T Clark, 1960), 582. Barth also suggests that the incarnation of Christ has rendered the Priestly Blessing obsolete.

the practice of enjoining such blessings upon Christian worshipers would be frowned upon by Christians."[74]

Since Christian use of the Priestly Blessing is not based on unbroken continuity of practice, any additional justification it needs might be developed on analogy with the theological tradition of a "third use of the law" (*tertius usus legis*), in which the spiritual guidance of Old Testament law is available for Christians in a spirit of grace rather than compulsion. It is striking to see how Luther names Old Testament examples as directly applicable to the worship situation of his own day.[75] Despite his contrast between law and gospel, Luther did not question the relevance of Old Testament texts for Christian worship and instead sought to draw out their significance. Indeed, for Luther the Old Testament was not identical to the "law," which existed for him in both Testaments.[76] At Vatican II, the Priestly Blessing was officially sanctioned for Catholics as one of five possible endings to the mass.[77]

Today the opposite question has more force: Does Christian use of the Priestly Blessing unfairly appropriate a practice that properly belongs to Judaism? Edna Brocke argues that the biblical text assigns the blessing exclusively to the Aaronite priesthood and the historical people of Israel.[78] The question of whether Judaism will view Christian use of the Priestly Blessing as a beneficial expansion of its traditional witness to God or an improper appropriation of its heritage is finally something that Jews must answer for themselves. But from a Christian vantage point, the Priestly Blessing can certainly be

---

74. Richard S. Briggs, *Theological Hermeneutics and the Book of Numbers as Christian Scripture* (Notre Dame, IN: University of Notre Dame Press, 2018), 229.

75. Luther, "Order of Mass," 21, 26, cites, e.g., 1 Sam. 5:2 and 2 Kings 16:10–14 as scriptural warrants.

76. Maurice E. Schild, "Gospel and Canon in Luther's Bible Prefaces," *LTJ* 49, no. 2 (2015): 60–73.

77. Don E. Saliers, "Aaronic Blessing," *RPP* 1:4.

78. Edna Brocke, "Von den 'Schriften' zum 'Alten Testament'—und zurück? Jüdische Fragen zur christlichen Suche einer 'Mitte der Schrift,'" in *Die Hebräische Bibel und ihre zweifache Nachgeschichte: Festschrift für Rolf Rendtorff zum 65. Geburtstag*, ed. Erhard Blum, Christian Macholz, and Ekkehard W. Stegemann (Neukirchen-Vluyn: Neukirchener, 1990), 581–94 (here 591–92). Since Jewish tradition mandates reciting the Priesty Blessing only in Hebrew (m. Megillah 4:10), it could be argued that from a Jewish perspective it is also illegitimate to say it in any other language.

used without a spirit of displacement (as if the blessing now obtains only for Christians and no longer for Jews). Indeed, the words can be heard in an expansive sense, as extending to all humankind (cf. Gen. 5:2; Isa. 19:24–25).

Jews may also feel, more than Christians do, that there is a disenfranchisement of a priestly prerogative in the Christian practice, since Jewish tradition has limited the recitation of the blessing to priests. But some Christian traditions have also restricted the recitation of the blessing to clergy (especially when used as a post-eucharistic benediction).[79] The Apostolic Constitutions already stipulate: "Neither do we permit the laity to perform any of the offices belonging to the priesthood; as, for instance, neither the sacrifice, nor baptism, nor the laying on of hands nor the blessing. . . . For such sacred offices are conferred by the laying on of the hands of the bishop" (3.10).[80] There is thus a historic link in Christianity between blessing and priestly, even episcopal, authority.

The Christian tradition did not abolish Israel's priesthood and its prerogatives but maintained them, while also eventually extending them—if not always in practice, at least in principle—to the laity. Protestants have spoken since the Reformation of the "priesthood of believers" and Catholics, particularly after Vatican II, have endorsed a baptismal as well as a ministerial priesthood.[81] So Christian use of the Priestly Blessing does not have to be viewed, and has not functioned, as a disenfranchisement of the priestly role. To the contrary, many Christian traditions would affirm that the act of blessing belongs centrally to the work of ordained clergy and lies close to the heart of the ministerial vocation—even as they would affirm the right and the responsibility of every Christian to bless whenever it is possible and appropriate to do so (1 Pet. 3:8–9).

---

79. Daniel G. Van Slyke, "Toward a Theology of Blessings: Agents and Recipients of Benedictions," *Antiphon* 15, no. 1 (2011): 57–59; John D. Witvliet, "On Ordination and Worship Leadership," *RW* 69 (2003): 42–43.

80. *ANF* 7:429.

81. See the Vatican II statement on the baptismal or common priesthood and the special priesthood in *Lumen Gentium* (section 10). For discussion, see Jean-Pierre Torrell, *A Priestly People: Baptismal Priesthood and Priestly Ministry* (New York: Paulist Press, 2011), 128–37.

2

The Blessing's Thesis

> The LORD spoke to Moses, saying:
> Speak to Aaron and his sons, saying,
> Thus you shall bless the Israelites:
> You shall say to them,
>
> The LORD bless you and keep you.
>
> —Numbers 6:22–24 (NRSV modified)

In this chapter and the next, the Priestly Blessing will be examined phrase by phrase and word by word. Such an approach is a hallmark of the Touchstone Texts series, of which this volume is a part. But the more important reason to follow this pattern is to demonstrate just how rich the language of the Priestly Blessing is, and how a slower, more patient exploration of its words will reveal unsuspected theological depths.

The twentieth-century philosopher Ludwig Wittgenstein went so far as to assert that a relationship exists between understanding and the pace of apprehension. Drawing an analogy from music, he wrote: "I think it is an important and remarkable fact that a musical theme alters its *character* if it is played at (very) different tempi."[1] In a similar

---

1. Ludwig Wittgenstein, *Culture and Value*, ed. G. H. von Wright, trans. Peter Winch (Chicago: University of Chicago Press, 1980), 75e (emphasis original).

fashion, the rate of reading can affect how a reader understands the words. Wittgenstein confessed that he wanted his own writing to be read slowly and so he used "copious punctuation marks" to retard his reader.[2] Some things can be read quickly, and perhaps they are even better read quickly. But some things need to be read slowly for them to make a certain kind of sense.[3]

The biblical literature is by its very nature communal, contemplative literature, with a long history of devotional reflection, critical study, and liturgical use. It is a religious literature that continually repays close examination and benefits from careful attention to its details. Even if something originally got into the Bible for fortuitous or accidental reasons, it has since been drawn into a common nucleus of readerly attention by virtue of its placement within the biblical canon. The Bible's readers have studied, questioned, debated, and meditated on its every detail for centuries. The Bible is not merely a random assortment of ancient remembrances. It was compiled to be, and was faithfully transmitted as, a *scripture*.[4] That is why a slow reading of it is best.[5]

Nor is such reading merely a conversation or dialogue between text and reader. There is a unique quality to "instruction through texts," which requires not only critical consideration but imaginative assent.[6] To read a rich, literary text well entails provisionally agreeing with it, prior to critiquing it—"trying it on for size." Otherwise it will not be

---

2. Wittgenstein, *Culture and Value*, 68e.

3. See Thomas Newkirk, *The Art of Slow Reading* (Portsmouth, NH: Heinemann, 2011). And not only reading. The burlesque dancer Gypsy Rose Lee is supposed to have said, "If a thing is worth doing, it is worth doing slowly . . . very slowly."

4. I use this term here in a phenomenological rather than a theological sense. See Wilfred Cantwell Smith, *What Is Scripture? A Comparative Approach* (Minneapolis: Fortress, 1993). A "scripture" is a body of literature to which a particular community looks for a certain kind of guidance. A crucial failing of modern biblical studies has been its inability to recognize the type of thing the Bible actually is.

5. See K. Jo-Ann Badley and Ken Badley, "Slow Reading: Reading along Lectio Lines," *Journal of Education & Christian Belief* 15, no. 1 (2011): 29–42; David Mikics, *Slow Reading in a Hurried Age* (Cambridge, MA: Belknap, 2013); Eugene H. Peterson, "Words to Savor: Slow Down, You Read Too Fast," *ChrCent* 119, no. 25 (Dec. 4–17, 2002): 18–23.

6. See Paul Ricoeur, "Naming God," trans. David Pellauer, in *Rhetorical Invention and Religious Inquiry*, ed. Walter Jost and Wendy Olmstead (New Haven: Yale University Press, 2000), 162–81.

understood adequately and cannot be evaluated wisely.[7] This is why faithful Jews and Christians have traditionally read Scripture aloud, so that Scripture actualizes its own sound, its own audible voice.[8] Historically, the "voice" of Scripture was never a pure metaphor. The voice of Scripture was a living reality within the worshiping community.

The Literary Context of the Blessing

In biblical interpretation, it often proves helpful to think about literary context as a series of concentric circles, beginning with the immediate context of a particular text in its present location and moving out ever more widely. With the Priestly Blessing, that means beginning with its location in the book of Numbers, and then expanding to consider its location within the Pentateuch, the Old Testament, and finally the entire Christian Bible. In what follows, I will focus on Numbers and the Pentateuch, reserving comments on the broader biblical context of the Priestly Blessing for subsequent chapters.

Excursus on Method

Attentive readers will note how I am privileging literary over historical context. It is quite intentional. In the modern era "context" in biblical studies has become equated with a reconstructed history, which pries individual texts out of their literary setting and effectively recontextualizes them according to an alternate scale of reference. While historical criticism of the Bible continues to have value, its true merit emerges from the way it can help to inform the literary-canonical setting of biblical texts—rather than using it to dissolve that setting. Although the great historicist confidence that dominated the field in the mid-twentieth century has receded significantly,[9]

---

7. Cf. Paul Ricoeur, *Freud and Philosophy: An Essay in Interpretation*, trans. Denis Savage (New Haven: Yale University Press, 1970), 525: "We must believe in order to understand and understand in order to believe."

8. John Burgess, *Why Scripture Matters: Reading the Bible in a Time of Church Conflict* (Louisville: Westminster John Knox, 1998), 58–64.

9. For the issues at stake, see Robert D. Hume, *Reconstructing Contexts: The Aims and Principles of Archaeo-Historicism* (Oxford: Oxford University Press, 1999);

biblical scholarship continues to underestimate the challenges and overvalue the benefits of placing a biblical text within a single historical setting. A crucial aspect of this problem has to do with the philosophical obstacles to discerning causation in history.[10] On what basis is one thing said to be caused by another?[11] The identification of a "cause" and an "effect" already introduces a hierarchy of values. The "results" of the procedure typically only reaffirm the values adopted at the outset of the investigation.

In Num. 6, there is a clear literary frame around the blessing proper.[12] Its introduction (v. 22) and conclusion (v. 27) correspond to each other by presenting the blessing as a statement by God to Moses. The blessing is described as a task for the Aaronite priests to perform (v. 23), which is why it is sometimes called the Aaronic (or Levitical) Blessing. As to the wording of the blessing itself, there is no preamble, no if-then formula, no specification of a particular time or context. Its words just *are*. The blessing is an unconditional statement without requirements or contingencies.[13] Its words appear as words of sheer grace. Remarkably, they are the only liturgical words provided for any of the regular priestly activities described in Leviticus and Numbers, which otherwise focus exclusively on priestly actions.[14] Israel Knohl calls attention to this aspect of the priestly legislation with his phrase "the sanctuary of silence."[15] In

---

David Perkins, *Is Literary History Possible?* (Baltimore: Johns Hopkins University Press, 1992).

10. Clayton Roberts, *The Logic of Historical Explanation* (University Park: Pennsylvania State University Press, 1996).

11. S. H. Rigby, "Historical Causation: Is One Thing More Important than Another?," *History* 80 (1995): 227–42.

12. Michael Fishbane, "Form and Reformulation of the Biblical Priestly Blessing," *JAOS* 103, no. 1 (1983): 115–21.

13. Angelika Berlejung, "Der gesegnete Mensch: Text und Kontext von Num 6,22–27 und den Silberamuletten von Ketef Hinnom," in *Mensch und König: Studien zur Anthropologie des Alten Testament; Rüdiger Lux zum 60. Geburtstag*, ed. Angelika Berlejung and Raik Heckl (Freiburg: Herder, 2008), 58.

14. The only other time the priests speak is in Num. 5:19–22, which is not part of the regular daily service.

15. Israel Knohl, *The Sanctuary of Silence: The Priestly Torah and the Holiness School* (Minneapolis: Augsburg Fortress, 1995), 148–52. The phrase was introduced by Yehezkel Kaufmann. Knohl acknowledges that this portrait of worship is an idealized one, and he draws a distinction between the Priestly material generating it and the

the Priestly Blessing, Israel's priests are finally given a script to speak to the assembled worshipers, an indication of its climactic force.[16]

The blessing consists of three phrases, all foregrounding the divine name. Each use of the name appears together with two divine benefits.[17] The phrases increase in length, from three to five to seven Hebrew words, for a total of fifteen. If each letter of the Hebrew alphabet is assigned an ascending numerical value, as is done in traditional Jewish numerology, known as gematria, the numerical value of YHWH (fifteen) is identical to the total number of words in the blessing.[18] This numerical symbolism is a clue to the importance of the divine name in the blessing. Moreover, this expanding, threefold rhythmic pattern provides a sense of symmetry, a feeling of acceleration, and a satisfying climax.[19] After the words of the blessing are concluded, a final word of instruction characterizes the blessing as an act in which God's name is effectively put or placed on the people (v. 27).

Although God is initially speaking only to Moses (v. 22), the instructions for the blessing are given in the plural (to Aaron and his sons): "Thus shall you [pl.] bless the Israelites, saying to them . . ." (v. 23b, my trans.). However, the blessing itself then uses second-person singular verb forms, even though they are directed to the (pl.) Israelites (vv. 23b, 27). This small detail of the language could

---

contributions of the Holiness school, often credited with producing Lev. 17–26. On the similarities between this school and the Priestly Blessing, see Mark A. Awabdy, "The Holiness Composition of the Priestly Blessing," *Biblica* 99, no. 1 (2018): 29–49.

16. Robert D. Macina, *The LORD's Service: A Ritual Analysis of the Order, Function, and Purpose of the Daily Divine Service in the Pentateuch* (Eugene, OR: Pickwick, 2019), 158–59.

17. Macina, *LORD's Service*, 164–65. Each phrase consists of two clauses. The first clause begins in Hebrew with a prefixed verb and the divine name, followed by the second clause with *waw* + another prefixed verb. For a technical analysis, see Marjo C. A. Korpel, "The Priestly Blessing Revisited (Num. 6:22–27)," in *Unit Delimitation in Biblical Hebrew and Northwest Semitic Literature*, ed. Marjo C. A. Korpel and Josef M. Oesch, Pericope (Assen: Van Gorcum, 2003), 61–81.

18. Raik Heckl, "The Aaronic Blessing (Numbers 6): Its Intention and Place in the Concept of the Pentateuch," in *On Dating Biblical Texts to the Persian Period*, ed. Richard J. Bautch and Mark Lackowski, FAT 2/101 (Tübingen: Mohr Siebeck, 2019), 132.

19. Macina, *LORD's Service*, 164, also notes that the threefold form is suggestive of the superlative.

be viewed as an inconsistency or a historical holdover from the blessing's prehistory. But in its present context, the mixed second-person forms bring greater attention to the narrative context of the blessing and invite reflection on how the intended narrative recipients of the blessing are being conceived. The blessing is also presented as a set formula ("thus [*kōh*] you shall bless," v. 23b).

More broadly, Num. 5 and 6 contain a series of instructions for the priestly camp in the wilderness. Within this next most proximate literary context, the Priestly Blessing ends these instructions and therefore this section of Numbers. Most biblical scholars have felt unable to pinpoint any connecting structure or theme within this material.[20] Thomas Dozeman suggests that the context relates blessing to purity, even as it clarifies that God (rather than the priests) is the one who truly blesses Israel.[21] It is hard to imagine that this second point was seriously in doubt, since even everyday blessing formulas referred to God as the agent of blessing (stated explicitly or implied; see Ruth 2:4; 1 Sam. 15:13; 2 Kings 4:29). Nevertheless, the concluding phrase of Num. 6:27 is emphatic in Hebrew ("and I *myself* will bless them," my trans.).[22] Jacob Milgrom suggests a contrast at this point to a supposed priestly welcome formula—"*We* bless you from the house of the LORD" (Ps. 118:26b)[23]—but there is no explicit evidence of any confusion. Even the first part of that same psalm verse maintains such blessing occurs "in the name of the LORD" (Ps. 118:26a).

Yet Dozeman's connection between blessing and purity is generative. He sees a natural progression within Num. 5–6, moving from practices of expulsion (5:1–4) through three examples of defiling relationships (fraud, 5:5–10; adultery, 5:11–31; violations of the Nazirite vow, 6:1–21). Because the appropriate remedies for these defilements narrow spatially, from consulting a priest anywhere (Num. 5:9, 15) to consulting a priest at the door of the tabernacle (Num. 6:10, 13),

---

20. E.g., Jacob Milgrom, *Numbers*, JPS Torah Commentary (Philadelphia: Jewish Publication Society, 1990), 51, concludes that "a satisfactory explanation of the occurrence of the Priestly Benediction in its present setting has yet to be found."

21. Thomas Dozeman, "The Book of Numbers: Introduction, Commentary, and Reflections," *NIB* 2:3–268 (here 66).

22. I.e., the independent pronoun is used with the verb. This emphasis is lacking in the NRSV and NJPS translations, which both simply render "and I will bless them."

23. Milgrom, *Numbers*, 50–51 (emphasis added).

Dozeman argues that the material moves from an outer to an inner orbit centered on the tabernacle. Accordingly, the Priestly Blessing could be understood as representing an ultimate remedy for defilement, even as it serves as a reminder that the priestly camp features the tabernacle and therefore has God's blessing at its innermost core.[24] Milgrom reports that the medieval scholar Ibn Ezra similarly perceived an "associative reasoning" at work in the combination of Nazirite and priestly traditions in Num. 6, since both the Nazirite and the priest were holy.[25] A modern alternative is to view the material in Num. 5–6 as merely detailing various functions for priests.[26] Either way, the thrust of the whole section moves toward a reliance on God's blessing, which could in context be understood as a response to impurity and the epitome of holiness.[27]

The next wider circle of contextual association occurs within the Sinai legislation of the Pentateuch as a whole. In terms of its present shape, the Pentateuch is formed by five books of somewhat different lengths and characters. There are 20,611 words in Genesis, 16,712 words in Exodus, 11,950 words in Leviticus, 16,413 words in Numbers, and 14,294 words in Deuteronomy.[28] Genesis is significantly longer than the other books and stands apart by its focus on Israel's pre-Mosaic story. The three internal books—Exodus, Leviticus, and Numbers—share a predominant focus on the Sinai event and its legislation. Their approximate word counts of 16,000–12,000–16,000

---

24. For arguments against purity as a common theme in this material, see Eryl W. Davies, *Numbers*, NCBC (Grand Rapids: Eerdmans, 1995), 43.

25. Milgrom, *Numbers*, 51.

26. Thus Horst Seebass, "YHWH's Name in the Aaronic Blessing (Num 6:22–27)," in *The Revelation of the Name YHWH to Moses: Perspectives from Judaism, the Pagan Graeco-Roman World and Early Christianity*, ed. George H. van Kooten (Leiden: Brill, 2006), 51.

27. The most common critical view is still to reject any connection at all between the blessing and its literary context. Klaus Seybold, *Der aaronitische Segen: Studien zu Numeri 6,22–27* (Neukirchen-Vluyn: Neukirchener, 1977), 54, styles this section of Numbers a literary *Rumpelkammer* ("junk room"). On blessing as a prominent theme throughout the entire book of Numbers, see Josef Forsling, *The Theology of the Book of Numbers*, OTT (Cambridge: Cambridge University Press, forthcoming).

28. Following the count of Konrad Schmid, *Genesis and the Moses Story: Israel's Dual Origins in the Hebrew Bible*, trans. James D. Nogalski, Siphrut 3 (Winona Lake, IN: Eisenbrauns, 2010), 28.

immediately suggest an envelope structure consisting of two outer panels (Exodus and Numbers) sandwiching a third (Leviticus), like a triptych. Deuteronomy presents a substantial Mosaic postscript in which Israel is no longer at Sinai but in Moab, forty years later, having completed its wilderness wanderings and now on the brink of entering the land of Canaan.

The Pentateuch can therefore be read as possessing a Sinaitic core with a Genesis prelude and a Deuteronomy postlude.[29] Genesis not only details Israel's history before Sinai; it explicitly looks ahead and tells its story with an eye toward the future (Gen. 15:12–16; 50:24; cf. 12:10–20). Analogously, Deuteronomy not only tells what happened after Sinai but refers back to the Sinai event and retells it (Deut. 1:1–5; 4:44–49). The interpretation of Exodus–Leviticus–Numbers as having a common focus is supported by historical-critical work on the literary formation of these three books, whose contents have apparently come from different hands at different times but now primarily recount the Sinaitic tradition. Their compositional development seems to have been shared to some degree, although it has proven elusive to work out exactly how. There is nevertheless much agreement in biblical scholarship that the material, whatever its ultimate origins, was broadly transmitted in a priestly milieu.

Major blessings appear at the end of Genesis (Gen. 49) and the end of Deuteronomy (Deut. 33), like bookends to the Pentateuch. Moreover, these blessings share similar themes and metaphors, even specific phrases.[30] These and other features suggest that the Pentateuch has been shaped according to a large-scale structure of curse and blessing, from the blessings and curses of Gen. 1–3 right down to the curses and blessings of Deut. 27–28 (cf. Deut. 30:1–5).[31] From this bird's-eye view, the Priestly Blessing occupies something like a

---

29. See Stephen B. Chapman, "The Pentateuch as Canon," in *Canon Formation: Tracing the Role of Sub-Collections in the Biblical Canon*, ed. W. Edward Glenny and Darian R. Lockett (London: Bloomsbury T&T Clark, 2023), 101–19.

30. Compare Gen. 49:25 with Deut. 33:13, and Gen. 49:26 with Deut. 33:15–16.

31. Stephen B. Chapman, "Pentateuch and Blessing," in *T&T Clark Handbook of the Doctrine of Creation*, ed. Jason Goroncy (London: Bloomsbury Academic, 2024), 44–55; cf. Olivier Artus, "The Pentateuch: Five Books, One Canon," in *The Oxford Handbook of the Pentateuch*, ed. Joel S. Baden and Jeffrey Stackert (New York: Oxford University Press, 2021), 32, 37.

position at the Pentateuch's center. It closes a loop back to Lev. 9:22, which reports how Aaron blessed the people at the tabernacle, and it completes the sanctuary building program begun in Exodus.[32]

Biblical scholars have long seen how Num. 6:22–27 reads like a script specifically for Lev. 9:22.[33] Some have ventured a diachronic explanation: that Num. 6:24–26 once appeared right after Lev. 9:22 but was subsequently displaced by additional material inserted between them.[34] Such a historical reconstruction is possible but not the only way of understanding a relationship between the two passages—and anyway impossible to prove.

More valuable for contemporary readers is how the connection between Lev. 9:22 and Num. 6:24–26 signals a broader literary structure extending beyond the (loose) narrative format of Numbers. In its own literary context, Lev. 9 functions as something of an initial conclusion to the Sinai event, which is then further extended by subsequent descriptions of additional priestly activity—including readying the people in the first part of Numbers to move on from Sinai into the wilderness (Num. 10:11–12).[35] In its present location, Num. 6 comes at the very end of the tabernacle building account (cf. Num. 7:1) and is thus a "literary capstone."[36]

---

32. Heckl, "Aaronic Blessing," 127.

33. In the following verse (Lev. 9:23), Moses and Aaron deliver a second blessing outside the tent of meeting. Gary A. Anderson, "The Tabernacle Narrative as Christan Scripture," in *The Identity of Israel's God in Christian Scripture*, ed. Don Collett, Mark Elliott, Mark Gignilliat, and Ephraim Radner, Resources for Bible Study 96 (Atlanta: SBL Press, 2020), 91–95, calls attention to how Lev. 9:24 then not only provisionally concludes the tabernacle narrative that begins in Exod. 25 but echoes, both materially and formally, the theophany at the end of Exod. 40. Both Lev. 9 and Exod. 40 were understood by ancient interpreters as describing the same event, which also underscores how the Sinai material has been expanded—sometimes through an extended chronological framework and sometimes without a strict sense of chronological sequence. See Gary A. Anderson, *That I May Dwell among Them: Incarnation and Atonement in the Tabernacle Narrative* (Grand Rapids: Eerdmans, 2023), 19–48. Cf. Seebass, "YHWH's Name," 48.

34. This proposal already appears in Ibn Ezra. Milgrom, *Numbers*, 51.

35. Cf. Horst Seebass, "Moses' Preparation of the March to the Holy Land: A Dialogue with Rolf P. Knierim on Numbers 1:1–10:10," in *Land of Israel in the Bible, History, and Theology: Studies in Honor of Ed Noort*, ed. Jacques van Ruiten and Jacobus C. de Vos, VTSup 124 (Leiden: Brill, 2009), 99–100.

36. Heckl, "Aaronic Blessing," 137.

So the Priestly Blessing appears in the Pentateuch in a concluding liturgical position, just as it did in worship at the Jerusalem temple.[37] With Num. 6, the pentateuchal narrative begins its shift from Sinai to the world beyond Sinai. The Priestly Blessing is literarily both a crowning point of priestly instruction and a priestly word of "traveling mercy" as Israel goes forth into the world.[38]

The Logic of the Blessing

Dozeman also argues that the blessing's verbs should be read as three pairs rather than six separate actions.[39] He further proposes that in each case the second verb reports the purpose or result of God's action in the first verb.[40] The syntax of the blessing supports his first proposal but not his second.

Grammatically, the Priestly Blessing is not in the indicative mood. If it were, it would read "The LORD *blesses* you." It would then be a simple statement of fact, a description of God's ongoing action. The blessing is instead a *volitive* statement, an expression of the speaker's will. This distinction is crucial for understanding the blessing, indeed all blessings, and so it will benefit from further scrutiny, even though such scrutiny will necessarily involve a discussion of semantics. However, the action of the second verb in each pair should not be read as specifying the purpose or result of the first verb, as Dozeman suggests. While two volitional verbs in a row, connected by *waw*, may sometimes carry an implication of result or purpose (e.g., 2 Sam. 19:38; Jer. 40:15), sometimes they do not (Gen. 9:27; 17:2; 1 Kings 18:41).[41] The syntax of the blessing does present all of

---

37. Rolf P. Knierim and George W. Coats, *Numbers*, FOTL 4 (Grand Rapids: Eerdmans, 2005), 96.
38. Seybold, *Der aaronitische Segen*, 68.
39. Dozeman, "Book of Numbers," 66.
40. Cf. Macina, *LORD's Service*, 164–65n404; Martin Noth, *Numbers: A Commentary*, trans. James D. Martin, OTL (Philadelphia: Westminster, 1968), 58.
41. See Bruce K. Waltke and Michael O'Connor, *An Introduction to Biblical Hebrew Syntax* (Winona Lake, IN: Eisenbrauns, 1990), comparing sections 33.4, 39.2.2, and 39.2.5. As they note, "It is often difficult to distinguish examples of this [purpose] construction from cases with two volitional forms in a row" (650). They

its verbs as prefixed forms, but these verbs are best rendered not as conjunctive-sequential but conjunctive-nonsequential. There is no compelling reason to understand the second verb in each phrase as describing a purpose or result of the first verb, and doing so introduces difficulties in interpretation.

It does seem that the second verb in each phrase mirrors and extends the sense of the first verb in some way. Because the subject of the first verb carries over to the second (whose subject is otherwise unspecified), reading the verbs as paired makes good sense.[42] A close analogy exists here with the parallelism of biblical Hebrew poetry. The two terms in each phrase of the blessing are treated almost as synonyms of each other and yet are also distinct, opening up fresh possibilities for analogical reflection. How is "blessing" both like and unlike "keeping"? How is the "shining of God's face" like and unlike God's "grace"? How is the "lifting up of God's countenance" like and unlike God's "peace"?

It is worth noting that Dozeman's paraphrase of the blessing does not fully observe the pattern of his own analysis. Instead of saying that "keeping" is the *result* of God's blessing (i.e., God's blessing results in people being secure), Dozeman merely says that the first phrase of the blessing "emphasizes concrete gifts." With regard to the second phrase, he makes more of an effort to adhere to his theory, suggesting that it expresses "the hope that God will be well disposed toward the person . . . and *thus* temper judgment with mercy." But this makes it sound as if the favor of God is a condition of God's mercy. So too with the third phrase, which Dozeman glosses as "God will pay attention (lift his face), *thus* providing fullness of life (peace)."[43] Not only is there an insufficient syntactical basis for this insinuation of a result clause, the ensuing sense of the blessing is theologically problematic ("the LORD bless you *so that* the LORD will keep you"?). On the basis of syntax and sense, it is better to read the six verbs

---

also warn against "a tendency, both in translation and commentary, to assign to the conjunctive *waw* a more logically distinct value" than warranted (653).

42. On this point, see Patrick D. Miller, "The Blessing of God," *Int* 29, no. 3 (1975): 240–51.

43. All three quotations are from Dozeman, "Book of Numbers," 66 (emphasis added).

of the blessing as three paired actions,[44] with six actions in all, but without an implication of sequence ("first God does *x*, and [only] then God will do *y*") or result ("God does *x*, which thus creates the further possibility of God's doing *y*").

"(May)"

Indo-European languages, of which English is one, originally had four grammatical moods: the indicative, the subjunctive, the imperative, and the optative. The indicative describes how things are. The other moods all describe how the speaker wants them to be. (To this extent, one can argue that there are fundamentally just two moods, the indicative and the volitive.)

In modern English (as in biblical Hebrew), there is no longer a distinct optative verbal paradigm, which is one of the non-indicative moods for describing a wish or desire. An optative sense can still be conveyed through modal verbs and periphrastic constructions (e.g., "if only," "would that"). But the optative now functions largely as a subset of the subjunctive mood, which is used for an even broader range of volitional nuances, from wish to mild command. The subjunctive expresses not what is, but what could have been or could be. The English subjunctive is denoted by an uninflected or "bare" verbal form: "your kingdom *come*" (subjunctive) rather than "your kingdom comes" (indicative). Other well-known examples are: "God *be* with you" (not "God is with you") and "God *forbid*" (not "God forbids"). These subjunctive expressions are not simple statements of fact but requests, pleas, or claims. If unspoken, "may" is implied. The imperative is also a subset of the volitive and is used for second-person commands (e.g., "Come here!").

In biblical Hebrew, there are three main subjunctive or volitive verbal forms: the first-person cohortative, the second-person imperative, and the (mostly) third-person jussive.[45] A cohortative verbal form

---

44. So too P. Miller, "Blessing of God," 243.
45. For further details, qualifications, and exceptions, see Paul Joüon and Takamitsu Muraoka, *A Grammar of Biblical Hebrew*, 2nd ed., Subsidia Biblica 27 (Rome: Gregorian and Biblical Press, 2011), 127–28, 130–32.

is often translated as beginning "let us," while the jussive is usually translated "let him/her/them." These forms are familiar and biblical sounding because they are prominent in many passages of the Bible, such as the first chapter of Genesis (e.g., Gen. 1:3, "Let there be light"; 1:26, "Let us make humankind"). In certain cases the spelling (or morphology) of jussive Hebrew verb forms is distinct from the regular imperfect and then considered "marked." But usually a jussive is spelled the same as the indicative verb, in which case the context has to decide.

Since the Hebrew imperative is the form for positive second-person commands, it is noteworthy that the standard Hebrew convention is to use the jussive with the negative particle *'al* (and sometimes *lō'*) for negative commands. Technically, there is no negative imperative in Hebrew (although English translations may legitimately translate the negative jussive as if it is a negative imperative in English). The language cannot actually say "Do not come here," only "Let you not come here." This convention points to a close linguistic relationship between the imperative and the jussive, and it reinforces the way in which the jussive can express an urgent request as well as a wish or a hope. All of this grammatical information may seem obscure, but it is crucial for understanding biblical blessings because blessings are volitive statements in Hebrew (as in English). They are not simple statements of fact. They are statements that testify to what could be.

The Priestly Blessing uses jussive verb forms. Only two of its six verbs are marked as jussives morphologically (*yā'ēr* in v. 25a and *yāśēm* in v. 26b). The other four verbs are spelled in such a way that they could be either regular indicative third-person imperfects or jussives. But the context determines, and the context of blessing is decisive.[46] In fact, this linguistic feature goes to the heart of what

---

46. Occasionally it has been argued that the verbal forms in the Priestly Blessing are not jussives: e.g., H. Jagersma, "Some Remarks on the Jussive in Numbers 6,24–26," in *Von Kanaan bis Kerala: Festschrift für Prof. Mag. Dr. Dr. J. P. M. van der Ploeg O.P. zur Vollendung des siebzigsten Lebensjahres am 4. Juli 1979*, ed. W. C. Delsman et al., AOAT 211 (Neukirchen-Vluyn: Neukirchener, 1982), 131–36. However, Jagersma's argument relies on his judgment that "it is hardly thinkable that the priest spoke out a word of blessing over the pilgrims or over the assembled congregation in the form of a wish" (135). His concern can be addressed through a better understanding of the jussive form itself—which, after all, is marked twice in the form of

blessing is. Perhaps it is not quite right to say that blessing as a volitive statement is not a statement of fact. Volitives are statements of contrary facts. They are statements expressing the vantage point of a speaker who views things differently and is expressing a type of counterfactual statement. The speaker-orientation is also crucial. In the example of one Hebrew grammar, "Let him arise" does not mean "*He* wants to arise," it means that the *speaker* wants this person to arise.[47] Similarly, "Let/may God bless you" does not technically mean that *God* wishes to bless you—although it presumes that possibility. First and foremost, it means the *speaker* wishes that God will bless you. So the Priestly Blessing is a statement by a human speaker in which God's blessing is invoked, described, and conferred upon its hearers.

This last aspect of blessing—its conferral—is also part of what is signaled by the jussive, which does not merely express a wish or a hope. Here again the close relationship between the jussive and the imperative is important. The jussive can be more of a command, and (even though it is weaker than the imperative) the jussive still initiates performative speech.[48] If a judge says of a prisoner, "Let her go free," it not only expresses a wish but also frees a person from jail. It introduces a new social situation, with specific conventions and rules. The condition of the prisoner is altered. The judge's statement is not easily ignored or withdrawn. Such a statement is "performative" because it not only says something, it does something.

Blessing in this sense is performative speech. It does something. It inaugurates a new reality, a different set of facts, and by virtue of its pronouncement it helps to bring that reality into fuller realization. Blessing is testimony to an Otherwise.

Klaus Seybold argues against interpreting the Priestly Blessing as performative speech, insisting that in such a context perfect verb

---

the blessing found in the Masoretic text—and the genre of blessing. It is true that jussive forms are sometimes improbable in the Hebrew Bible and that the context can require the indicative; see Joüon and Muraoka, *Grammar of Biblical Hebrew*, 349. But nothing in Num. 6:24–26 requires the indicative. Instead, the blessing genre requires the jussive.

47. Joüon and Muraoka, *Grammar of Biblical Hebrew*, 347.
48. On performative speech, see J. L. Austin, *How to Do Things with Words*, 2nd ed. (Cambridge, MA: Harvard University Press, 1976).

forms would be used in Hebrew, and in the first person (= "I hereby bless you").[49] It is true that the Priestly Blessing makes a request of a superior third party, and in that sense it cannot take the purely declarative form that Seybold envisions. But his understanding of performative speech is overly narrow. Speech act theory has described a range of performative formulas, with differing degrees of urgency and varying modes of performativity.[50] The Priestly Blessing has the character of a confident request, and one that sets in motion the changed reality it names.

Some biblical scholars and theologians have resisted the notion that blessing is performative speech because they worry that such an understanding brings blessing too close to magic.[51] There are different definitions of magic, many of them unfairly pejorative. "Magic" is often assumed to be, in effect, what other people do.[52] Yet quite a few approaches would stress how verbal formulations in magic ("spells" or "incantations") are thought to possess the power to change ordinary outcomes, whether in nature or interpersonal relations.[53] In this sense, magic is extra-human power over creation. Because such power seems theologically blasphemous, competing with God, it is often denied to blessing, which then becomes only the expression of a pious wish or devout hope. But this reductionistic move fatally

49. Seybold, *Der aaronitische Segen*, 22. So too Magdalene L. Frettlöh, *Theologie des Segens: Biblische und dogmatische Wahrnehmungen*, 2nd ed. (Gütersloh: Kaiser, 1998), 377. Cf. *hiqdaštî* in 1 Kings 9:3.

50. Austin, *How to Do Things with Words*, 159, describes multiple subsets of performative utterances. He classes blessings and curses as "behabitives" or statements describing someone's present or future condition.

51. Anthony C. Thiselton, "The Supposed Power of Words in the Biblical Writings," *JTS* 25 (1974): 283–99, has written scathingly of "word magic," insisting that performative speech operates by virtue of the personal authority and institutional power possessed by the speaker. However, Thiselton still considers biblical blessings, including the Priestly Blessing, to represent a "special category of performative utterances." See also his *Promise and Prayer: The Biblical Writings in the Light of Speech-Act Theory* (Eugene, OR; Cascade Books, 2020), 13–15, 79.

52. This was already the tendency in antiquity. See Sarah Iles Johnston, "Magic," in *Religions of the Ancient World: A Guide*, ed. Sarah Iles Johnston (Cambridge, MA: Belknap, 2004), 139–52 (here 140).

53. Cf. John W. Hilber, "Prophecy, Divination, and Magic in the Ancient Near East," in *Behind the Scenes of the Old Testament*, ed. Jonathan S. Greer, John W. Hilber, and John H. Walton (Grand Rapids: Baker Academic, 2018), 368–74 (here 369).

weakens the biblical understanding of blessing, in which blessing does possess genuine power.[54]

There is a ditch on either side of this road. On the one side is the impoverished modern understanding of blessing as just a nice thing to say.[55] On the other side is the robust but quasi-magical notion of blessing perhaps most familiar today from prosperity gospel teaching. In this type of ecclesial context, blessings are celebrated and advocated as a practical means of creating new personal outcomes, whether in the form of health or love or success or wealth. "Name it and claim it" is a familiar motto in this part of the contemporary church. Believers are encouraged to understand that God has given them a power to control what happens to them in their lives, and they are sometimes chastised or made to feel guilty for not taking full advantage of that power.[56]

Against the nonperformative notion of blessing is the Hebrew jussive itself, along with those biblical stories in which blessings are portrayed as having reality-altering effects. Indeed, the Balaam stories, appearing later in the book of Numbers (Num. 22–24), highlight the genuine power of blessing and identify its source as the God of Israel, even when the blessing is spoken by a foreign prophet.[57] In the story about Jacob and Esau in Gen. 27, the blessings of Isaac are not only considered to be determinative for the respective futures of his two sons, they are also treated as irrevocable and objective. Like words of prophecy, they cannot be taken back (e.g., Gen. 27:35–37; cf. Num. 23:20). In line with these examples, a blessing is not merely an expression of goodwill or a future intention.

---

54. It is possible that the traditional magic word "abracadabra"—already known and used in ancient Rome—was derived from the Hebrew phrase *ha-brakah dabrah* (seemingly meaning something about saying a blessing). See Don C. Skemer, *Binding Words: Textual Amulets in the Middle Ages* (University Park: Pennsylvania State University Press, 2006), 25. There are other etymological possibilities.

55. Emily R. Brink, "Make Me a Blessing: Benedictions Are More Than Pious Wishes," *RW* 19 (1991): 2–3.

56. Some Christians invoke biblical verses like Deut. 8:18; 28:11; Ps. 37:4; and Rom. 11:29 in support of this idea. For an illuminating study, see Kate Bowler, *Blessed: A History of the American Prosperity Gospel* (New York: Oxford University Press, 2013).

57. See Forsling, *Theology of the Book of Numbers*, chap. 7.

It is a word of power that identifies and ratifies a God-originated reality.[58] Yet biblical blessings are not free-floating incantations for personal gain or professional advancement either. Blessings in the Old Testament are primarily for Israel as God's chosen people. In this sense, blessings articulate and reinforce Israel's election (Deut. 28:1–2).[59] They are closely associated with Israel's covenantal understanding. Individuals are blessed because they are members of Israel or because they are contributing in some fashion to God's destiny for Israel within the world.

So ultimately the difference between blessing and magic is not purely linguistic or conceptual but theological.[60] Blessing freely shares incantatory features with magic.[61] What sets blessing apart from magic in the biblical tradition is that blessing does not attempt to wrest power from God. It instead seeks to *participate* in God's power.[62] Biblical blessing occurs at God's direction and in God's name. God remains the guarantor of blessing, even though the blessing itself is uttered by a human speaker. Conversely, although God is the ultimate source of blessing, the role of the human speaker remains crucial, bold, and necessary. In some mysterious fashion, the human speaker cooperates with God, but only because God ordains and enables the act of doing so.[63] God is fully able to use what humans view as magic—for example, Jacob's rods in Gen. 30:37–43 (cf. 30:27); Joseph's cup in Gen. 44:5; Moses's serpent in Exod. 7:8–12; the *magi* in Matt. 2:1–12; Paul's handkerchiefs in Acts 19:11–12. Even some of Jesus's actions were apparently viewed as magical acts (e.g., Luke 11:14–23; cf. Matt. 8:16; Mark 1:32–34;

---

58. Martin Luther, "Genesis, Chapters 26–30," in *Luther's Works (American Edition)*, vol. 5., trans. George V. Schick and Paul D. Pahl, ed. Jaroslav Pelikan (St. Louis: Concordia, 1968), 140: "In Holy Scripture, however, there are real blessings. They are more than mere wishes. They state facts and are effective. They actually bestow and bring what the words say."

59. Seebass, "YHWH's Name," 42.

60. Which is only to agree that "magic" is ultimately a normative and not an exclusively descriptive term; on this point, see Johnson, "Magic," 141.

61. Cf. Daniel Miller, "Another Look at the Magic Ritual for a Suspected Adulteress in Numbers 5:11–31," *Magic, Ritual, and Witchcraft* 5, no. 1 (2010): 1–16.

62. Andrew Davison, *Blessing*, Faith Going Deeper (Norwich: Canterbury, 2014), 23–24.

63. Frettlöh, *Theologie des Segens*, 378–403.

9:25; Luke 4:31–37).[64] After all, God can enlist any kind of human practice to communicate and redeem (e.g., 1 Sam. 28). In both the Old Testament and the New, there is a close link between divine power and human use of the divine name (e.g., Acts 4:7, 30).[65] God is the one who acts, but human figures may invite God's actions by pronouncing the name of God.

The Priestly Blessing illustrates this dynamic not only by beginning each of its three blessing statements with God's name, but also by its framing as priestly instruction: "Thus you shall bless. . . . You shall say to them . . ." (Num. 6:23). The act of pronouncing the Priestly Blessing is an act of faithful obedience rather than a Promethean effort to purloin cosmic power for the self.

There is a closeness at this point to other biblical commands, especially those that issue forth into liturgy and spiritual practices. The Lord's Supper is viewed as a response to Jesus's injunction to "do this" (Luke 22:19). Lots of other things happen in the Lord's Supper from a liturgical or sociological or anthropological point of view. But Christians engage in the practice primarily as an expression of obedience to their Lord. They do it because Christ said to do it. The well-known magical formula "hocus pocus" is sometimes said to have arisen from mishearing the Latin phrase *hoc est corpus meum* (this is my body) in the medieval Eucharist.[66] The turning of bread and wine into the body and blood of Jesus Christ could understandably be viewed, from an external vantage point, as an instance of magic.[67] If the Eucharist is magic, however, then it is divine magic. It is "magic" that God in Jesus Christ authorizes and performs. The difference between magic and miracle is not exclusively in the event itself or the language used to describe it, but in the source of the event and the One who guides

---

64. Morton Smith, *Jesus the Magician* (San Francisco: Harper & Row, 1978); Graham H. Twelftree, "Jesus, Magician or Miracle Worker?," *BibAn* 10, no. 3 (2020): 405–36. On magic in early Christianity, see David E. Aune, *Apocalypticism, Prophecy and Magic in Early Christianity: Collected Essays*, WUNT 199 (Tübingen: Mohr Siebeck, 2006), 385–401.

65. Aune, *Apocalypticism, Prophecy and Magic*, 407–11. The story of the sons of Sceva in Acts 19:13–16 provides further evidence for this connection and a warning about its limits.

66. There are alternative explanations.

67. Morton Smith, *Jesus the Magician*, 122.

its unfolding. The identity of the Guarantor of Israel's blessing creates a distinction in how its blessing-magic should be understood.

Rather than the power of brute force, the power of blessing is subjunctive power. Blessing invites, appeals, encourages, summons, confesses, and persuades. Blessing does not constrain, force, oblige, compel, dictate, or impose. Cynthia Jarvis has suggested that this type of subjunctive stance is instructive for all of Christian ministry. "Mastering" divinity is, after all, the purest arrogance, and the gendered implication of the terminology ("master") should therefore occasion no surprise.[68] By contrast, Jarvis describes ministry in the subjunctive as characterized not so much by assured truths and ironclad doctrines but by "faith and hope and the kenotic work of love that is the Incarnation."[69] For Jarvis, the subjunctive aspect of ministry emerges mostly as an ability to embrace uncertainty and doubt in contrast to insisting on indicative facts. As she relates it, even Christian truths like the resurrection require a new understanding of what may be real and objective, so that there is a counterfactual quality to them. Ministry imagines the whole world "otherwise."[70] Faced with the brokenness of the world and the reality of evil, the faithful can nevertheless perceive hints that damage and decay are not ultimate truths, and that a deeper reality exists behind present appearances, or even within those appearances—a spiritual reality seeking to break forth and flourish.

Yet God will not use brute force to achieve such ends. John Caputo has similarly written of "the subjunctive power of God," of how coercion is profane and therefore *cannot* be God's power.[71] He summarizes:

> The kingdom of God does not exist; it *insists*. The kingdom of God does not exist; it calls. It is what is being dreamt of, prayed for, called

---

68. Cynthia A. Jarvis, "Ministry in the Subjunctive Mood," *ThTo* 66 (2010): 445–58. While Jarvis acknowledges that she has known men in ministry who have favored a subjunctive style, she argues that women in ministry are more likely to adopt such an approach.
69. Jarvis, "Ministry in the Subjunctive Mood," 448.
70. Jarvis, "Ministry in the Subjunctive Mood," 446. Cf. John S. McClure, *Otherwise Preaching: A Postmodern Ethic for Homiletics* (St. Louis: Chalice, 2001).
71. John D. Caputo, "The Subjunctive Power of God," *Concilium* 3 (2020): 12–21.

for. . . . The realm of God does not refer to a *different world* but to a poetic vision of how *this world* would be *different*, how it *would look*, in the subjunctive, if the powerless power of God held sway.[72]

Blessing does not force, and neither should ministry force, because God does not force. Rather than reflecting a lack of certitude or conviction, this resistance to force is in place because God has given human beings the gift of freedom. God does desire obedience, but only a willing obedience. God will not enforce the divine purpose in any way that obliterates, diminishes, or negates human freedom (Gal. 5:1). This freedom must have great value in the eyes of God because its cost seems quite steep. The price of human freedom is human sin and the brokenness of the world.

In sum, blessing must be understood as performative speech—against the idea that a blessing is only an encouraging word. Blessing can even be considered a kind of magic, so long as it is understood to be *God's* magic. Blessing is an invitation to participate in God's ongoing work of redemption, not a human effort to force God's hand. For this reason, it is helpful to imagine that the word "may" stands at the head of the Priestly Blessing and introduces each of the following five clauses.[73] "*May* the LORD bless you. The subjunctive quality of the Priestly Blessing signals that God's blessing is being faithfully invoked. The priestly blessers are in effect saying, "We make bold to convey Your blessing to this people." Thanks to God's promissory faithfulness, and God's faithfulness alone, this blessing can be spoken and heard in full confidence that what it affirms comes with a divine guarantee.

▪ "The LORD"

God's name appears at the beginning of each of the three phrases in the Priestly Blessing. Many people think of the word "God" as

---

72. Caputo, "Subjunctive Power of God," 19 (emphasis original).
73. As in David Noel Freedman, "The Aaronic Benediction (Numbers 6:24–26)," in *No Famine in the Land: Studies in Honor of John L. McKenzie*, ed. James W. Flanagan and Anita Weisbrod Robinson (Missoula, MT: Scholars Press, 1975), 35–48. Also Milgrom, *Numbers*, 51.

God's name, so it bears reminding that "God" is not actually a name but a generic term.[74] In English, it is conventionally capitalized when it refers to the God of the Bible or the God of Jews and Christians, because then it denotes a particular deity. But although people pray to "God," that is not God's personal name.[75] God's name is YHWH.

In what follows, I will spend some time discussing the latest scholarship on the history of this name and early YHWH-belief in ancient Israel. My goal is not to seek "the answer" to the historical question of YHWH's origin or an essence of YHWH-belief to be used as a key in unlocking the meaning of the Priestly Blessing. My hope is instead to: (1) sketch the contours of current knowledge for pastors and other readers who are interested in these questions but do not know where to learn about them; (2) remind readers that YHWH-belief did emerge and develop historically, even while underscoring the genuine limitations of present historical knowledge about it; (3) counter persisting misperceptions of the nature of the divine name and the character of YHWH-belief; (4) emphasize the centrality of the divine name to the distinctive character of Old Testament theology; and (5) amplify what it means to say that YHWH is God's personal name. I will then argue that this name lies at the heart of the Priestly Blessing and is ultimately its most important feature. But it remains the case that the full significance of the divine name is to be found not in its history or etymology but in its biblical usage.

A prime component of Old Testament teaching is that God does indeed have a personal name, and that this name is more than a historical accident. This name, as related in at least one biblical tradition, was not always known by Israel (Exod. 6:2–3; but cf. Gen. 4:26). In time, God revealed God's name as a gift. The classic narrative

---

74. For discussion of how this situation arose historically and what its theological implications are, see Ingolf U. Dalferth and Philipp Stoellger, "Einleitung: Die Namen Gottes, 'Gott' als Name und der Name Gottes," in *Gott Nennen: Gottes Namen und Gott als Name*, ed. Ingolf U. Dalferth and Philipp Stoellger, Religion and Philosophy and Theology 35 (Tübingen: Mohr Siebeck, 2008), 1–20, esp. 14–17. The basic problem is that "God" has become an abstraction and that utilizing a proper name for God, despite the importance of this idea in the biblical tradition, is no longer thought to be necessary or even appropriate.

75. "God" (*'ĕlōhîm*) can be used as a proper name in the Bible, as it is today. But it is not presented in the Bible as God's personal name.

account of the revelation of God's name occurs in the episode of the burning bush, when Moses encounters God on Mount Horeb (Exod. 3:1–4:17). This story turns on how Moses already knows of God as "the God of your ancestors" (3:13), "the God of Abraham, the God of Isaac, and the God of Jacob" (3:6, 15), but not as YHWH, the name that God now gives to Moses and, through Moses, to Israel.

Excursus on Y(a)HW(e)H

The consonantal name YHWH is typically transcribed in full as "Yahweh" because of ancient evidence for this vowel pattern. Neo-Babylonian and Achaemenid vocalizations render the name as *ia-a-ḫu-û* and *ia-a-ma*.[76] Some later Greek and Latin spellings are similar: for example, Clement of Alexandria gives the name in Greek as *Iaoue* (*Stromata* V 6.34.5).[77] Yet the available evidence is less than conclusive. It is usually thought that the Masoretic Text of the Hebrew Bible adds the vowels for the Hebrew word *'ădōnāy* (the Lord) to the consonants Y-H-W-H (known as the Tetragram) as a signal that the divine name should not be pronounced aloud, and that *Adonai* should be spoken instead. For this reason, most English translations render YHWH as Lord, but this convention also hides the term YHWH. Bible readers need to remember that YHWH probably appears in the Hebrew text whenever Lord (capital/small capitals) appears in their English Bibles. Misunderstanding the Hebrew reading convention led to a mixed form consisting of the consonants of the Tetragram plus the vowels of *Adonai* (= "Jehovah"; *Y* became *J* because of German-language influence, and the initial short *a* changed to an *e* vowel due to the *J* consonant).[78] Recent historical evidence indicates that an even earlier substitution for YHWH was Aramaic *šəmā'* (name; cf. *haššēm* in Lev. 24:11; cf. 24:16).[79] Many modern Jews continue this tradition by

---

76. See Josef Tropper, "The Divine Name *Yahwa*," in *The Origins of Yahwism*, ed. Jürgen van Oorshot and Markus Witte, BZAW 484 (Berlin: De Gruyter, 2017), 1–21.

77. For further examples, see Martin Rose, *Jahwe: Zum Streit um den alttestamentlichen Gottesname* (Zurich: Theologischer Verlag, 1978), 6–16.

78. Karel van der Toorn, "Yahweh," *DDD*, 910–19 (here 910).

79. See Kristin de Troyer, "The Pronunciation of the Names of God," in *Gott Nennen: Gottes Namen und Gott als Name*, ed. Ingolf U. Dalferth and Philipp Stoellger,

saying the Hebrew term *ha-Shem* (the Name) instead of pronouncing YHWH out loud. A great reluctance to speak the name YHWH or write it out in full continues to exist within contemporary Judaism. Many non-Jews also avoid doing so and thereby giving unintended offense. Partly for that reason, I avoid vocalizing the Tetragram when possible. I also avoid it, however, because I think the reticence serves as an important reminder not to be cavalier with God's name. I always remember the comment of a rabbi after she met with my divinity students. "They speak very casually of God," she said. Should we really be so free in stating what we believe God "thinks" and "wants"?[80]

The burning bush story also interprets the name YHWH, but its interpretation is just that: an interpretation, a play on words, rather than a genuine definition or etymology of the name. The phrase "I am who I am" treats YHWH as if it is a verbal form based on the Hebrew root *h-y-h*, "to be." YHWH would presumably be a third-person singular verbal form ("he is" or "he will be"), and yet in this passage the name is paralleled with a first-person form of the same verb. The literal result is God's self-declaration "I am 'I am.'" Moses is to tell the Israelites that this "I am" has sent him (Exod. 3:14).

In Exod. 3–4, knowledge of God's personal name is treated as both a special revelation and an empowering gift. God's name YHWH is a divinely provided sign that will embolden the Israelites and strengthen them in their quest for freedom from Egyptian bondage. They are to petition for their liberation using this name of God (3:16–18). The name YHWH is thus associated from the outset with Israel's desire for justice and God's promise of freedom. If "the God of your ancestors" (3:13) broadly aligns with land, family, and the past, the name

---

Religion in Philosophy and Theology 35 (Tübingen: Mohr Siebeck, 2008), 143–72 (here 145).

80. For further reflection, see R. Kendall Soulen, "'Hallowed Be Thy Name!': The Theological Significance of the Avoidance of God's Name in the New Testament," in *Strangers in a Strange Land: A Festschrift in Honor of Bruce C. Birch upon His Retirement as Academic Dean of Wesley Theological Seminary*, ed. Lucy Lind Hogan and D. William Faupel (Lexington: Emeth, 2009), 145–49; Johanna W. H. van Wijk-Bos, "Writing on Water: The Ineffable Name of God," in *Jews, Christians, and the Theology of the Hebrew Scriptures*, ed. Alice Ogden Bellis and Joel Kaminsky, SymS 8 (Atlanta: Society of Biblical Literature, 2000), 45–59.

YHWH carries with it the spirit of social change, a new land, and an expanded sense of peoplehood.

Remarkably, these narrative associations with the name YHWH mirror certain findings that have emerged from historical investigation. There are still genuine puzzles. Why are there not any ancient place names (toponyms) in the land of Israel which include the name (or part of the name) YHWH?[81] A number of place names containing references to other gods like 'El or Ba'al exist (e.g., Beth-el, "the house of 'El"). It is especially strange that "Israel" is formed with 'El's name rather than YHWH's.[82] And why is there no definitive evidence for a deity named YHWH outside the land of Israel?[83] Despite an intensive search, YHWH-belief appears to have been unique to ancient Israel and, unlike belief in other deities in the ancient Near Eastern pantheon, not shared across multiple cultures and people groups.[84] Even so, the lack of YHWH-formulated toponyms does suggest that YHWH-belief came into the land of Israel from someplace else.

The nonindigenous character of YHWH-belief is especially strange now that archaeological work has moved in the direction of viewing the ancient Israelites themselves as indigenous to the land of Canaan. Older views of Israel's emergence in the land tended to endorse in varying degrees the main narrative thread of the Pentateuch and Joshua, in which the early Israelites mostly came to Canaan from Egypt, and more or less at one time as part of a unified military campaign. But the material culture of early Israelite communities has been shown to be more akin to Canaanite culture than different from it. Today, archaeologists work with a basic presumption that Israel

---

81. Martin Leuenberger, "YHWH's Provenance from the South," in *The Origins of Yahwism*, ed. Jürgen van Oorschot and Markus Witte, BZAW 484 (Berlin: De Gruyter, 2017), 157–79 (here 163): "There is no Yahwistic toponym from Palestine at all."

82. Jörg Jeremias, "Three Theses on the Early History of Israel," in *The Origins of Yahwism*, ed. Jürgen van Oorschot and Markus Witte, BZAW 484 (Berlin: De Gruyter, 2017), 145–56 (here 145).

83. Lester L. Grabbe, "'Many Nations Will Be Joined to Yhwh in That Day': The Question of Yhwh outside Judah," in *Religious Diversity in Ancient Israel and Judah*, ed. Francesca Stavrakopoulou and John Barton (London: T&T Clark, 2010), 175–87.

84. For a discussion of some possible references outside of Israel, see Robert D. Miller II, *Yahweh: Origin of a Desert God*, FRLANT 284 (Göttingen: Vandenhoeck & Ruprecht, 2018), 69–78.

was formed by multiple streams of events over a lengthier period of time, and that the early Israelites were, for the most part, Canaanites.[85] Even stranger, then, that these indigenous Canaanite-Israelites possessed an imported deity. Despite occasional suggestions to the contrary, there is no clear indication of YHWH in the earlier Canaanite culture of Ugarit either.[86] So, just as in the Exodus account, there appears to be less of a link between Israel's God and the land of Israel than is standard in other cultures in the ancient Near East.[87]

It is frequently speculated, however, that YHWH may have been known earlier in northwestern Arabia. Two Egyptian temple inscriptions, one at the temple of Soleb from the time of Amenhotep III (ca. 1370 BCE) and another from the temple of Amara-West from the time of Ramses II (ca. 1250 BCE), include references to "Yahu in the land of the Shasu" and "the land of the Shasu of Yahu."[88] In both instances, the reference is usually thought to be to a place name "Yahu" rather than the name of a deity.[89] But a reference to a deity, perhaps as an expansion of a place name (or vice versa), cannot be ruled out. One of the main theories of YHWH's origins suggests that Yahu, which apparently refers to an area somewhere to the southeast of the land of Israel, in the region of Midian, became identified with a certain deity who later migrated into Israelite territory and culture.[90] The Exodus account provides indirect evidence for this reconstruction

---

85. Christian Frevel, *History of Ancient Israel*, ABS 32 (Atlanta: SBL Press, 2023), 75–76.

86. Grabbe, "Many Nations," 178.

87. One hint of such an understanding may exist in Deut. 32:8–9. Here it is ʿElyôn (the Most High) who has established the nations' boundaries and their respective deities, even as YHWH is professed to be the deity assigned to Jacob. The designation ʿElyôn may have originally referred to ʾEl, but here it has been largely subsumed into a Yahwistic framework.

88. Leuenberger, "YHWH's Provenance," 169. It has long been supposed that the desert bedouin known as Shasu could represent one of the ancestral groups from which the Israelites emerged.

89. Van der Toorn, "Yahweh," 910–11. For problems with the place name reading, see Faried Adrom and Matthias Müller, "The Tetragrammaton in Egyptian Sources: Facts and Fiction," in *The Origins of Yahwism*, ed. Jürgen van Oorschot and Markus Witte, BZAW 484 (Berlin: De Gruyter, 2017), 93–113.

90. On the challenge of locating Midian geographically, see R. Miller, *Yahweh*, 23–24. He argues for an area clustered around the Gulf of Aqaba and extending east from there.

by relating how Jethro, Moses's father-in-law, was a priest of Midian (Exod. 2:16; 3:1; 18:1). Interestingly, Jethro is presented as being highly receptive to YHWH (Exod. 18:8–12) or possibly as having already been a committed YHWH worshiper even before Moses's arrival in Midian.[91]

The southern provenance of YHWH is also supported by scattered references throughout the Hebrew Bible to Edom and Seir as YHWH's home (esp. Deut. 33:2; Judg. 5:4–5; Ps. 68:7–8 [8–9H]; Hab. 3:3). These biblical references are matched by the inscriptional references to "Yahweh of Teman" found at Kuntillet ʿAjrud.[92] Such evidence reinforces the likelihood of a Midianite origin for YHWH, sometimes known as the "Kenite hypothesis."[93] (According to Judg. 1:16 and 4:11, the Kenites were the part of the Midianite people group to which Jethro, known in this tradition by the alternate name Hobab, had belonged; cf. Num. 10:29.[94]) There is also evidence for widespread trading activity by Midianite caravanners (e.g., Gen. 37:28), who could well provide the missing historical link between YHWH's Midianite origins and YHWH-belief in the land of Israel.[95] Another possible pathway might have existed via copper mining and the trade in precious metals.[96] There remains as well the biblical testimony to a familial link between Jethro and Moses, and it is entirely possible that the introduction of YHWH into Israelite culture was transmitted through tribal relationships and personal interactions—but such a

---

91. The biblical text does not explicitly describe Jethro as a priest of YHWH, but Moses's encounter with YHWH in Midian suggests complementarity rather than conflict with regard to the religious beliefs of Jethro.

92. Van der Toorn, "Yahweh," 912. See Zeev Meshel, *Kuntillet ʿAjrud (Ḥorvat Teman): An Iron Age II Religious Site on the Judah-Sinai Border* (Jerusalem: Israel Museum, 2012).

93. Joseph Blenkinsopp, "The Midianite-Kenite Hypothesis Revisited and the Origins of Judah," *JSOT* 33, no. 2 (2008): 131–53.

94. R. Miller, *Yahweh*, 30–41. Jeremias, "Three Theses," 146, points out that the Kenites are counted as Judahites in 1 Sam. 27:10; 30:29.

95. J. David Schloen, "Caravans, Kenites, and *Casus belli*: Enmity and Alliance in the Song of Deborah," *CBQ* 55, no. 1 (1993): 18–38.

96. See S. N. Amzallag, "Yahweh, the Canaanite God of Metallurgy," *JSOT* 33 (2009): 387–404; Erez Ben-Yosef, ed., *Mining for Ancient Copper: Essays in Memory of Beno Rothenberg* (University Park, PA: Eisenbrauns, 2018). In this connection, it is also of interest that the term "Kenite" is related to the word for "smith" and the name "Cain." See R. Miller, *Yahweh*, 25.

prospect moves beyond the type of history that can be reconstructed on the basis of archaeological and inscriptional evidence.[97]

If the YHWH tradition did come from the south,[98] it will affect how the name itself is understood. Usually, YHWH has been explained as either a basic (*qal*) or causative (*hiphil*) third masculine singular verbal form based on the Hebrew root *h-y-h* (or in early Hebrew *h-w-y*): either "he is/will be" or "he makes/causes to be."[99] But this sense of the verb, the kind on which the account in Exod. 3:13–15 is also based, imputes a West Semitic meaning to what is evidently a South Semitic verbal form.[100] For this reason, many scholars now look to Arabic for a better understanding of the divine name, and the leading possibility is "to blow" (cf. Syriac *hawwē*, "wind").[101] The form could still be basic or causative ("he blows" or "he causes to blow"). Either way, its meaning would match and reinforce the early biblical profile of YHWH as a storm god (e.g., Judg. 5:4–5; Pss. 18:6–15 [7–16H]; 68:7–8 [8–9H]), with "blow" being understood to relate to wind and other storm-like phenomena (rain, hail, thunder, etc.).

The earliest phases of YHWH-belief and YHWH's introduction into Israelite culture are thus veiled in mystery. Indeed, it is possible, even likely, that the ancient Israelites themselves may not have known what the word "YHWH" originally meant or how earlier YHWH-worship had been conducted. But by the time of the Israelite monarchy there are signs that YHWH had become established as Israel's official, if not exclusive, deity. A lack of complete exclusivity is apparent both from the many biblical narratives that detail conflicts arising from the worship of multiple deities within Israel, and

---

97. For an investigation into the history of YHWH with similar conclusions, see Friedhelm Hartenstein, "Die Geschichte JHWHs im Spiegel seiner Name," in *Gott Nennen: Gottes Namen und Gott als Name*, ed. Ingolf U. Dalferth and Philipp Stoellger, Religion in Philosophy and Theology 35 (Tübingen: Mohr Siebeck, 2008), 73–95.

98. There presently appears to be a fairly strong consensus favoring YHWH's southern origin. The main holdouts are representatives of what is sometimes called a "Berlin school" favoring either an origin in Jerusalem itself or in the northern Levant/Syria. See Leuenberger, "YHWH's Provenance," 159–60.

99. R. Miller, *Yahweh*, 18. For an argument that YHWH is instead a nominal form, see Tropper, "Divine Name."

100. Van der Toorn, "Yahweh," 915; Ernst Axel Knauf, "Yahwe," *VT* 34 (1984): 467–72.

101. Van der Toorn, "Yahweh," 916.

from the tradition of YHWH's *desire for* exclusivity. Thus, the name YHWH is paralleled with the name Jealous (Exod. 34:14, "his name is Jealous," *qannā' šəmô*; cf. Exod. 20:5//Deut. 5:9). Even the commandment not to have any other gods "before me" (lit., "before my face," *ʿal-pānāy*) in Exod. 20:3//Deut. 5:7 presumes that worshiping other gods is a real possibility. Yet the official status of YHWH-belief is not only registered by biblical references to YHWH as the God of Israel (Deut. 32:8–9), but also the prevalence of personal names with Yahwistic elements during the monarchic period.[102]

Moreover, there is eventually a heightened theological understanding of YHWH's name itself—of the fact that YHWH has a name and can be represented by it. This understanding is particularly emphasized in the book of Deuteronomy. The core of that book, basically Deut. 12–26, was long thought to have been the product and expression of a religious reform movement during the seventh-century reign of King Josiah. It was held to be the "book of the law" that had been discovered when repairs were made on the Jerusalem temple (2 Kings 22–23).[103] This reconstruction has now unraveled, partly because the archaeological evidence for a widespread reform of worship practices is lacking,[104] and partly because the historical accuracy of the account in Kings has itself been called into question.[105] Deuteronomy not only insists on the centralization of all sacrificial worship in Jerusalem (Deut. 12), it also promotes an apparently new understanding of the temple as the house of—not God per se—but God's *name*. For Deuteronomy, God's name is the form of God's presence residing in the Jerusalem temple.

Within historical-critical Old Testament scholarship, a basic difference has accordingly been postulated between Priestly and

---

102. Jeffrey H. Tigay, *You Shall Have No Other Gods: Israelite Religion in the Light of Hebrew Inscriptions*, HSS 31 (Atlanta: Scholars Press, 1986).

103. See Paul B. Harvey Jr. and Baruch Halpern, "W. M. L. de Wette's 'Dissertatio Critica . . .': Context and Translation," *ZABR* 14 (2008): 47–85.

104. See Lisbeth S. Fried, "The High Places (*bāmôt*) and the Reforms of Hezekiah and Josiah: An Archaeological Investigation," *JAOS* 122, no. 3 (2002): 437–65.

105. Juha Pakkala, "Why the Cult Reforms in Judah Probably Did Not Happen," in *One God–One Cult–One Nation: Archaeological and Biblical Perspectives*, ed. Reinhard G. Kratz and Hermann Spieckermann, BZAW 405 (Berlin: De Gruyter, 2010), 201–35.

non-Priestly, especially Deuteronomic, views of divine presence. The classic statement was that of Gerhard von Rad, who distinguished between, on the one hand, a Priestly tradition in which the God of Israel had a form and could be seen, and, on the other hand, a Deuteronomic tradition that rejected both the idea that God had a form and the notion that God could be apprehended visually.

In von Rad's account, the book of Deuteronomy not only sought to centralize Israelite worship, it intended to purify Israelite worship with a heightened, more abstract, view of God's presence. As he puts it: "Deuteronomy is replacing the old crude idea of Jahweh's presence and dwelling at the shrine by a theologically sublimated idea."[106] For von Rad, Deuteronomy marks a transition in Israel's beliefs from an older, immanent conception of God to a transcendent one. In the Deuteronomic program of worship reform, the temple's holy of holies would not feature any sort of cult statue; instead, it would hold the ark of the covenant containing God's words, the tablets with the Ten Commandments (Deut. 10:1–2). Indeed, what the Deuteronomists did was to replace older notions of YHWH's visible form with the name of God as a divine symbol and substitute. As such, the name represented a *reduced* understanding of God's presence from what had obtained previously, according to von Rad.[107]

Here a key chapter is Deut. 4, which many critical scholars regard as a series of later supplements to the earlier base text of Deuteronomy.[108] Deuteronomy 4 retells the Sinai event, insisting that the Israelites "saw no form" of God but only heard "the sound of words" as God spoke "out of the fire" (v. 12). The fire-motif in this passage corresponds to the divine fire-tradition of ancient Near Eastern theophanies (cf. Deut. 9:3; Ps. 97:3; Isa. 30:27, 33; 33:11; 65:5).[109] The

---

106. Gerhard von Rad, *Studies in Deuteronomy*, SBT 9 (London: SCM, 1953), 38–39.
107. But see Ian Wilson, "Merely a Container? The Ark in Deuteronomy," in *Temple and Worship in Biblical Israel*, ed. John Day, LHBOTS 422 (New York: T&T Clark, 2007), 212–49.
108. For an overview, see Knut Holter, "Literary Studies of Deut 4: Some Criteriological Remarks," *BN* 81 (1996): 91–103.
109. *Pace* Ian Wilson, *Out of the Midst of the Fire: Divine Presence in Deuteronomy*, SBLDS 151 (Atlanta: Scholars Press, 1995).

shapeliness of idols, which Israel is commanded to avoid, appears to be pitted against the shapelessness of YHWH (Deut. 4:15–19).

Of particular interest has been the "name formula" used seven times in Deuteronomy in relation to a central worship site (apparently the Jerusalem temple): "to put his name there to dwell" (*lāśûm 'et-šəmô šām ləšiknô*, Deut. 12:5) or "to establish his name there" (*ləšakkēn šəmô šām*, Deut. 12:11; 14:23; 16:2, 6, 11; 26:2). The first version of the formula is similar to the one in the concluding instruction of the Priestly Blessing (Num. 6:27) in that it employs the same Hebrew verb (*ś-y-m*, "put") and noun (*šēm*, "name"). However, the formula lacks the prepositional phase beginning with *'al* ("on the Israelites"). The Deuteronomic language, especially in the second formula, echoes a well-known cultic expression with Near Eastern linguistic cognates, designating the establishment of a cultic site.[110] For the Deuteronomic tradition it is God's name that not only establishes but dwells within the Jerusalem temple. This name is how God's presence is mediated to human worshipers.

The divine name tradition reverberates in later Deuteronomistic passages like 1 Kings 9:3, God's response to Solomon's construction of the first Jerusalem temple: "I consecrate this house that you have built, to put my name there forever [*lāśûm-šəmî šām 'ad-'ôlām*]; my eyes and my heart will be there for all the days [*kŏl-hayyāmîm*]." However, this passage actually undercuts von Rad's case that name theology offers a more abstract, distancing account of God's presence, because it parallels God's name with God's eyes and heart, as if they are synonymous.[111] A similar equation of God's name and God's personal presence appears in the account of Manasseh's idolatry in 2 Kings 21:4–7. There God's name as resident in the temple is endangered by the introduction of a physical cult statue of Asherah, suggesting they are equivalent competitors. Such passages support a

---

110. For the history of scholarship and further discussion, see Sandra L. Richter, *The Deuteronomistic History and the Name Theology: lᵉšakkēn šᵉmô šām in the Bible and the Ancient Near East*, BZAW 318 (Berlin: De Gruyter, 2002). Richter argues that the language indicates divine ownership rather than divine presence (with the possible exception of 1 Kings 8). However, the two need not be mutually exclusive.

111. Angelika Berlejung, "Divine Presence and Absence," in *The Oxford Handbook of Ritual and Worship in the Hebrew Bible*, ed. Samuel E. Balentine (New York: Oxford University Press, 2020), 355.

view that God's name is not conceived in the Deuteronomic tradition as less than God but in fact as God's real presence.[112]

Name Theology

Rather than a lesser divine replacement, as von Rad would have it, the divine name in the temple is presented by Deuteronomy as a theophanic manifestation, a divine hypostasis.[113] In this regard, it is worth noting that Deut. 4 does not actually say that God has no form, only that the people gathered at Sinai could not see it. It is an important distinction, echoed in other biblical witnesses (Exod. 24:9–11; Num. 12:8; 1 Kings 22:19; Ps. 17:15; Isa. 6:1–5; Ezek. 1:26–28; Amos 9:1). Moreover, it is not as if the people see nothing. They see God's "great fire," explicitly described as a localized and material appearance of God on earth while God is speaking from heaven (Deut. 4:36).[114] Rather than a diminished substitute, the name of God functions in Deuteronomy as a concentrated expression of divine presence and power.[115]

The counterargument emphasizes a number of references in Deuteronomy to God as residing in the heavens (Deut. 4:36; 26:15; cf.

---

112. Theodore J. Lewis, *The Origin and Character of God: Ancient Israelite Religion through the Lens of Divinity* (New York: Oxford University Press, 2020), 385.

113. I use "hypostasis" to mean an essential form of a deity but not a separate deity. To be fair, von Rad, *Studies in Deuteronomy*, 38–39, says that the name conception in Deuteronomy "verges closely upon a hypostasis." But he resists the notion of a full hypostasis because he views the Deuteronomic understanding of God to be a corrective to older, anthropomorphic accounts of the divine in which God was present without remainder. By contrast, see A. D. H. Mayes, *Deuteronomy*, NCB (London: Oliphants, 1979), 59–60: "The name and the reality signified thereby are not distinguishable; when Yahweh is said to have caused his name to dwell at a sanctuary, the intention is to indicate the real and effective presence of Yahweh himself at that sanctuary." Cf. Charles A. Gieschen, "The Divine Name in Ante-Nicene Christology," *VC* 57, no. 2 (2003): 115–58 (123); Roberto Ouro, "Divine Presence Theology versus Name Theology in Deuteronomy," *AUSS* 52, no. 1 (2014): 5–29.

114. Lewis, *Origin and Character of God*, 384; I. Wilson, *Out of the Midst*, 92–93.

115. Berlejung, "Divine Presence and Absence," 355: "Surely not a downgrade of YHWH's divine presence but a full embodiment of his essence (1 Kgs 9:3)." Berlejung also holds, however, that name theology "de-materializes YHWH's presence," and that is less clear to me.

1 Kings 8:30, 32, 34, 36, 39, 43, 45, 49; cf. 8:22, 54).[116] Some scholars have interpreted this motif as expressing a conviction that God is not in two places at once, and on this basis they have again understood Deuteronomy as promoting a more abstract deity. Yet a verse like Deut. 4:36 ("From heaven he made you hear his voice to discipline you. On earth he showed you his great fire, while you heard his words coming out of the fire") demonstrates that God could be conceived as living in heaven and nevertheless taking on material earthly forms. What has frequently seemed to modernist scholars like an either/or was instead a both/and. Michael Hundley has reviewed the ancient Near Eastern evidence and concludes that YHWH was believed to be in heaven and on earth simultaneously, just as Amun was thought in Egypt to occupy various holy places at once and Baal to be present at his temples in Ugarit as well as in his storm cloud.[117] It bears reminding in this connection that "heaven" was not conceived as outside the created world but part of it (Gen. 1:1).

However, Hundley then treats the divine name as a divine *attribute*, concluding that the divine name functions as a metonym for God but not as a full and genuine hypostasis. In reaching this conclusion, Hundley stresses that the divine name in Deuteronomic tradition, much like the divine *kābôd* (glory) in Priestly tradition, can suggest God's presence but is also distinguishable from God.[118] He works with a part-for-the-whole understanding of metonymy,[119] suggesting that "name" refers to "some of the divine essence yet does not encapsulate the whole."[120] The one distinction he posits is that while the

---

116. In 1 Kings 8:22 and 54, Solomon's hands stretched out to heaven may also imply that heaven is God's place of residence.

117. Michael Hundley, "To Be or Not to Be: A Reexamination of Name Language in Deuteronomy and the Deuteronomistic History," *VT* 59 (2009): 533–55 (here 539–40n28). See also his *Gods in Dwellings: Temples and Divine Presence in the Ancient Near East* (Atlanta: Society of Biblical Literature, 2013).

118. Hundley, "To Be or Not to Be," 550–51.

119. Technically, synecdoche is the figure of speech that exploits the part-whole relationship; it is a subset of metonymy, in which other kinds of figural substitutions may be employed. See D. Brent Sandy, *Plowshares and Pruning Hooks: Rethinking the Language of Biblical Prophecy and Apocalyptic* (Downers Grove, IL: InterVarsity, 2002), 74. E.g., "he is a question mark" or "she has a short fuse" engages in metonymic substitution without invoking the part-whole logic of synecdoche.

120. Hundley, "To Be or Not to Be," 554.

divine name is conceived as being present in the temple, worshipers are never said to serve, sacrifice to, or bow down to the name, only to God.[121] However, parallel constructions in Deuteronomy and elsewhere weaken such a distinction between God's name and God.[122]

For Hundley, "name" is a conceptual abstraction, and so it represents an ambiguous understanding of God's presence.[123] The purpose of the abstraction is to preserve God's "ineffability."[124] Yet the opposite interpretation is more probably the case, especially if one considers how the divine name was traditionally understood in Judaism as *only* to be pronounced at the Jerusalem temple in the Priestly Blessing and by the high priest on the Day of Atonement (m. Yoma 6:2; m. Tamid 3:8; 7:2). The name of God was likely believed to reside at the temple (Jer. 7:12–14; Ezra 6:12; Neh. 1:9) because that is where the name was regularly spoken and heard.[125] In other words, the divine name was no abstraction but instead a marker of God's *effability*.

In fact, quite a bit of evidence exists for a hypostatic understanding of divine representations in the ancient Near East, including divine names as divine hypostases. As Theodore Lewis notes, the inclusion of the word for "name" *within* divine names would seem to supply definitive proof. So, for instance, there are deities such as 'Athartu-Name-of-Ba'lu in Ugarit, Name-of-'El at Kuntillet 'Ajrud, Eshem-Bethel in Elephantine, and the deity Ashima mentioned in 2 Kings 17:30.[126] Here the names of deities *are* deities. Human names can also feature the term "name" as a divine or theophoric element (e.g., Samuel = name of + 'El).[127]

The name of God appears in other parts of the Old Testament as a divine hypostasis as well. In Exod. 23:20–24, God's angel—itself a divine hypostasis, which will guide the Israelites into the promised

---

121. Hundley, "To Be or Not to Be," 551n74.
122. See Deut. 28:58; Exod. 34:14; 1 Chron. 16:29; Pss. 29:2; 66:4; 86:9; Jer. 3:17; 23:27. In Jer. 3:17, the NRSV translates "name of the Lord" as "presence of the Lord."
123. Hundley, "To Be or Not to Be," 552.
124. Hundley, "To Be or Not to Be," 553.
125. Gordon J. Wenham, "Deuteronomy and the Central Sanctuary," *TynBul* 22 (1971): 103–18.
126. Lewis, *Origin and Character of God*, 387.
127. Lewis, *Origin and Character of God*, 387.

land and whose voice is said to be the same as God's own (v. 22)—has God's name "in him" (*bəqirbô*, v. 21).[128] The three main theophanies in Exodus (the burning bush episode in Exod. 3–4, the Sinai revelation in Exod. 19–20, and the cleft of the rock encounter in Exod. 33–34) all feature a provision of YHWH's name (Exod. 3:14; 20:2; 33:19; 34:5–7). As Katherine Sonderegger insightfully perceives, "This Name is the great explosion at the very center of Scripture."[129]

Within the Priestly tradition, it is noteworthy that the frontlet worn on Aaron's forehead (Lev. 8:9) bears the inscription "holy to YHWH" (Exod. 28:36–38), leading to perceptions in the Second Temple period (i.e., the time of the postexilic Jerusalem temple) of both the divine name and the high priest as theophanic manifestations (cf. Sir. 45:6–22).[130] The high priest bore the names of Israel's twelve tribes on his jeweled chest plate and shoulder epaulets, which not only underscored the representative nature of the high priest's role but also transformed the priestly body into a priestly text.[131]

The clearest example of the divine name as a divine hypostasis is found in Isa. 30:27: "See the name of YHWH comes from far away, burning with his anger and in thick rising smoke." Here the divine name again possesses some of the traditional ancient Near Eastern characteristics of theophany (e.g., fire, smoke) and is even personified as the agent of an action (it "comes"; cf. Ps. 124:8; Prov. 18:10). Verses in the Old Testament referring to "the glory of his name" might also be considered (e.g., Pss. 29:2; 66:2; 96:8; cf. 1 Chron. 16:29). They combine the traditional theophanic term "glory" (*kābôd*) with "name," once more signaling that the presence of God's name is a theophanic manifestation of God's self.

References to the "name" of God are sometimes explained as euphemistic avoidances of God's actual name (as represented by the Tetragram). Historical-critical scholars have tended to locate the

---

128. See Jarl E. Fossum, *The Name of God and the Angel of the Lord*, WUNT 36 (Tübingen: Mohr Siebeck, 1985), 87–106.

129. Katherine Sonderegger, *Systematic Theology*, vol. 1, *The Doctrine of God* (Minneapolis: Fortress, 2015), 221.

130. Crispin H. T. Fletcher-Louis, *All the Glory of Adam: Liturgical Anthropology in the Dead Sea Scrolls*, STDJ 42 (Leiden: Brill, 2002), 93–94, 223–48.

131. Alice Mandell, "Writing as a Source of Ritual Authority: The High Priest's Body as a Priestly Text in the Tabernacle-Building Story," *JBL* 141, no. 1 (2022): 43–64.

custom of avoiding the utterance of God's name in the later Second Temple period, perhaps beginning in the third century BCE.[132] Prior to that point, the divine name was likely spoken aloud fairly commonly, even in daily greetings (e.g., Ruth 1:8–9; 2:4, 20; 1 Sam. 15:13; Ps. 129:8; cf. m. Berakhot 9:5). Its restriction appears to have been the result of a gradual and lengthy process. Over time, pronouncing the name became increasingly restricted.[133] As use of the divine name was limited, euphemisms for God became more prevalent.

Yet euphemistic usage is obviously not going on in Isa. 30:27, since "name" is used together *with* the Tetragram (*šēm-yhwh*) rather than as a substitute for it. In fact, the NJPS translation renders the phrase not as "the name of the LORD" but "the LORD Himself." Also of significance is how the compound subject "name of YHWH" is used in this verse in combination with the term *hinneh* (*hinnê šēm-yhwh*, "behold, the name of YHWH"), which could indicate something perceptible by the senses (cf. Isa. 56:6; 60:9).[134]

Indeed, a substantive distinction between God and God's name is difficult to draw on the basis of the canonical Old Testament witnesses. In Deut. 28:58, Moses enjoins his hearers to observe "all the words of this law that are written in this book, fearing this glorious and awesome name, the LORD your God." Not only is the term "name" followed here by the Tetragram as an explanatory or epexegetical specification (= "that is, YHWH your God"), the name itself is said to be "glorious and awesome." In the Psalms, praise is directed toward both YHWH and the name of YHWH as parallel terms. Thus, in Ps. 20: "The LORD answer you in the day of trouble! / The name of the God of Jacob protect you!" (v. 1 [2H]). Here protection or security (*ś-g-b*, *piel*, "to set securely on high") comes from

---

132. Berlejung, "Divine Presence and Absence," 355; cf. Gieschen, "Divine Name," 123.

133. Ephraim Urbach, *Sages: Their Concepts and Beliefs*, trans. Israel Abrahams (Cambridge, MA: Harvard University Press, 1979), 126–28. For additional evidence, see Hans Beitenhard, "*onoma*," *TDNT* 5:243–83 (here 268–69); Sean M. McDonough, *YHWH at Patmos: Rev. 1:4 in Its Hellenistic and Early Jewish Setting*, WUNT 2/107 (Tübingen: Mohr Siebeck, 1999), 58–122.

134. However, I have not been able to locate an instance in either Testament in which a *verb* of visual perception (e.g., "see") appears with God's name as its object (e.g., "to see the [divine] name"). Isa. 30:27 nevertheless comes close.

God's name. Or in Ps. 68, "Sing to God, sing praises to his name; / lift up a song to him who rides upon the clouds— / his name is the LORD— / be exultant before him" (v. 4 [5H]).[135] This last example is especially interesting because Ps. 68 is often considered to be a very early psalm. Its divine epithet "cloud rider" (*rkb ʿrpt*) appears in the Ugaritic literature as a standard epithet of Baal. In Ps. 69:30 (31H), the psalmist praises the name of God with a song. In Ps. 86:9, bowing down to YHWH and glorifying God's name again appear in synonymous parallelism. A final well-known example is Ps. 103: "Bless the LORD, O my soul, and all that is in me bless his holy name" (v. 1). In each of these instances, God's "name" is used as an alternative reference for God's self.

What becomes evident from this historical review is that the God of the Priestly Blessing is not, first of all, the "God of the philosophers," a heavenly inference imagined to be the best of all there is, but is instead the scandalously concrete and distinctive God of the Jews, a specific deity with whom one stands in an existential relation. In the words of Emil Brunner, "God is not an 'It' but a 'Thou' who addresses us."[136] The provision of God's name enables and invites such communication. But neither is this God a God who was simply "there" already, like the indigenous gods of Canaan (Hosea 2:8 [10H]).[137] The biblical presentation insists that God freely chose to establish a special form of communion with Israel; it was not an aboriginal, geographical bond.[138] Retaining a robust sense of God's holy name—even when it remains unspoken—is therefore crucial to biblical faith and perhaps the most important way that gentile Christians "take hold of a Jew, grasping his garment and saying 'Let us go with you, for we have

---

135. The translation "on the clouds," widely accepted, requires emending MT *bāʿărābôt* to *bāʿărāpôt*.

136. Emil Brunner, *The Christian Doctrine of God: Dogmatics*, vol. 1, trans. Olive Wyon (London: Lutterworth, 1949), 120.

137. Brunner, *Christian Doctrine of God*, 138. Brunner unfortunately then goes on to insist that once this point had been made in Israel's history, God's proper name could justifiably disappear.

138. For an effort to work this out historically, along with criticism of the Kenite hypothesis, see Daniel E. Fleming, *Yahweh before Israel: Glimpses of History in a Divine Name* (Cambridge: Cambridge University Press, 2021).

heard that God is with you'" (Zech. 8:23).[139] YHWH *is* his name (Jer. 33:2; Amos 5:8; 9:6).

In contrast to much twentieth-century scholarship, my review thus rejects the understanding of Deuteronomic theology that considers the divine name to be a lesser, more abstract form of God's presence, and it narrows the distance between Deuteronomic and Priestly theologies of divine presence. Against this differently sketched exegetical-historical backdrop, the Priestly Blessing in Num. 6:24–26 becomes a particularly intriguing example of the close relationship between God's beneficent presence and God's name. As noted in the first chapter, each line of the blessing begins with YHWH as its subject, and its total Hebrew word count is identical to the numerical value of YHWH. So although the blessing goes on to describe different kinds of actions and characteristics of YHWH, the most important performative aspect of the blessing consists precisely in the verbal proclamation of YHWH's name. As Kendall Soulen eloquently writes of the Priestly Blessing:

> The threefold repetition of God's name anchors the blessing in the affirmation of God's uniqueness even as each line pours it out like so many streams of luxurious perfumed oil. God's blessing is also God's keeping, which is also God's shining face, which is also God's grace, which is also God's countenance lifted up, which is also God's peace. And all of these together brim over with the riches of "my name."[140]

The blessing as a whole pronounces and simultaneously explicates the name YHWH.[141]

The Priestly Blessing *is* what the name YHWH means. It not only identifies God as the source of the blessing, it also explains who God is. Even though it will proceed to assert and confirm additional qualities of God's protective care, the blessing in its present literary-canonical form is most fundamentally an act of speaking

---

139. Cf. R. Kendall Soulen, *The Divine Name(s) and the Holy Trinity*, vol. 1, *Distinguishing the Voices* (Louisville: Westminster John Knox, 2011), 9: "This is the name that unites Jews and Christians, if they are united at all."
140. Soulen, *Divine Name(s) and the Holy Trinity*, 152.
141. Seebass, "YHWH's Name," 52.

forth God's name, of saying what became ordinarily unsayable, of placing God's name before the worshipers of Israel as an expression of God's invitational presence. In this sense, the Priestly Blessing is a type of divine greeting: "God is now here, and this is who God is and what God will do." Seybold uses a nice German expression for this feature of the blessing by describing it as *bezogen auf das Du* or "all about the you" (i.e., about the relationship between the worshiper and God).[142] Here the word *Du* is also the familiar word for "you" in German, the word used for family and friends (rather than the formal *Sie*). This distinction emphasizes how blessing is intimate and relational, even though its wording is relatively general and metaphorical. Seybold suggests that worshipers would therefore have needed to fill in the content of the blessing with what they already knew about YHWH, even as YHWH was exegeted, one might say, by the blessing. In this sense too, the Priestly Blessing is fundamentally about YHWH and encountering YHWH in worship.

The Priestly Blessing proclaims and confirms YHWH's identity as the God of Israel. YHWH is the One who is in relationship with Israel. Israel is YHWH's people and YHWH is Israel's God. In the Old Testament, the gracious provision of God's name does not merely add ideational content about who God is and what God is up to, it supplies a reliable means of relating to God. To use Christian language, God's name is itself an incarnational form of God's presence in the world. This Old Testament tradition carries over into the New Testament, which likewise insists on the importance of the divine name as synonymous with divine identity and power. Jesus came "in the name of the Lord" (Matt. 21:9). Early Christians preached and performed miracles in the name of Jesus (Acts 4:7, 30). As Paul writes in Rom. 10:13 (citing Joel 2:32 [3:5H]), "For, 'Everyone who calls on the name of the Lord shall be saved.'" Throughout the New Testament, the divine name retains its salvific power. As Phil. 2:9–11 says, "Therefore God also highly exalted him and gave him the name that is above every name, so that at the name of Jesus every knee should bend, in heaven and on earth and under the earth, and every

---

142. Seybold, *Der aaronitische Segen*, 36.

tongue should confess that Jesus Christ is Lord, to the glory of God the Father."

Rather than being a sort of magical formula that supposedly operates mechanically and on its own, what gives the divine name its power is instead the power of the One whom the name designates and invokes. "Hallowed be your *name*" (Matt. 6:9, emphasis added) is a crucial petition in the Lord's Prayer. It reminds all Christians of the importance of God's name and of their responsibility to honor that name with their words (Exod. 20:7) and deeds (John 13:7).

"Bless"

The Hebrew verb "bless" (*bērak*, *piel*) and its related noun form "blessing" (*bərākâ*) appear throughout the Old Testament with a variety of nuances. Because the root *b-r-k* can also mean "to kneel" in Arabic, and since there is a Hebrew *berek* (knee), some older linguistic scholarship interpreted the notion of blessing as arising from the act of kneeling.[143] The widely used but dated Hebrew dictionary known as *BDB* gives both meanings for the *b-r-k* root.[144] The Hebrew word for "pool" (*bərēkâ*) is similar as well. However, modern linguists are unconvinced that all of these terms have arisen from the same Semitic root.[145] Some of the ways that older reference works sought to combine "blessing," "knee," and "pool" are quite imaginative, but clearly go beyond any available evidence.[146] More closely related to the Hebrew word for bless is the Akkadian verb *karābu*, which also means bless and possesses the same three consonants (although the first and third are reversed).[147]

---

143. See the discussion in J. K. Aitken, *The Semantics of Blessing and Cursing in Ancient Hebrew*, ANESSup 23 (Leiden: Peeters, 2007), 93–94.

144. *BDB*, 138–40.

145. Aitken, *Semantics of Blessing and Cursing*, 94.

146. There does appear to be a play on words between "knees" and "bless" in 1 Kings 8:54–56, but it may turn on a folk etymology rather than a genuine linguistic connection. See Matthew Richard Schlimm, *Hebrew Words Every Christian Should Know* (Nashville: Abingdon, 2018), 70.

147. In Babylon this term may have referred primarily, if not exclusively, to greeting formulas. See E. J. Bickerman, *Studies in Jewish and Christian History*, ed. Amram Tropper, 2 vols., AJEC 68 (Leiden: Brill, 2007), 2:587.

Claus Westermann deserves enduring credit for bringing renewed attention in modern scholarship to the significance of blessing in the Bible.[148] Writing in response to salvation-historical approaches to the Bible in the mid-twentieth century Biblical Theology Movement, in which "the mighty acts of God" were viewed as the proper subject matter of biblical theology,[149] Westermann described the presence of a second through-line in Scripture. This trajectory emphasizes fertility, descendants, genealogies, agricultural bounty, and communal well-being. The divine work of redemption came about not just in dramatic deeds but also in the routine occurrences of daily life and the seasonal workings of creation. Salvation was not only an event but a condition and a process. In retrospect, it is clear that Westermann's work offered a healthy corrective to an overemphasis in the Biblical Theology Movement,[150] which later eroded anyway as subsequent research undercut its arguments for a unique Israelite understanding of history.[151] But many scholars since Westermann have criticized him for introducing the idea of two separate spheres of divine activity in ancient Israel, one focused on "saving" and another on "blessing."[152] Today, salvation-historical approaches are enjoying something of a comeback and Westermann's crucial insight is in danger of becoming lost.[153]

Because God is always the direct or indirect agent of blessing in the Bible,[154] it is logical again to think of the human act of blessing as par-

---

148. Claus Westermann, *Blessing in the Bible and the Life of the Church*, trans. Keith Crim, OBT (Philadelphia: Fortress, 1978).

149. E.g., Oscar Cullmann, *Salvation in History*, trans. Sidney G. Sowers, NTL (London: SCM, 1967); G. Ernest Wright, *God Who Acts: Biblical Theology as Recital*, SBT 8 (London: SCM, 1952).

150. Tryggve N. D. Mettinger, *In Search of God: The Meaning and Message of the Everlasting Names*, ed. Frederick H. Cryer (Philadelphia: Fortress, 1988), 3.

151. See Bertil Albrektson, *History and the Gods: An Essay on the Idea of Historical Events as Divine Manifestations in the Ancient Near East and in Israel*, ConBOT 1 (Lund: Gleerup, 1967).

152. See Christopher Wright Mitchell, *The Meaning of* BRK *"to Bless" in the Old Testament*, SBLDS 95 (Atlanta: Scholars Press, 1987), 177–79.

153. For evidence of this trend and a critique, see Darian Lockett, "Limitations of a Purely Salvation-Historical Approach to Biblical Theology," *HBT* 39, no. 2 (2017): 211–31.

154. Horst Dietrich Preuss, *Old Testament Theology*, 2 vols., OTL (Louisville: Westminster John Knox, 1995–96), 1:180.

ticipation in God's holiness, which describes God's nature and way with the world.[155] Human blessing, which characteristically consists of both word and rite,[156] verbally incorporates both the speaker and the hearer within an alternative reality, a different way of seeing and thinking about the world—God's way.[157] In this act of redescription, there is a pedagogical effect: "By becoming people who bless and are blessed, and a church that blesses and is blessed, we are taught to look at the world in certain terms."[158] There is also eschatological insight, since in blessing people will come to "understand the will of God as being for all things to be set apart, consecrated, made holy, [and] conformed to him."[159] Blessing is the way of the kingdom of God. It is like a mustard seed, a tiny, beautiful sign of God's creational goodness that grows organically to an unanticipated height (Matt. 13:31–32).

Blessing therefore names both the origin of all things (Gen. 1:1–2:3) and their final disposition (Eph. 1:3–10; Rev. 22:3–4). In blessing, things are re-narrated as elements in God's world, thereby taking on a new significance. Andrew Davison puts it this way:

> When we bless something we change its orientation. We direct it towards God, not so as to imply that it was not already God's or that God was not already the One in whom the fulfillment of all things is to be found, but so as to make this explicit and, in a certain sense, to underline it. . . . We do not treat a blessed object or person, or anything else, in quite the same way as it was before.[160]

Accordingly, we might also think of blessing as a ceremonial "placing," in which something or someone is "re-placed" into a relationship

---

155. Davison, *Blessing*, 23–24. Also see Andrew Davison, *Participation in God: A Study in Christian Doctrine and Metaphysics* (Cambridge: Cambridge University Press, 2019).
156. Westermann, *Blessing in the Bible*, 43.
157. Cf. Gordon Lathrop, *Holy Ground: A Liturgical Cosmology* (Minneapolis: Fortress, 2003), 86: "A thing or person is 'blessed' by gathering that thing or person verbally into the story of God."
158. Davison, *Blessing*, 21.
159. Davison, *Blessing*, 25.
160. Davison, *Blessing*, 110.

with God as primary and constitutive to its being and character.[161] To bless is thus to claim something for God.

This fundamental aspect of blessing helps to explain the close relationship between "blessing" and "praise" in biblical discourse, with the two actions often appearing in parallel (e.g., Pss. 34:1 [2H]; 145:2; cf. Neh. 9:5; 1 Chron. 16:35–36). In light of the parallelism, some scholars have concluded that when the object of the verb "bless" is God, it simply means "praise" (e.g., Gen. 24:48).[162] But the equation is somewhat tendentious and has been influenced by certain theological concerns about the limits of human agency and the sovereignty of God. The theological concern becomes clearer when the sense of *b-r-k* is said to be "declarative" if God is the subject of the verb, but "expressive" when a human being is the subject.[163] Crediting human beings with the possibility of blessing, especially blessing God, might seem to imply that God can gain something in blessing that God did not already have, a theologically problematic notion.[164]

However, blessing is not in fact reducible to praise when the object of blessing is God, because the linguistic profile of blessing is not entirely identical with that of praise. Blessing maintains its own distinctive content and range.[165] If blessing something is to claim it for God, then that sort of attribution is closely related to the identity of God and rightly named with gratitude and thanksgiving. However, blessing is understood in the Bible as *consignment* as well as acknowledgment. Blessing not only confesses something that is true about God's nature but also entrusts it to God in the confident expectation that God's followers can continue to rely on it.[166] Blessing

---

161. Davison, *Blessing*, 111–12.

162. Aitken, *Semantics of Blessing and Cursing*, 113.

163. Aitken, *Semantics of Blessing and Cursing*, 116. Cf. Mitchell, *Meaning of BRK*, 146–50, 170–71.

164. E.g., Daniel G. Van Slyke, "Toward a Theology of Blessings: Agents and Recipients of Benedictions," *Antiphon* 15, no. 1 (2011): 49: "God, being impassible, does not benefit from any blessing."

165. See Stephen B. Chapman, "Psalm 115 and the Logic of Blessing," *HBT* 44, no. 1 (2022): 47–63. Cf. William P. Brown, "What Does It Mean to Bless God?," *Call to Worship* 52, no. 2 (2018): 16–22; Stephen B. Dawes, "'Bless the Lord': An Invitation to Affirm the Living God," *ExpTim* 106, no. 10 (July 1995): 293–96.

166. Cf. Helen Oppenheimer, "Blessing," in *The Weight of Glory: A Vision and Practice for Christian Faith*, ed. D. W. Hardy and P. H. Sedgwick (Edinburgh: T&T

God ascribes the worshipers themselves to God in a way that even praise does not. Blessing actually *does* that. Not to recognize this productive aspect of blessing reduces blessing to encouraging speech.[167]

To use the language of speech act theory, blessing is not only a locution (a saying) but an illocution (a saying that accomplishes something, like saying "I do" in response to a prompt for a promise). The biblical tradition understands God to be the ultimate source of blessing, but that does not mean human beings are not actually blessing when they say they are, or only expressing a hope that God will bless. In the Priestly Blessing, the jussive verbal forms signal that the intention of the *speaker* is being communicated. Typically, the passive participle *bārûk* is used in blessing ("blessed be"), which likely does represent a lessening of human agency.[168] But it does not eliminate human agency all together. The activity of blessing is one in which there is a mysterious form of *cooperation* between God and human beings, as in biblical prophecy (in which prophets even use the first person "I" in speaking on God's behalf).[169] To bless God is not only to acknowledge God's power, as in praise, but also to reaffirm God's "powerless," subjunctive way of using that power within creation and recommitting to it.[170]

It is true that Hebrew *b-r-k* is consistently translated in the Greek Bible with the Greek verb *eulogeō* (to speak well of). For this reason, blessing is often said to mean "good speaking." But on this point, it

---

Clark, 1991), 224: "not of course conferring blessing or greatness upon Him, but ascribing them to Him with gratitude, hoping to come into the orbit of the blessedness of the power that they ascribe."

167. E.g., Lathrop, *Saving Images*, 147: "The core biblical tradition understands blessing simply as *our good words before God*" (emphasis original). He goes on to say, confusingly, "Of course, 'blessing' is also and especially what the Bible calls the good words spoken *by God*." He neither explains why the first is the "core" tradition nor how these two aspects of blessing relate to each other.

168. Cf. Bickerman, *Studies in Jewish and Christian History*, 588: "The human person does not 'send' his blessing; he does not claim to transmit his own stream of blessing in the direction of divinity. All he does is to affirm that the divinity is 'blessed,' i.e. full of effective kindness."

169. On the contemporary ecclesial abuse of performative speech, see Brent A. Strawn, *The Old Testament Is Dying: A Diagnosis and Recommended Treatment* (Grand Rapids: Baker Academic, 2017), 133–38.

170. Caputo, "Subjunctive Power of God," 19.

is important to note that LXX *eulogeō* is itself a Hebraism, a word whose meaning has been shaped more by the context of ancient Judaism than its usage in the Greco-Roman world.[171] So rather than the Greek term indicating how to understand Hebrew *b-r-k*, Hebrew *b-r-k* indicates how *eulogeō* is to be understood in the Greek Bible. Hebrew *b-r-k* does indicate a type of "good speaking," but it is "good speaking" in the sense of promising divinely sourced well-being.[172]

"You (singular)"

In interpreting the Bible, one of the most important words to examine exegetically is always the deceptively simple word "you," especially for English-language speakers. The history of the second-person pronoun in English is a fascinating one, and mostly unfamiliar to contemporary speakers of the language.[173] Yet there are important implications in this history for pastors and worship leaders.

Like many languages, English once had two basic forms of the second-person pronoun, a formal one and an informal one. The *formal* pronoun was "you/your" while the *informal* pronoun was "thee/thou/thy/thine." Over time, use of the formal pronoun expanded and displaced the informal pronoun.[174] Some traditionalist groups (like the Quakers) held on to "thee" and its related forms, which they

---

171. Aitken, *Semantics of Blessing and Cursing*, 104.

172. Marguerite Harl, *La Genèse: Traduction du texte de la Septante; Introduction et notes*, La Bible d'Alexandrie 1 (Paris: Cerf, 1986), 56.

173. The contemporary discussion of this phenomenon was initiated by Roger Brown and Albert Gilman, "The Pronouns of Power and Solidarity," in *Style in Language*, ed. Thomas A. Sebeok (Cambridge, MA: Massachusetts Institute of Technology Press, 1960), 253–76.

174. This may have occurred because "thee" came to be perceived as a mode of address for those of lower status, even a sign of condescension or contempt. The expansion of "you" as the standard second-person form would then have had appeal as a means of gaining status, especially for the rising middle class in early modern England. The leveling out of "thee" by "you" was largely complete by the eighteenth century. As noted by Reggie Siriwardena, *Addressing the Other: A Three Language Study in Power, Personal Relations and Second Person Pronouns* (Colombo, Sri Lanka: International Centre for Ethnic Studies, 1992), 56, class distinctions were nevertheless maintained by use of titles and honorifics (e.g., "sir," "madam") and other verbal designations.

continued to use in informal address (i.e., for family and friends), sometimes even as a replacement for "you" altogether.[175] "Thee" also survived in Christian liturgy, which tends to retain traditional language. In contemporary culture, "thee" sounds old-fashioned, and it is. But it also sounds formal, which is only a modern misperception.

This point is crucial for congregations to understand, to avoid the false impression that language like "Thy will be done" in the Lord's Prayer is formal language, and that it is used because formal language is appropriate in church. In fact, the opposite is the case. "Thee" was traditionally used when speaking to God because the *informal* mode of address was considered appropriate. Relationship with God was intimate and personal, on par with the relations that one had with family and friends. This is still true in Germany. As a non-native German speaker, it was quite striking for me to use the standard *Sie* (formal)/*Du* (informal) distinction when I lived there—taking care to refer politely to a new acquaintance as "Sie" but then saying "Du" to God in prayers at church. Modern German speakers probably do not even think about it, because it is such a familiar convention. But for me it was a powerful signal of something deep and true about prayer.

Traditionally, "you" in English was also a singular form; the plural form was "ye." Here again, the range of "you (sg.)" has expanded and "ye" is no longer used, except in certain idiomatic phrases (e.g., "O ye of little faith"). In contemporary English, "you" is employed in both formal and informal modes of address and can refer to a single individual ("you") or a group of individuals ("you"). Sometimes the context still pushes for a numerical distinction, which is why Southerners may use "y'all" for "you (pl.)," residents of Appalachia say "you'uns," and people in Pittsburgh have come up with "yinz." In eastern Pennsylvania, New Jersey, and New York, the preferred colloquial form is "youse." In the Midwest (and all over), it is "you guys."

Biblical Hebrew does not have a formal/informal difference with regard to the second person, but it does have a singular/plural distinction. Both with independent pronouns and verbal forms,

---

175. See George Fox, *The Journal*, ed. Nigel Smith (London: Penguin, 1998), 36: "Moreover, when the Lord sent me forth into the world, he forbade me to put off my hat to any, high or low. And I was required to 'thee' and 'thou' all men and women, without any respect to rich or poor, great or small."

Hebrew distinguishes between speaking to individuals and speaking to groups. But it is also important to note that this distinction is a subjective rather than an objective one; that is, it again expresses how the speaker is *conceiving* of the addressees rather than how many people are in fact being addressed. Sometimes there is no meaningful difference. The speaker conceives of the addressee as a single individual because there is only one person listening. But sometimes a singular form can be used when a speaker is addressing a group of people. An example is the Ten Commandments (Exod. 20:1–17; Deut. 5:6–21), which in their narrative context are addressed to a group (Exod. 19:25; Deut. 5:1–5) but use the singular form of second-person address. So the "you" of "you shall not kill" is a singular "you."[176] This does not mean that only one person is involved, it means that there is a nuance of personal responsibility to what is being said.[177] These commandments are not only for Israel as a political entity to observe and enforce, they are the responsibility of every Israelite.[178] English translations mask this nuance because they no longer differentiate between "you (sg.)" and "you (pl.)." It has been estimated that there are 4,720 verses in the Bible in which "you" should be read as "you (pl.)."[179] In this way, the Bible is much more communal than many English speakers ordinarily recognize. Thus, the current English language itself helps to create the individualistic misunderstanding of the Bible

---

176. "Thou" was used in the KJV to indicate "you (sg.)" in verses like this one.

177. The danger of taking this aspect of the language too literally is illustrated in David J. A. Clines, "The Ten Commandments: Reading from Left to Right," in *Words Remembered, Texts Renewed: Essays in Honor of John F. A. Sawyer*, ed. Jon Davies, Graham Harvey, and Wilfred G. E. Watson, JSOTSup 195 (Sheffield: Sheffield Academic, 1995), 97–112.

178. Brevard S. Childs, *Exodus: A Critical, Theological Commentary*, OTL (Philadelphia: Westminster, 1974): 399–400: "The Decalogue is not addressed to a specific segment of the population, to the priestly class, or a prophetic office within Israel, but to every man." A similar nuance of language occurs in the traditional *Credo* of the Latin mass, which begins "I believe" rather than "We believe," even though it is a statement of Christian doctrine for the entire church and spoken by the congregation together.

179. Matthew Schmitz, "Texas Bible Converts 'You' to 'Y'all,'" http://www.firstthings.com/texas-bible-converts-you-to-yall/. This count includes the New Testament, because Greek also makes a sg.-pl. distinction.

prevailing in contemporary US society and creates many false biblical interpretations.[180]

Just the opposite is the case in the Sermon on the Mount in Matt. 5–7, also remembered as the Sermon on the Plain in Luke 6:17–49. Once again the narrative setting indicates that Jesus is addressing a group (Matt. 5:1; 7:28–29; cf. Luke 6:17–19), which is now clearly the gathered crowd but was perhaps originally the disciples.[181] Here the second-person references are prevailingly plural in Greek, although there are significant variations.[182] For instance, the second-person reference in "for yours is the kingdom of God" (Luke 6:20b) is plural (*hymetera*).[183] The misunderstanding to be avoided comes not only from hearing the Beatitudes as moral demands, rather than identity statements, but as individual rather than *communal* identity descriptions.[184] The Sermon on the Mount is not an individual ethic; it is a community manifesto. English translations abet this mistake by translating the plural Greek forms simply as "you." In this instance, it might be better if they instead offered "all of you" or "you all." Preachers might at least do so in their sermons to draw out a proper understanding of this central biblical passage. "You are, *all together*, the light of the world" is a description of the church's mission, not the vocation of the individual Christian.[185]

---

180. See Robert N. Bellah et al., *Habits of the Heart: Individualism and Commitment in American Life* (Berkeley: University of California Press, 1985).

181. Robert Guelich, *The Sermon on the Mount: A Foundation for Understanding* (Waco: Word, 1982), 59–60.

182. On the variations, see Paul Ellingworth, "'Thou' and 'You' in the Sermon on the Mount," *BT* 58, no. 1 (2007): 11–19. Cf. the conclusion of Angus Paddison, "How We Should Read the Sermon on the Mount," *ExpTim* 121, no. 12 (2010): 617–19 (here 619): "The pronouns in this reading [Luke 6:20–31] are plural and the thrust is overwhelmingly corporate."

183. Matt. 5:3 instead reads "for theirs is the kingdom of heaven," which is also plural but in the third person.

184. See, however, the cautionary note offered by Gerald W. Peterman, "Plural You: On the Use and Abuse of the Second Person," *BBR* 20, no. 2 (2010): 201–14, who emphasizes the lack of a "neat one-to-one correspondence" between pronouns and their referents. Even in contemporary colloquial English, "How are we feeling today?" could be directed to an individual. In other words, use of the plural should not be assumed to exclude individual hearers or individual application (and vice versa).

185. Paddison, "How We Should Read," 619: "Who we were called to be is found firmly within the context of the church, not in some solo effort."

It is also important to note that English translations obscure the Greek text by translating the Beatitudes as consisting of blessing formulations, when in fact the underlying Greek word usually translated as "blessed" is *makarioi* (Matt. 5:3; Luke 6:20). While some scholars have argued that "beatitudes" or makarisms are a type of blessing-saying, most now agree that their character and function are different. Important for this discussion is the Old Testament background of the form, which lies not in *bərākôt* but *'ašrê* statements (e.g., Pss. 1:1; 32:1 [2H]; 40:4 [5H]; 84:4–5, 12 [5–6, 13H]; 119:1).[186] A better translation would be "Fortunate are those who . . ." or "Happy are those who . . ."[187] On the one hand, the traditional translation "blessed" helps to counteract a mistakenly moralistic interpretation of the discourse. But on the other hand, translating the Beatitudes as blessing statements muddies the profile of both the Beatitudes and biblical blessings. It reinforces the impression that blessings are primarily or exclusively about speaking encouraging words.[188]

There is a final second-person distinction in Hebrew that is obscured in English translations, and that is a gender distinction between male and female addressees. Feminist scholarship has been especially productive in drawing new attention to this phenomenon. The Hebrew language has distinct forms for "you (masc. sg.)" and "you (fem. sg.)," along with "you (masc. pl.)" and "you (fem. pl.)." As in English, Hebrew apparently used masculine forms as a grammatical default, so that mixed gender groups are sometimes addressed by using masculine forms. The result is that the presence and role of women in biblical texts (and in ancient Israel) is frequently underacknowledged and incorrectly devalued. An example of an important corrective in this regard is provided by Wilda Gafney, whose work

---

186. Waldemar Janzen, "'*AŠRÉ* in the Old Testament," *HTR* 58, no. 2 (1965): 215–26.

187. Guelich, *Sermon on the Mount*, 67, even suggests "congratulations to" as the best way of catching the Greek nuance in English.

188. Cf. Guelich, *Sermon on the Mount*, 110–11: "The failure on the practical level stems from the misunderstanding of the Beatitudes as a literary form. Although beatitudes in a Wisdom context may have a more exhortative or paranetic [*sic*] function . . . , the Beatitudes of 5:3–12 do not promise well-being and success. They are much closer to the function of the beatitude in prophetic/apocalyptic writings. They address those who already *are* what they are identified as being" (emphasis original).

on the prophetic tradition offers multiple examples of how mixed gender prophetic groups are described with plural masculine forms.[189] Prophecy in the Hebrew Bible is a more egalitarian tradition than has often been realized.

To turn to the Ten Commandments again, their addressee is not only "you (sg.)" but "you (masc. sg.)," which also helps explain the way certain individual commandments are framed (e.g., Exod. 20:17b, "You shall not covet your neighbor's wife"). But in literary terms, this specification only relates directly to the narratee of the text, not its implied audience or real audience. That is, a text in theory can be geared to a specific addressee in the narrative (= narratee) but at the same time also be intended for a wider hearing (or "overhearing") by the narrative's readers. The narratee, the implied audience, and the actual audience of a text are not necessarily the same.[190] We cannot say for sure, in purely literary terms, just who the original (historical) audience of Exod. 20:1–17 was, or even who it was intended to be. It seems quite likely that the received literary form of Exod. 20:1–17 has a broader understanding of its implied audience. But the narratee of the Ten Commandments is unmistakably "you (masc. sg.)."

The upshot of this deep dive into language is that English is particularly impoverished when it comes to the second person. There appears to be a strong desire among English speakers to maintain an egalitarian posture in which everyone is addressed the same way. While no doubt commendable in some respects, it can also disguise the differences that exist in lived experience—differences that are routinely acknowledged more openly in other linguistic cultures, including the cultures of the Bible. So English speakers must be particularly careful not to read the word "you" in the Bible without posing important questions: *Who* is "you" in a particular biblical text? Singular or plural? Masculine or feminine? The answers can shed much light on the sense of a given biblical passage, sometimes in surprising ways.

---

189. Wilda Gafney, *Daughters of Miriam: Women Prophets in Ancient Israel* (Minneapolis: Fortress, 2008).

190. Gerald Prince, "Introduction to the Study of the Narratee," in *Narratology: An Introduction*, ed. Susana Onega and José Angel García Landa (London: Longman, 1996), 190–202.

The "you" of the Priestly Blessing, like the "you" of the Ten Commandments, is "you (sg.)," while the context makes clear that its narratee is a group. More precisely, the Priestly Blessing consists of a speech nested within a speech, a common occurrence within the Pentateuch. God tells Moses to speak to Aaron and his sons—a plural addressee. They are directed in turn to bless the people of Israel—another plural addressee. So the words of the Priestly Blessing are spoken by God to be spoken by Moses to be spoken by Aaron and his sons to the Israelites. Yet all the verbal formulations of the blessing itself are composed in the singular, while the context would seem to call for the plural. The Priestly Blessing therefore holds open the possibility of being heard as directed either to a collective or an individual.[191] It is Israel's blessing, but it also comes to each citizen of Israel as a personal word from God.[192] It is above all in this individual commitment from God to every Israelite that God's name is "placed" or "put" on the people, and yet it is the people as a whole who are blessed (Num. 6:27, "and I will bless *them*").

"Keep"

What does it mean to ask God to "keep" someone? The term is familiar and poetic. But it no longer adequately conveys in English what it needs to. Today people tend to think of the word "keep" in two ways: either in the durative sense of "keeping up" and "keeping on" (with its nuance of persistent effort) or "keeping" in the possessive, caretaking sense (e.g., to "keep" chickens). The older sense of "keep" as sustaining and protective action, as in the traditional translation of Priestly Blessing, is no longer widely employed, except in a phrase like "keep me safe from harm." But "keep" alone, without any verbal complement ("safe from harm"), normally lacks such a

---

191. Noth, *Numbers*, 58. For the collective understanding, see Baruch A. Levine, *Numbers 1–20: A New Translation with Introduction and Commentary*, AB 4A (New York: Doubleday, 1993), 227.
192. Heckl, "Aaronic Blessing," 129: "The wish of being blessed is meant for each and every individual but, thereby, it also reaches the present collective and the entire group indicated as the people of Israel."

meaning. Changed English usage therefore pushes toward finding a more suitable alternative for the Hebrew term.

The Hebrew verb *šāmar* is widely distributed throughout the Old Testament, appearing over 450 times, often as a verb or a verbal noun (= "keeper," "guard"), and sometimes as a verbal complement.[193] It is most frequently found in the Deuteronomistic stream of tradition (i.e., Deuteronomy and the books of the Former Prophets), but its second-most frequent location is in Priestly texts (including Psalms and Ezekiel). The verb has a close association with the theological notion of covenant, since "keeping the covenant" is a known idiom (e.g., Gen. 17:9–10; Exod. 19:5; Deut. 7:9), and this suggests that its range of usage in the Old Testament includes law (Exod. 20:6// Deut. 5:10) as well as worship (Exod. 20:8). The verb is employed in relation to both individuals and the community of Israel as a whole. It can exhibit "secular" as well as "sacred" meanings. In the Psalms, where the term's religious sense is prominent, the subject of the verb is most frequently God.[194]

Suggested dictionary glosses for the verb in English are "watch," "guard," "keep," and "protect." Such commonly used English verbs offer an important reminder that *šāmar* is an ordinary Hebrew word.[195] It has a strong religious meaning in the Priestly Blessing, since God is the proclaimed agent of the action being described. Yet it is not the kind of religious word that exists in isolation from everyday activities and concerns. To the contrary, *šāmar* is an unexceptional term that is taken up in the act of worship as a reminder that God, the God of Israel, is not far off and disconnected from the daily life but intimately concerned with ordinary things.

One basic use of the word relates to the shepherding activities of guarding and protecting, as is evident in the use of *šāmar* for "watching over" a flock of animals (e.g., Gen. 30:31; Jer. 31:10; Hosea 12:12 [13H]). A somewhat similar use appears in narratives about the valuables residing at the temple and palace, which must be "watched over" or guarded (e.g., 2 Sam. 15:16; 16:21; 20:3; 1 Kings 14:27; 2 Kings

---

193. F. García López, "*šāmar*," *TDOT* 15:279–305; G. Sauer, "*šmr*," *TLOT* 3:1380–84.
194. García López, "*šāmar*," *TDOT* 15:286.
195. García López, "*šāmar*," *TDOT* 15:286.

11:5–6).[196] The normal occupational term "guard" (*šōmēr*) is a verbal noun constructed from this same Hebrew root. Very often in Hebrew usage, a verbal form will appear together with a second verb or an object further specifying exactly what is to be guarded and/or how such guarding will transpire. For instance, "keep to do" (= observe diligently) is a common phrase in Deuteronomy (e.g., Deut. 5:1, 32; 6:3, 25; 7:11; 8:1).[197]

If the stress in the Deuteronomistic tradition is perhaps more on obedience, the emphasis in the Priestly tradition is on reassurance and God's promises. The term still appears in priestly injunctions to "keep" God's commandments, but these injunctions are frequently found together with divine identity formulas like "I am YHWH your God" or "I am YHWH" (e.g., Lev. 18:4–5, 26–30; 19:37; 20:22–24).[198] So in Israel's liturgical tradition there is a close connection between the identity of YHWH and the divine activity of "guarding" (e.g., "The LORD is your keeper," Ps. 121:5). In other words, "guarding" is one of the characteristic activities of Israel's God.[199] The term can also refer to a guardian appointed by God. The archetypal instance of Israel's protection occurs in the exodus, when Israel is guarded by Moses (Hosea 12:13 [14H]). Such a person is understood to be a "keeper," in the dual sense of being a good steward of God's creation and being responsible for other creatures (Gen. 2:15; 4:9). In this way, the priests, especially the Levitical priests (Num. 1:53; 3:28, 32), are considered not only divinely appointed guards but also emblematic human "keepers," stewards of God's presence in the world. They stand guard at the threshold of the temple (2 Kings 12:9 [10H]; 23:4; 25:18).

Because of the military connotations of "guard" in contemporary English, the translation of *šāmar* as "protect" should be preferred in the Priestly Blessing: "(May) the LORD bless you and protect you." This powerful, combined pronouncement is at once both the thesis statement and the essence of the Priestly Blessing

---

196. García López, "*šāmar*," *TDOT* 15:288.
197. García López, "*šāmar*," *TDOT* 15:284.
198. García López, "*šāmar*," *TDOT* 15:299.
199. García López, "*šāmar*," *TDOT* 15:301.

as a whole.[200] What follows in the blessing will build on but not significantly alter what this forthright statement sets out: God will bless and protect. These twin verbs are not merely poetic synonyms but two discrete actions, with each one nevertheless implying and supporting the other. God not only blesses but protects. God not only protects; God blesses. God's blessing is protective, even as God's protection is filled with blessing. A blessing lacking in protection is not the kind of blessing that God generously offers. Protection apart from blessing is not the type of protection freely available from God.

Contemporary worshipers might imagine blessing and protection as the two hands of God, who reaches toward them in the Priestly Blessing with both these hands at once. Moreover, the two actions together offer a profound expression of God's own character, as signified by God's personal name. Blessing and protection are not only what God does but who God is. They define God's very name. To rely on God's blessing is therefore to trust confidently and expectantly in the "otherwise" of Israel's God.

---

200. P. Miller, "Blessing of God," 243, also concludes that God's commitment to bless and keep is "the basic, all-inclusive petition" of the Priestly Blessing. So too Knierim and Coats, *Numbers*, 94 ("basic statement").

3

Unpacking the Thesis

> The LORD make his face to shine upon you, and be gracious to you;
> The LORD lift up his countenance upon you, and give you peace.
>
> So they shall put my name on the Israelites, and I will bless them.
> —Numbers 6:25–27

The remainder of the blessing offers a further description of divine blessing and protection, followed by a concluding direction to the priests. The second and third phrases of the blessing, with their common motif of God's face or countenance, are broadly synonymous and yet also expand on the nature of God's identity and activity. Together, these two subsequent phrases explicate the blessing's first phrase, which announces God's protective blessing and stands at the head of the Priestly Blessing as its basic thesis. Because of the repeated subject YHWH at the beginning of each line, the phrases "make his face to shine" and "lift up his countenance" echo and unfold the core actions ascribed to God in the first line. The final priestly instruction in verse 27 closes the frame introduced in verses 22–23 by returning to divine speech ("my name"), which interprets the blessing even as it completes the ritual of pronouncing it.

"Make Shine"

The traditional translation is cumbersome: "make shine." It is an effort to translate the causative form (*hiphil*) of the stative verb "to be light" (*'-w-r*), with a sense of "enlighten" or "brighten." This same phrase appears eight times in the Old Testament as a volitive verb with God's face as the subject, as in the Priestly Blessing.[1] The jussive form ("let your face shine") is used twice: once here in Num. 6:25, and again in Ps. 67:1 (2H), with both these verses articulating a shared understanding of blessing. The imperative is used in the other six occurrences, but the sentiment is similar: "make your face shine" (e.g., Pss. 31:16 [17H]; 80:3, 7, 19 [4, 8, 20H]; 119:135; Dan. 9:17). In Pss. 31 and 80, the verb is consistently paired with the verb *y-š-ʿ* (to "deliver" or "save"), suggesting that the light emanating from God be understood as God's salvific attention (cf. Pss. 27:1; 43:3; Isa. 9:2 [1H]).

Mayer Gruber argues that the noun phrase "light of face" or "shining face" (*'ôr pānîm*) basically had two related meanings: the happiness of the one whose face has brightened and the "kind disposition" extended toward the viewer of that face.[2] Gruber glosses the meaning of the first as "smile," offering as examples Job 29:24 ("I smiled on them") and Prov. 16:15 ("in a king's smile there is life" [his trans.]). He glosses the second meaning as "favor" and points to Ps. 4:6–7 (7–8H) and Ps. 44:3 (4H).

A proposed alternative is to take the verbal form "make shine" as a judicial metaphor, perhaps relating to solar worship. (The sun god was widely regarded as the source of justice in the ancient Near East; cf. Deut. 33:2; Zeph. 3:5; Mal. 1:11; 4:1–2 [3:19–20H].)[3] For instance, Ps. 67 uses language similar to the Priestly Blessing and then goes on to describe God's righteous activity as a judge (Ps. 67:4 [5H]). On this view, the expression "make shine" indicates a divine offer of mercy (as opposed to punishment). But this interpretation

---

1. H. Simian-Yofre, "*pānîm*," *TDOT* 11:589–615 (599).
2. Mayer I. Gruber, *Aspects of Nonverbal Communication in the Ancient Near East*, StPohl 121.I–II (Rome: Biblical Institute Press, 1982), 557–62.
3. See Raik Heckl, "The Aaronic Blessing (Numbers 6): Its Intention and Place in the Concept of the Pentateuch," in *On Dating Biblical Texts to the Persian Period*, ed. Richard J. Bautch and Mark Lackowski, FAT 2/101 (Tübingen: Mohr Siebeck, 2019), 130–31; further, B. F. Batto, "Zedeq," *DDD*, 929–34.

threatens to make the Priestly Blessing more about forgiveness and atonement than seems warranted.[4] Atonement has to be imported into the blessing from somewhere else, since the rest of its words do not require or suggest it. There is no mention in the blessing of conditions or judgment or punishment at all.[5]

Given the close association in the ancient world between deities and visible light, the "shine" language carries a more literal valence than modern hearers will likely realize. This light is more than a metaphor. For Israel, light is a characteristic mode of God's appearance, symbolizing salvation (e.g., Pss. 4:6 [7H]; 18:28; 84:11 [12H]; 89:15 [16H]; 90:8; Isa. 60:1).[6] God is clothed in light (Ps. 104:2), even as God's word and law are illuminated by divine radiance (Ps. 119:105; Prov. 6:23). God made light in the first act of creation (Gen. 1:3). Jesus is identified by John's Gospel as both a witness to and a representative of that light (John 1:7–9). Jesus is the light of the world (John 8:12). Christian worshipers can therefore hear the Priestly Blessing as affirming God's benevolent guidance of historic Israel as well as adumbrating Christ's person and work.

A shining face can exist in isolation but normally occurs when it is viewed by another. It appears in the hope of being reflected in the face of the other. Faces "brighten" to be seen and shared. Smiles are contagious. God's shining face intends not only to be observed or registered by human worshipers; it aims to become reflected in their own faces. Michael Emlet nicely glosses "make shine" in Num. 6:25 as "beam," noting how "he beamed at her" is a way of describing an affectionate gaze in English.[7] "Beam" is especially suggestive in this context because "beam" can also mean "ray" (e.g., as in "sunbeam"),

---

4. E.g., Hermann Spieckermann, "'YHWH Bless You and Keep You': The Relation of History of Israelite Religion and Old Testament Theology Reconsidered," *SJOT* 23, no. 2 (2009): 165–82 (here 179), describes peace as being gained in the Priestly Blessing through "God's atoning act."

5. As compared with, say, Exod. 34:6–7. See Horst Seebass, "YHWH's Name in the Aaronic Blessing (Num 6:22–27)," in *The Revelation of the Name YHWH to Moses: Perspectives from Judaism, the Pagan Graeco-Roman World and Early Christianity*, ed. George H. van Kooten (Leiden: Brill, 2006), 41.

6. Magne Sæbø, "'ôr," *TLOT* 1:63–67 (here 66).

7. Michael R. Emlet, "Benediction: Living under God's Good Word," *Journal of Pastoral Counseling* 35, no. 3 (2021): 2–12 (here 3).

and the idea of divine light beaming forth recalls visual art in the ancient Mesopotamian *melammu* tradition.

In this tradition, well-known from ancient iconography, Mesopotamian deities and kings (and sometimes monsters/mythic creatures, illnesses/demons, weapons, and buildings) are conceived as luminous or radiant.[8] They can be depicted with rays or wings of light extending from their bodies or around their heads. This nimbus phenomenon, which has persisted into the modern era in the form of saints' halos, has long been recognized as having analogues in the Old Testament as well (e.g., Prov. 16:15: "In the light of a king's face there is life"). Divine luminosity was known in the Akkadian language as *melammu*, and it produced a fearful response on the part of those who encountered it. The response was known as *puluḫtu* (cf. Exod. 23:27).[9] Perhaps the closest biblical analogue is the description of God in Ps. 104:1–2, proclaiming that God is "clothed with honor and majesty, wrapped in light as with a garment." Within an ancient Near Eastern context, it is entirely understandable that Israel would have envisioned YHWH as a light-like deity. Biblical scholars have also pointed to the similarity between the *melammu* conception and biblical attributes of God such as splendor (*hādār*), majesty (*hôd*), and glory (*kābôd*), all of which are finally related and can even be combined (Ps. 145:5, "the glorious splendor of your majesty").[10]

However, Shawn Zelig Aster has mounted an important qualification to prior research. Aster argues that radiance did not become the chief characteristic of *melammu* in Mesopotamia until the latter part of the eighth century BCE. Prior to that point, the root quality of the phenomenon was instead what Aster terms "overwhelming and overpowering strength."[11] It could be represented by rays as early as the second millennium BCE but was even more basically understood as the outer appearance or "covering" of a person or deity, an idea perhaps partly rooted in the golden ornaments sewn onto the

---

8. Shawn Zelig Aster, *The Unbeatable Light: Melammu and Its Biblical Parallels*, AOAT 384 (Munster: Ugarit-Verlag, 2012), 59–66.
9. Aster, *Unbeatable Light*, 81–85.
10. Theodore J. Lewis, *The Origin and Character of God: Ancient Israelite Religion through the Lens of Divinity* (New York: Oxford University Press, 2020), 344–79.
11. Aster, *Unbeatable Light*, 352.

ceremonial garments of kings and idols, which would shimmer in the light.[12] Early on, the *melammu* seems in fact to have been conceived as physical in nature.[13] So *melammu* was not always understood to mean "radiance" per se but did refer consistently to dazzling power.[14]

There are many biblical texts testifying to the radiant appearance of Israel's God (e.g., Hab. 3:3–4). Most of these text traditions, according to Aster, do not represent direct borrowings of the *melammu* tradition, but testify to a notion of YHWH's radiance that may be native to the Israelite tradition and grounded in a root association of YHWH with fire (Exod. 3:1–6; Deut. 4:11, 24; 9:3; 2 Sam. 22//Ps. 18; Jer. 20:9; Amos 5:6).[15] God's light is both creational (Gen. 1:3) and cosmic (Isa. 60:19–20). All light comes from God and mirrors God's light (Ps. 36:9 [10H]). This light is in turn to be reflected by Israel to the nations (Isa. 42:6; 49:6).

In the New Testament, Paul similarly writes of how Christians, "seeing the glory of the Lord as though reflected in a mirror, are being transformed into the same image" (2 Cor. 3:18; cf. Exod. 34:29–35). This emphasis on transformation further expands the notion of God's reflective light. Thus, Douglas Knight insists that Christians are not only to be light-reflective but "light-generating":

> There is no strong distinction to be made here between the face, the light it radiates, and the image it casts. Christ is the face that shines its own light with such brightness that it not only reflects off other faces but also heats their fire, making it not their fire but his, so that it is not merely their exteriors that shine Christ's light but their interiors that host his fire.[16]

---

12. A. Leo Oppenheim, "The Golden Garments of the Gods," *JNES* 8, no. 3 (1949): 179–93. It is also possible that masks played a role in ancient worship ceremonies. See Raz Kletter, "To Cast an Image: Masks from Iron Age Judah and the Biblical Masekah," in *"Up to the Gates of Ekron": Essays on the Archaeology and History of the Eastern Mediterranean in Honor of Seymour Gitlin*, ed. S. W. Crawford et al. (Jerusalem: W. F. Albright Institute, 2007), 189–208.

13. Aster, *Unbeatable Light*, 38.

14. Aster, *Unbeatable Light*, 352.

15. See also Ian Wilson, *Out of the Midst of the Fire: Divine Presence in Deuteronomy*, SBLDS 151 (Atlanta: Scholars Press, 1995).

16. Douglas H. Knight, *The Eschatological Economy: Time and the Hospitality of God* (Grand Rapids: Eerdmans, 2006), 164.

Christ's light is to be embodied by the Christian community (Matt. 5:14–16).

In contemporary English, "shine" best conveys this imagery and can sustain the Bible's rich intertextual discourse about divine light. Throughout the Bible, God's face is pictured as seeking and reaching the human faces that turn expectantly toward God. A good translation of this clause of the blessing is therefore: "(May) God's face shine upon you." The Hebrew idiom actually uses the preposition "to" ("[May] God's face shine *to* you"), a unique construction in the Hebrew Bible,[17] but to reproduce this idiom literally in English would be awkward and perhaps sound too much like "take a shine to," implying something casual and fortuitous.

"Face"

"Face" (*pānîm*) is one of the most common words in the Old Testament, used over two thousand times.[18] It is for the most part just an ordinary noun, which perhaps surprisingly—at least for modern Bible readers—is also employed in describing God. Modern readers tend to treat such language as an archaic anthropomorphism. In biblical Hebrew, however, the noun has figurative as well as literal senses. It can be used spatially to mean "facing" or "toward"—or even temporally ("with his face toward war," 2 Chron. 32:2, my trans.). As with many body parts, it can be used metonymically to refer to an entire person or presence (e.g., Gen. 33:10; Exod. 10:28–29). An example appears in 2 Sam. 17:11, when Hushai counsels "your face" ("you" NRSV; i.e., the king) to go into battle. Moreover, the term sometimes is used with reference to impersonal objects, such as the "facing" or facade of the temple (e.g., Ezek. 41:14–21) or the "face" or surface of the earth (e.g., Gen. 2:6; 8:13).[19] Similar to "name," "face" can also be treated as a hypostasis of YHWH, a particular manifestation of the divine presence.[20]

---

17. Seebass, "YHWH's Name," 39n11.
18. A. S. van der Woude, "*pānîm*," *TLOT* 2:995–1014 (here 996).
19. See Mayer I. Gruber, "The Many Faces of Hebrew *nāśā' pānîm* 'lift up the face,'" *ZAW* 95, no. 2 (1983): 252–60.
20. C. L. Seow, "Face," *DDD*, 322–25 (322).

A striking example occurs in Exod. 33:14–16, with God telling Moses, "My face ["presence" NRSV] will go with you, and I will give you rest."

Of particular interest is the way that *pānîm* expressions are used to convey emotions, intentions, and desires. Just as in contemporary experience, biblical faces can express anger, fear, shame, empathy, or agreement. Faces can also register a change of emotion (e.g., 1 Sam. 1:18). The divine face is likewise capable of showing judgment and rejection (e.g., Pss. 34:16 [17H]; 80:16 [17H]; Lam. 4:16) as well as approval.

"Face" is furthermore used in the context of Israel's worship before the ark or altar.[21] Worship is directed toward God's "face" (Pss. 22:27 [28H]; 24:6; 68:4)—although when "face" is employed in the prepositional phrases *'al pənê* and *lipnê* ("before," lit., "to the face of"), it no longer seems to have as much of a personal character and is often treated as just one part of a compound preposition.[22] Psalm 63:2 (3H) employs such language visually in relation to worship at a holy site: "So I have looked upon you [lit., your face] in the sanctuary." Here "face" has become primarily a spatial designation, with some scholars arguing that the literal, personal dimension of the term "face" is entirely lost. But as Hans Urs von Balthasar notes, an exclusively spatial treatment of the language is finally too thin and reductionistic.[23] The biblical rhetoric of "God's face" is not only about the location of the divine presence but the quality of that presence, which is God's own self (Exod. 23:15, 17; 34:24; Deut. 16:16; 31:11; Isa. 1:12).

God's face can turn toward or away from those who seek God. God's face must be sought (Pss. 27:8; 105:4). God can also hide God's face (Pss. 13:1 [2H]; 102:2 [3H]; 143:7). To "seek" God's face is not merely to attempt to discern God's presence but to secure God's favor, to confirm that one stands before God and remains in good standing with God.[24] The Priestly Blessing explicitly pairs the sight of God's face with "grace" or "favor" (*ḥēn*).

---

21. E.g., Mark S. Smith, "'Seeing God' in the Psalms: The Background to the Beatific Vision in the Hebrew Bible," *CBQ* 50, no. 2 (1988): 171–83.

22. Mervyn D. Fowler, "The Meaning of *lipnê* YHWH in the Old Testament," *ZAW* 99, no. 3 (1987): 384–90.

23. Hans Urs von Balthasar, *The Glory of the Lord: A Theological Aesthetics*, 7 vols. (San Francisco: Ignatius, 1991), 6:71. Cf. I. Wilson, *Out of the Midst*, 204–5.

24. George Martin, "Seeking the Face of God," *TBT* 52, no. 2 (2014): 75–81.

David Ford suggestively describes the deeper logic of the metaphor:

> A face is a distillation of time and memory. Think of the face of someone important to us and it conjures up past events, stories and associations, a world of meaning. It can reach into the future too, with plans, hopes and fears. Imaginatively, we rehearse our lives and intentions before the faces of those we respect, fear, love or otherwise take special notice of or want to impress. What faces do we have in our hearts? Might that be one of the best clues to our identity?[25]

Here Ford identifies the crucial significance of "face" for self-understanding. "Face" is not only one metaphor among many. It turns out to be a particularly important metaphor for the construction and maintenance of personal identity.[26]

However, "seeing God's face" is usually treated in modernity as only a metaphor. After all, people say, God does not actually have a "face." Yet the biblical idiom unproblematically uses "face" as a metonym for God. When God says, "My face will go before you" (Exod. 33:14), the expression means that God will go before the Israelites. The reference to "the angel of his face" in Isa. 63:9 means God's angel. Still, there is also the inner-biblical problem of how some biblical texts commend seeing God's face and other biblical texts reject that possibility out of hand.[27] So "seeing God/God's face" is central to the heart of faith in a variety of biblical texts (Pss. 11:7; 17:15; 27:4, 8; 42:2 [3H]; 2 Cor. 4:6). Yet counter-testimonies also

---

25. David F. Ford, *Self and Salvation: Being Transformed* (Cambridge: Cambridge University Press, 1999), 18. For more on faces and the Priestly Blessing, see Michael J. Glodo, *The Lord Bless You and Keep You: The Promise of the Gospel in the Aaronic Blessing* (Wheaton, IL: Crossway, 2023).

26. Another aspect of the face's importance lies in its ambiguity and plastic ability to convey multiple messages at once, something emphasized in the work of Emmanuel Levinas. See Bernard Waldenfels, "Levinas and the Face of the Other," in *The Cambridge Companion to Levinas*, ed. Simon Critchley and Robert Bernasconi (Cambridge: Cambridge University Press, 2002), 63–81. Struggling to understand a face necessarily involves the viewer in existential questions and an ongoing task of identity formation.

27. From a Jewish perspective, see Steven Kepnes, "Seeing and Not Seeing the Face of God: Overcoming the Law of Contradiction in Biblical Theology," *European Journal for Philosophy of Religion* 12, no. 2 (2020): 133–47.

appear in both Testaments—for example, "No one shall see me and live" (Exod. 33:20; cf. Gen. 32:30; Judg. 6:22–23; John 1:18) and "the invisible God" (Col. 1:15). Alongside the desire for God's face is Israel's persistent reluctance to describe or depict it, as well as Israel's fear that God's face could be mortally dangerous.[28]

So however this tension is negotiated, it is wise not to assume that such "face" talk is purely metaphorical. Much recent historical work has emphasized how ancient conceptions of deities did not necessarily insist on their invisibility or ontological discontinuity with human beings—how, in other words, ancient gods had bodies (cf. Exod. 15:3, 6, 8; 24:9–11; Dan. 7:9).[29] This ancient understanding has been obscured by the Greek philosophical tradition, with its suspicion of the material, the visible, and the body, as well as its preference for conceptual abstraction.[30] Another interpretive possibility was charted in the modern era by Karl Barth, who instead approached the biblical idiom realistically, radically reversing the flow of modern assumptions.

A bold example comes in a late sermon of his on Ps. 31, "My Time Is Secure in Your Hands (31 December 1960)."

> Yes, you may ask me, but does God have hands? Yes indeed, God has hands, quite different ones from these claws of ours, much better, much more skilful, much stronger hands. What does it mean to say: God's hands? Let me put it this way first of all: God's hands are his deeds,

---

28. See William G. Dever, "Archaeology and Ancient Israelite Iconography: Did Yahweh Have a Face?," in *"I Will Speak the Riddles of Ancient Times": Archaeological and Historical Studies in Honor of Amihai Mazar on the Occasion of His Sixtieth Birthday*, ed. Aren Maeir and Pierre de Miroschedji (Winona Lake, IN: Eisenbrauns, 2006), 461–75.

29. See Howard Schwartz, "Does God Have a Body? The Problem of Metaphor and Literal Language in Biblical Interpretation," in *Bodies, Embodiment, and Theology of the Hebrew Bible*, ed. S. Tamar Kamionkowski and Wonil Kim, LHBOTS 465 (New York: T&T Clark, 2010), 201–37; Benjamin Sommer, *The Bodies of God and the World of Ancient Israel* (Cambridge: Cambridge University Press, 2009); Brittany E. Wilson, *The Embodied God: Seeing the Divine in Luke-Acts and the Early Church* (Oxford: Oxford University Press, 2021).

30. Kallistos Ware, "'My Helper and My Enemy': The Body in Greek Christianity," in *Religion and the Body*, ed. Sarah Coakley (Cambridge: Cambridge University Press, 1997), 90–110; Robert Renehan, "On the Greek Origins of the Concepts Incorporeality and Immateriality," *Roman and Byzantine Studies* 21, no. 2 (1980): 105–38.

his works, his words, which, whether we know it and want it or not, surround and embrace, bear and sustain us all on all sides. But after all, that could be said and understood merely figuratively, symbolically. There is a place where the figurative and symbolic ceases, where the question of God's hands becomes quite literally serious . . . these are the hands of our Savior Jesus Christ.[31]

While Barth is sensitive to the figurative dimension of biblical language, he refuses to limit it to an abstract metaphor.[32] He instead attempts to read more literally but also more typologically. God's hands are in fact real, more real than human hands, and Christians ultimately recognize God's hands in the hands of Christ (which were and are real, and not purely metaphorical hands). Simply saying that God's hands are more real than ours, or are the "true" hands, could become an abstract, quasi-Platonic ideal. But Barth likewise resists that move in favor of a concrete referent, extended over time. God's hands are more real not only because they are perfect hands, but because they became Christ's hands in the flesh. Barth's sermon demonstrates how what is needed is not so much a reenchantment of the biblical language but a more robust understanding of biblical figuration.

For Christians, a similar move can be made with the "face" of God in the Priestly Blessing. God's face is a real face, and can be recognized as such, because it ultimately came and comes to them in the form of Christ's face.[33] As Paul wrote, "For it is the God who said, 'Let light shine out of darkness,' who has shone in our hearts to give us the light of the knowledge of the glory of God in the face of Jesus Christ" (2 Cor. 4:6). The face of Christ is not a metaphor (Matt. 26:67). "For now we see in a mirror, dimly, but then we will see face to face" (1 Cor. 13:12).

---

31. Karl Barth, *Call for God*, trans. A. T. Mackay (New York: Harper & Row, 1967), 39–47 (here 44).
32. As in Barbara Brown Taylor, *An Altar in the World: A Geography of Faith* (New York: HarperOne, 2009), 201: "God has no hands but ours."
33. For a rich historical account of how central to Christian understanding this notion has been, see Hans Boersma, *Seeing God: The Beatific Vision in Christian Tradition* (Grand Rapids: Eerdmans, 2018).

"Countenance" in the final phrase of the Priestly Blessing is an attempt to vary the wording of the English translation, a poetic variation used in William Tyndale's 1530 translation of the Pentateuch and continued in the NRSV. It obscures the fact that the Hebrew word in both the second and third phrases of the blessing is precisely the same: "face" (*pānîm*).[34] Not only is "countenance" overly formal and basically archaic, it also obscures the verbal parallelism of the two phrases and prevents hearers from recognizing the blessing's repeated emphasis on God's face. The NIV appropriately uses "face" in both lines. The repetition is a key part of what makes the blessing so powerful: it accentuates the unmediated relationality of God. Although some other biblical traditions are resolute in maintaining the distance between God and human beings, stressing that God is finally beyond human sight and may not be visually captured, the Priestly Blessing affirms that God does indeed have a face, a face that actively seeks direct face-to-face contact, a face that can be sought and beheld.

Biblical discourse lifts up this kind of contact as the ideal in the divine-human relationship by using the terminology of "face to face" (Gen. 32:30 [31H]; Exod. 33:11; Deut. 5:4; 34:10; Judg. 6:22; Ezek. 20:35; 1 Cor. 13:12). As these passages indicate, a face-to-face relationship with God can result in judgment as well as benevolence. Yet in Exod. 33:11, positive facial contact with God is further described with the phrase "as one speaks to a friend," making clear that favorable "face time" with God is a chief goal of the faithful life and lies at the core of what it is to be a human being.[35]

▪ "Be Gracious"

What does it mean to be "gracious"? In discussing this Hebrew root (*ḥ-n-n*), David Noel Freedman and J. R. Lundbom make the

---

34. Richard S. Briggs, *Theological Hermeneutics and the Book of Numbers as Christian Scripture* (Notre Dame, IN: University of Notre Dame Press, 2018), 226.
35. In Gregory of Nyssa, *The Life of Moses* (New York: HarperOne, 2006), 131–32, the goal of the entire Christian life is finally summarized as friendship with God, drawing especially from Exod. 33:11.

important observation that its nominal form (*ḥēn*) possesses two related senses.[36] It can be used to describe someone or something as beautiful. It can also be used to describe the effect of such beauty on someone. Freedman and Lundbom conclude that *ḥēn* is "the pleasing impression made upon one individual by another."[37] English speakers will not be likely to recognize this important *visual* aspect in the traditional translation of the term as "gracious" (although they might register that aspect in the related term "graceful"). Moreover, English speakers will not be apt to pick up on the term's *relational* nature in Hebrew.

The Hebrew verb form appears frequently within the context of interpersonal relationships. On the one hand, the verbal root *ḥ-n-n* can describe a personal regard that is ordinary and conventional. But in some cases *ḥ-n-n* describes an exceptional degree or quality of affection and kindness. Freedman and Lundbom, however, rule out a comparative sense of *ḥ-n-n*. They insist: "In Hebrew, *ḥnn* does not imply preferential treatment, a favoring of A over B."[38] So while the term can signal that someone receives something "extra," exceeding usual expectations and norms, it does not entail the corollary that someone else receives less. This is a significant linguistic point for understanding the Priestly Blessing, which expresses and confers divine favor within God's relationship with Israel, yet without an implication of "favoritism." Interestingly, this Hebrew root is found nowhere else in the Priestly texts of the Hebrew Bible.[39]

The Hebrew term for "face" (*pānîm*) can itself connote favor (Ps. 119:58; Zech. 7:2; Mal. 1:9). So the Priestly Blessing is centered on the provision of favor even beyond the reference to *ḥ-n-n*. Freedman and Lundbom make the further point that favor, while relational, is nevertheless not mutual. It is extended by one party to another and may be continued or ended whenever that party chooses. In this sense, then, grace or favor is always a gift rather than a possession or

---

36. D. N. Freedman and J. R. Lundbom, "*ḥānan*," *TDOT* 5:22–36.
37. Freedman and Lundbom, "*ḥānan*," *TDOT* 5:22. The connection is made explicit in the common Hebrew expression "to find favor in someone's eyes."
38. Freedman and Lundbom, "*ḥānan*," *TDOT* 5:24.
39. Jacob Milgrom, *Numbers*, JPS Torah Commentary (Philadelphia: Jewish Publication Society, 1990), 52.

a right, whether the favor involved is the ordinary grace that arises in normal personal interactions or a special grace that is conferred in addition to customary interpersonal regard. A good synonym for grace/favor is thus "generosity" or "benevolence," which can likewise embrace both ordinary and extraordinary kindness.

Such benevolence is provided by God's personal presence (Exod. 33:12–17) and results in divinely prompted prosperity and human flourishing (Gen. 33:1–11). The favor that comes from God can even make individuals sympathetic or favorable to other individuals (Gen. 39:21). This "favor" does not substitute for justice and the need for repentance, and in this respect God's favor is never automatic or to be taken for granted. But alongside repentance, Israel's call for God's gracious attentiveness is equal parts confession and proclamation of faith. Israel believes that God stands ready not only to forgive but also to respond with grace, particularly when Israel repents (e.g., Isa. 30:19; 33:2).

Because Christians often hear about grace in relation to salvation ("saved by grace"), there may be a tendency to treat the term "gracious" in the Priestly Blessing as a reference to salvation in an overly narrow, reduced form (= to be pardoned by God for sins in order to inherit eternal life). However, this is not the sense of *ḥ-n-n* in the context of the Priestly Blessing, which refers instead to God's present regard and ongoing, affirmative assistance. It would be better to conceive of "graciousness" here as something like the overflowing of divine benevolence, the wellspring of God's fundamental goodness. "My cup runs over," sings the psalmist (Ps. 23:5), as if in response. God *promotes* the best interests of those who acknowledge God.

Thus, the Bible speaks of "salvation" in a broader and richer fashion than many contemporary Christians apprehend.[40] Like blessing, salvation in the Bible is not exclusively individual or eschatological or religious or spiritual—but also communal, contemporary, political, and physical. Modernity has pushed for the privatizing and internalizing of religion, as if it is a purely subjective experience or emotion. But such an

---

40. See Terence E. Fretheim, "Salvation in the Bible vs. Salvation in the Church," *WW* 13, no. 4 (1993): 363–72; R. W. L. Moberly, "Salvation in the Old Testament," *JTI* 15, no. 2 (2021): 189–202.

account of religion is foreign to both Testaments of the Christian Bible. Indeed, there is not even a word for "religion" in the Old Testament.[41] Religion as it is known and understood today is basically a modern invention.[42] In the premodern world, religion was understood not as a discrete mental state or private disposition but as a holistic form of community life embracing politics, economics, cultures, and bodies.

Today religion has been reduced to a "spirituality" that has no ideational content or behavioral norms or corporate expression. Religion has become a mood or maybe a style. Rather than anachronistically reading this modern attenuation of religion back into the world of the Bible, contemporary believers can learn from the Bible—if they know to try—a keener understanding of their own religious accommodations to modernity, and they can take up the biblical challenge to think differently about their faith. Not only was *everything* in the Bible religious—the division of reality into "sacred" and "secular" realms is another modern invention[43]—religion had a much broader range of expression.

In the Hebrew Bible, the adjectival form of the root (*ḥannûn*, "gracious") is always (with a single exception in Ps. 112:4) employed to describe YHWH.[44] It is one of YHWH's chief characteristics and commonly appears in concert with other divine qualities (like "mercy," Exod. 33:19; 34:6). In the Old Testament, no one other than YHWH ever "gives favor" (*nātan ḥēn*). Moreover, YHWH never "seeks" favor; YHWH only gives it (Ps. 84:12).[45] However, human beings can and do "seek" favor within the Bible (e.g., Gen. 6:8), and the expression "be gracious to me" is a standard entreaty in the Psalter.[46]

---

41. It is sometimes suggested that the late Persian loan word *dāt* had this sense in the postexilic period, but that proposal in effect concedes the point.

42. See Daniel Dubuisson, *The Invention of Religions*, trans. Martha Cunningham (Bristol, CT: Equinox, 2019); Tomoko Masuzawa, *The Invention of World Religions, or, How European Universalism Was Preserved in the Language of Pluralism* (Chicago: University of Chicago Press, 2005).

43. See Talal Asad, *Formations of the Secular: Christianity, Islam, Modernity* (Stanford, CA: Stanford University Press, 2003); Craig Calhoun, Mark Juergensmeyer, and Jonathan VanAntwerpen, eds., *Rethinking Secularism* (Oxford: Oxford University Press, 2011).

44. Terence E. Fretheim, "*ḥānan*," NIDOTTE 2:203–6 (here 204).

45. H.-J. Fabry, "*ḥānan*," TDOT 5:22–36 (here 30).

46. Fabry, "*ḥānan*," TDOT 5:32.

The divine grace available in the Priestly Blessing is thus an instance of "special" favor. It is the superabundant divine benevolence that enriches and sustains the life of individuals and the entire community. Terence Fretheim describes it as "active kindness or generosity exhibited particularly toward those in need."[47] This grace is not exclusively "spiritual" in the modern sense, but—like blessing itself—it *materializes* in worldly aspects of human flourishing (prosperity, long life, fertility) as well as in a vibrant worship life and a vital apprehension of God.

"Lift Up"

This verb (*n-ś-'*) is another common one in biblical Hebrew, with a wide spectrum of uses. Its basic meaning covers a twofold sense: raising/lifting and bearing/carrying. It is used in everyday life as well as religious contexts. It is employed both literally and figuratively,[48] frequently indicating a physical gesture.[49] The specific idiom "to lift up (one's) face" sometimes just means "to look" (2 Kings 9:32), but sometimes means "to look with favor" or exhibit "a good conscience, confidence, favor, or acceptance" (e.g., Prov. 6:35; Job 11:15; 22:26; 32:21; 42:8–9).[50]

An instance of the "good conscience" sense of the idiom occurs as Abner attempts to dissuade Asahel from pursuing him: "Stop following me; why should I strike you down? How would I lift up my face to your brother Joab?" (2 Sam. 2:22, my trans.). However, when the expression is used with a transitive sense, it takes on the meaning "to be favorably disposed toward someone, gratify, show favor," as in Gen. 19:21; 32:21.[51] In Deut. 28:50 the idiom of "lifting the face" is doubled by the language of being "gracious" (*ḥ-n-n*), just as in the Priestly Blessing (Num. 6:25). The two expressions are essentially synonymous. Similar parallels occur with forms of the Hebrew roots

---

47. Fretheim, "*ḥānan*," *NIDOTTE* 2:204.
48. W. C. Kaiser, "*nś'*," *TWOT* 2:600–602 (here 600).
49. Simian-Yofre, "*pānîm*," *TDOT* 11:603–4.
50. Kaiser, "*nś'*," *TWOT* 2:600.
51. F. Stolz, "*nś'*," *TLOT* 2:769–74 (771).

r-ṣ-h ("to be pleased with," Mal. 1:8–9) and *n-b-ṭ* (*hiphil*, "to regard favorably," Lam. 4:16).[52]

Interestingly, the idiom "lifting the face" can be used with a negative as well as a positive meaning. In some cases, it is a way of expressing partisanship, unfair preferential treatment, or an inappropriate taking of sides (e.g., Mal. 2:9; Job 13:8, 10; Prov. 6:35).[53] But the same expression can also be used for the appropriate consideration of another (e.g., 2 Kings 3:14), and a participial form of the idiom ("lifted face," *nəśu' pānîm*) is employed to mean "well regarded" or "esteemed" (e.g., 2 Kings 5:1). So the basic sense of the phrase might be construed as paying close attention, with an understanding that such attention could be beneficial or harmful.

However, the phrase is never elsewhere used in the Hebrew Bible with God as the subject of the action, as the one lifting the face.[54] As with the verb "make shine," here again the Hebrew preposition is not "on" (*'al*) but "to" (*'el*), a unique construction.[55] Still, the raising of God's face can be said to indicate divine favor, insight, and guidance, as is evident in Ps. 4:6 [7H]: "There are many who say, 'O that we might see some good! Let the light of your face shine on us, O Lord!'" (cf. Pss. 27:1–4; 37:1–6). Based on this linguistic profile, it is preferable to understand the expression in Num. 6:26 as a statement about divine consideration and aid, not divine favoritism or preferential treatment (as can be the case in a legal context; see Lev. 19:15; Ps. 82:2; Prov. 18:5).[56] The Priestly Blessing is an affirmation that God's favor, which is available to all, will continue to be imparted in a special way to those who faithfully seek it. But because the best sense of the idiom in the context of Num. 6 is that of "consideration" and "favor," a better translation is "(May) the Lord's face look with favor." This translation avoids the overly formal term "countenance"

---

52. Stolz, "*nś'*," *TLOT* 2:771.
53. Stolz, "*nś'*," *TLOT* 2:771.
54. Timothy R. Ashley, *The Book of Numbers*, 2nd ed., NICOT (Grand Rapids: Eerdmans, 2022), 125; Seebass, "YHWH's Name," 39.
55. For further discussion, see Michaela Geiger, "Synergie zwischen priestlichem und göttlichem Handeln im Aaronitischen Segen (Num 6,22–27)," *VT* 68, no. 1 (2018): 51–72.
56. Simian-Yofre, "*pānîm*," *TDOT* 11:601.

and retains the duplication of "face" (*pānîm*) from the previous verse, as in the Hebrew text.

Another translational possibility appearing in some modern translations is "smile," either in the second phrase of the blessing ("May the LORD smile on you and be gracious to you," NLT) or perhaps the third (= "the LORD smile upon you and give you peace").[57] This type of translation receives a big boost from Eugene Peterson,[58] who uses it in his version of the Priestly Blessing:

> God bless you and keep you,
> God smile on you and gift you,
> God look you full in the face and make you prosper.
> (Num. 6:24–26 MSG)

Here "smile" substitutes for "face" in the second phrase, and the third phrase replaces God's face with the worshiper's face.[59]

One argument for the "smile" translation builds on the notion that the Hebrew idiom for a "fallen" face represents anger or disappointment (e.g., Gen. 4:5–6; Jer. 3:12), and thus a frown. By contrast then, a "lifted" face should indicate a smile. Of course, that applies to the third phrase of the blessing rather than the second. But the description of a "bright" face in the blessing's second phrase could also involve a smile. In Job 29:24, God's "smile" is paralleled with the light of God's (unfallen) face. In Jer. 3:12, God's fallen (*n-p-l*) face clearly indicates anger. A fallen face can generally indicate being angry or gloomy.[60] Yet in biblical discourse the opposite of a "lifted" face is not exclusively a frowning face but also a hidden or concealed face (e.g., Exod. 3:6; Isa. 50:6; 53:3).[61] For this reason, the cultic plea

---

57. Milgrom, *Numbers*, 52, acknowledges the possibility of such a translation for the blessing's third phrase.

58. As mentioned above, further advocacy for "smile" appears in Gruber's work. See especially his "Many Faces of Hebrew *nāśā' pānîm*," 253–54.

59. While I usually appreciate Peterson's work, the use of "gift" as a verb, with the corresponding loss of grace/favor, and the substitution of "give peace" with "prosper" seem like lapses in good judgment.

60. Simian-Yofre, "*pānîm*," *TDOT* 11:594; Gruber, *Aspects of Nonverbal Communication*, 350–79.

61. Simian-Yofre, "*pānîm*," *TDOT* 11:599.

"Do not hide your face" (e.g., Pss. 13:1; 44:24 [25H]; 69:17 [18H]; 88:14 [15H]) and the wish for God to "lift up" God's face are basically identical in intention and purpose. To "seek the face of God" is to desire God's blessing (2 Chron. 7:13–14).

Roy Gane rejects the "smile" translation as insufficient because for him it only refers to God's attitude and not God's action.[62] But smiles *are* actions. They communicate goodwill to others. A further objection is that Hebrew has another verb meaning "smile" (*b-l-g*), which therefore could have been used in the Priestly Blessing if that sense was wanted.[63] This objection and an even more fundamental complaint have been made by Claude Mariottini, who criticizes the "smile" translational choice as one that "trivializes the true intent of the blessing."[64] However, it is not clear to me that such a blanket verdict is appropriate. Yes, smiles can be trivial, and it is no doubt good to be suspicious of superficial cheeriness. But a smile can also be a powerful indication of kindness, forgiveness, and even love. The omnipresent smiley face is a trite emoji, to be sure. But a human smile can sometimes be profound. It is the chief reason that Leonardo da Vinci's *Mona Lisa* continues to fascinate its viewers.[65]

So I am not opposed to a "smile" translation in theory. For me, the more important consideration is to retain the double appearance of "face" in the blessing. Moreover, while either its second or third phrase might legitimately be translated "(May) the LORD's face smile," that move would tend to obscure the other important biblical resonances of a "shining" or "lifted" face. The Hebrew verb said properly to mean "smile" (*b-l-g*) is not a common verb (it only

---

62. Roy Gane, *Leviticus, Numbers*, NIVAC (Grand Rapids: Zondervan, 2004), 540. Gane views each paired phrase of the blessing as first specifying a divine attitude and then a corresponding divine action, but this distinction breaks down on closer inspection.

63. However, while this verb is glossed in *BDB* as "gleam, smile," it is glossed in *HALOT* not as "smile" but "become cheerful, brighten," based on Arabic cognates. The verb certainly does not mean "smile" in Amos 5:9; *HALOT* suggests "flash."

64. Claude Mariottini, "The LORD Make His Face to Shine upon You," https://claudemariottini.com/2018/12/10/the-lord-make-his-face-to-shine-upon-you/.

65. John B. Nici, *Famous Works of Art—And How They Got That Way* (Lanham, MD: Rowman & Littlefield, 2015), 85–100.

appears four times throughout the Hebrew Bible).[66] As Mariottini himself notes, it is also only ever used of human beings and not God. So the use of "smile" in translating the Priestly Blessing does not invite rich, intertextual connections with other biblical texts. In using "smile," the risk is to reduce the variegated meaning of either phrase to a statement of mere affirmation. Both the translations "shine" and "look with favor" additionally connote ongoing divine guidance, while "smile" does not.

As mentioned, the actual Hebrew idiom in verse 26 is "lift up his face *to* you." The NIV preserves the prepositional phrase but changes the verb to "turn" (= "the LORD turn his face toward you"), which suggests a horizontal instead of a vertical movement. The CEB keeps "lift up" but also tries to catch the prepositional phrase (= "lift up his face to you"). However, since the biblical idiom "to lift the face to" indicates possessing a clear conscience (2 Sam. 2:22; Job 11:15) or seeking approval (Job 22:26; Prov. 6:35),[67] both of which are out of place in the context of the Priestly Blessing, I favor the translation "look with favor *upon*."

"Give"

The Hebrew verb *ś-y-m* is thoroughly mundane. It commonly means "put" or "place" and is used in a wide variety of contexts.[68] In the Priestly Blessing, it is followed by "peace" and is therefore usually translated "grant" or "give" in English (= "give peace"), but it could just as easily be rendered as "put" (= "put peace").

In the context of the Priestly Blessing, two aspects of the verb deserve close attention. First, this same verb is not only used in the final phrase of the blessing as "give/put peace" but also in the next verse, in the concluding instruction to Aaron and his sons. In performing this blessing, they are to "give/put" (*ś-y-m*) God's name on the people. The shared term not only links together these two verses (i.e., the final phrase of the blessing and the closing priestly instruction), it

---

66. Ps. 39:14; Job 9:27; 10:20; Amos 5:9.
67. Stolz, "*nś'*," *TLOT* 2:771.
68. G. Vanoni, "*śym*," *TDOT* 14:89–112.

also operates as almost a play on words. In proclaiming the "giving" of peace, the priests are "giving" God's name to the Israelites. Or by "putting" God's peace on the people, the priests are "putting" God's name on them. The verbal link makes the closing instruction seem natural and epexegetical (= "and put peace on you; that is, put God's name on you"). In other words, the two statements are treated synonymously.

This language of "putting" also recalls the locative aspect of blessing, which "places" the worshiper within the framework of God's creation and ongoing nurture. If to bless is to claim something for God, it makes sense that blessing has an eye for specific recipients and their position in God's created world. Blessing can sometimes target categories of things (e.g., Gen. 1:22), but more typically blessing focuses on an individual person or object, whose place in creation is then re-narrated through the act of blessing. Blessing pushes toward specificity, which is why blessing is closely related to naming. When possible, blessing tends to single out "this" loaf of bread, "this" cup of wine, "this" person, and God's people gathered in "this" place.[69] To bless a particular person, object, or group is thus a way of affirming its position within God's creation and articulating how its well-being is intrinsic to and reliant on the well-being of all creation and the God who made creation. In this fashion, blessings are about *emplacement*.[70]

The second important aspect of the Hebrew verb *ś-y-m* in the context of the Priestly Blessing has to do with a particular nuance supported by comparative linguistic evidence. The related Akkadian verb *šamātu* is used for marking the name (or sign) of a deity on a cultic devotee or enslaved person.[71] Such markings would have been physical signs of ownership. The similarity with the closing priestly instruction

---

69. Stephen B. Chapman, "Psalm 115 and the Logic of Blessing," *HBT* 44, no. 1 (2022): 47–63.

70. Andrew Davison, *Blessing*, Faith Going Deeper (Norwich: Canterbury, 2014), 111–12.

71. Nili Fox, "Marked for Servitude: Mesopotamia and the Bible," in *A Common Cultural Heritage: Studies on Mesopotamia and the Biblical World in Honor of Barry L. Eichler*, ed. Grant Frame et al. (Bethesda, MD: CDL, 2011), 267–78; Sandra Jacobs, *The Body as Property: Physical Disfigurement in Biblical Law*, LHBOTS 582 (London: Bloomsbury T&T Clark, 2014), 214. Note that *ś-y-m* is also used in relation to Cain's mark (Gen. 4:15).

in Num. 6:27 is striking. It suggests not only that there may be a nuance of divine ownership in the administration of the Priestly Blessing, but that "putting" God's name on the people might have been understood more literally, even physically, than interpreters in the past have tended to assume. In fact, the "putting" of peace and the "putting" of God's name may convey a more material message than the disembodied spiritual message that twenty-first-century believers tend to hear. The Priestly Blessing is not only something to be heard and relied upon; it is something to be worn, like a new coat or a second skin.

"Peace"

This term has an even wider range in biblical Hebrew than it does in modern English.[72] In the Bible, peace or *shalom* is not only an absence of violence and strife, it is also the fullness of human flourishing. It is preponderantly something given and not made.[73] Peace comes from God and is available from God to those who follow God (Ps. 85:8 [9H]).[74] However, they must earnestly desire and pursue peace (e.g., Ps. 34:14 [15H]). Still, the term "peace" does have a very broad range of meanings and associations in the Bible, and it can be challenging to understand how its many uses stand in some type of relationship with one another. For instance, in 2 Sam. 11:7 David asks Uriah about the "peace [*šālôm*] of the war" (= "progress of the war"), a clear instance in which *shalom* means a general state or condition rather than war's absence.[75]

---

72. Shemaryahu Talmon, "The Signification of [*šlwm*] and Its Semantic Field in the Hebrew Bible," in *The Quest for Context and Meaning: Studies in Biblical Intertextuality in Honor of James A. Sanders*, ed. Craig A. Evans and Shemaryahu Talmon, BIS 28 (Leiden: Brill, 1997), 75–115.

73. Which is precisely why the term "peacemakers" in Matt. 5:9 is so distinctive (it is also absent from the Lukan version of the Beatitudes). Hugh M. Humphrey, "Matthew 5:9: 'Blessed Are the Peacemakers, for They Shall Be Called Sons of God,'" in *Blessed Are the Peacemakers: Biblical Perspectives on Peace and Its Social Foundations*, ed. Anthony J. Tambasco (New York: Paulist Press, 1989), 62–78.

74. Paul D. Hanson, "War and Peace in the Hebrew Bible," *Int* 38, no. 4 (1984): 341–62.

75. Ulrich Mauser, *The Gospel of Peace: A Scriptural Message for Today's World* (Louisville: Westminster John Knox, 1992), 15.

Johannes Pedersen influentially proposed a root meaning of "wholeness" for the Hebrew term, and Gerhard von Rad similarly favored "well-being."[76] Such abstractions are able to hold together the root's various uses in the Old Testament, although they lose in precision what they gain in comprehensiveness. Gillis Gerleman challenged Pedersen by arguing that the root should instead be given the basic sense of "repayment," based on the *piel* usage of the verbal root.[77] However, his argument has not gained wide acceptance.[78] If the proposals of Pedersen and von Rad are too general, Gerleman's is too narrow and unable to provide a convincing rationale for all the term's uses. A basic sense of well-being remains preferable, at least as a starting point.

The reference to *shalom* at the conclusion of the Priestly Blessing could be taken adverbially rather than objectively[79]—that is, "give peaceably" rather than "give peace" (cf. Mic. 2:3). The objective reading can turn "peace" into a static gift, most often heard by contemporary worshipers in a psychological sense. An adverbial reading might helpfully remind worshipers that peace has an active quality, that it describes a mode of action and a way of life (= "may God put you at peace" or "may God place you peaceably in the world"). But peace as a substantive is finally more powerful.

There has been a great deal of romantic talk over the years about peace in the Bible, but biblical peace is hardly an internal disposition or naïve, pie-in-the-sky political idealism. The superficiality of this idealized rhetoric is more evident now, thanks to current critiques of imperialism and colonialism. *Whose* peace? Who gets to decide what

---

76. Johannes Pedersen, *Israel: Its Life and Culture*, 2 vols., USFSHJ 28 (Atlanta: Scholars Press, 1999), 1:311; Gerhard von Rad, "*eirēnē* B.," *TDNT* 2:402–6.

77. Gillis Gerleman, "Die Wurzel *šlm*," *ZAW* 85, no. 1 (1973): 1–14.

78. See K. J. Illmann, "*šlm*," *TDOT* 15:97–104 (99); John Jarrick, "Shalom Affirmed: A Response to Gillis Gerleman," *LTJ* 20, no. 1 (1986): 2–9; Andrew Chin Hei Long, *A Cognitive Semantic Study of Biblical Hebrew: The Root* šlm *for Completeness-Balance*, Studies in Semitic Languages and Linguistics 104 (Leiden: Brill, 2021), 10–11.

79. On the adverbial accusative, see Bruce K. Waltke and Michael O'Connor, *An Introduction to Biblical Hebrew Syntax* (Winona Lake, IN: Eisenbrauns, 1990), 10.2.2. The use is characteristically anarthrous (i.e., without the definite article), as is the case with "peace" in the Priestly Blessing.

counts as "peace"? And is there truly room within a framework of "peace" for diverse inhabitants living in particular subcommunities? Or does "peace" not sometimes function as a cipher for conformity, hierarchy, and social control? The truth is that peace is often the cardinal virtue of those who hold power. Those without power, especially those who are financially, culturally, ethnically, and militarily disadvantaged, desire justice before peace.[80]

For instance, the famed *pax Romana* (or peace of Rome) was celebrated (cf. Acts 24:2–3) but also enforced militarily, and it embraced slavery as an accepted social convention. Yael Wilfand has explored how the rhetoric of peace was employed by Rome to justify and administer its empire, and how early Jewish scribes responded to that imperial reality.[81] The peace that was brought about within the earlier Assyrian Empire was also enforced through violence.[82] As these historical examples indicate, active work with an eye toward the ongoing need for decolonialization (both politically and epistemologically) is necessary to avoid a false, imperialistic account of peace and to ensure that *shalom* is rightly and productively understood.[83] Indigenous scholars have been particularly helpful in calling attention to this imperative in contemporary scholarship.[84] Even when

---

80. Patricia Hill Collins, *Fighting Words: Black Women and the Search for Justice* (Minneapolis: University of Minnesota Press, 1998), 248–49.

81. Yael Wilfand, "'How Great Is Peace': Tannaitic Thinking on Shalom and the Pax Romana," *JSJ* 50, no. 2 (2019): 223–51. Cf. Bruce W. Longenecker, "Peace, Prosperity, and Propaganda: Advertisement and Reality in the Early Roman Empire," in *An Introduction to Empire in the New Testament*, ed. Adam Winn (Atlanta: SBL Press, 2016), 15–46; Klaus Wengst, *Pax Romana and the Peace of Jesus Christ*, trans. John Bowden (Philadelphia: Fortress, 1987).

82. Frederick Mario Fales, "On *Pax Assyriaca* in the Eighth–Seventh Centuries BCE and Its Implications," in *Isaiah's Vision of Peace in Biblical and Modern International Relations: Swords into Plowshares*, ed. Raymond Cohen and Raymond Westbrook (New York: Palgrave Macmillan, 2008), 17–35. In ancient Egypt too, peace was not a mutual compact based on nonviolent interactions but capitulation to the pharaoh's authority. See Susanne Bickel, "Concepts of Peace in Ancient Egypt," in *Peace in the Ancient World: Concepts and Theories*, ed Kurt A. Raaflaub (Malden, MA: Wiley Blackwell, 2016), 43–66.

83. Atalia Omer, *Decolonizing Religion and Peacebuilding* (New York: Oxford University Press, 2023).

84. See Marcus Briggs-Cloud, "The United States as Imperial Peace: Decolonization and Indigenous Peoples," *Journal of Race, Ethnicity, and Religion* 1,

motivated by good intentions, the forced imposition of an imperial peace has never been fully successful.[85]

My go-to visual image of a peaceable society respectful of difference is the *salad bowl* rather than the melting pot.[86] The problem with the melting pot image, so central to the liberal political tradition in the US, is its antagonism toward cultural, ethnic, and religious particularity. It is an outgrowth of the Enlightenment presumption that ultimately everyone should be the same. Indeed, the tradition of Jewish particularism (often the prime target of anti-Jewish prejudice) offers a case study in why respect for particularity is essential within modern society.[87] Genuine peace requires a political framework that truly honors cultural and religious diversity within an overarching conception of society as a plurality of subcultures, rather than as a cultural homogeneity imposed by the most powerful. As Audre Lorde described in her well-known conference remarks about the limitations of working with "the master's tools," what is needed is not toleration but embodied difference.[88] Cultural diversity is not a threat but a blessing. It is the character of the people of God.

But the trickier question in the present context is whether *shalom* might have imperialistic connotations within the Bible itself. Various

---

no. 13 (2010) [online]; Randy Woodley, *Shalom and the Community of Creation: An Indigenous Vision* (Grand Rapids: Eerdmans, 2012).

85. Lauren Benton, *They Called It Peace: Worlds of Imperial Violence* (Princeton: Princeton University Press, 2024); Kimberly Zisk Marten, *Enforcing the Peace: Learning from the Imperial Past* (New York: Columbia University Press, 2004).

86. See Mohammed Berray, "A Critical Review of the Melting Pot and Salad Bowl: Assimilation and Integration Theories," *Journal of Ethnic and Cultural Studies* 6, no. 1 (2019): 142–51; Peter C. Wagner, "Should the Church Be a Melting Pot?," *CT* 22, no. 20 (August 18, 1978): 10–16; Sarah Wilson, *Melting-Pot Modernism* (Ithaca, NY: Cornell University Press, 2010). Sometimes the image of a quilt is used instead, but I am suspicious of the role of the stitching in that metaphor.

87. See Gordon Lafer, "Universalism and Particularism in Jewish Law: Making Sense of Political Loyalties," in *Jewish Identity*, ed. David Theo Goldberg and Michael Krausz (Philadelphia: Temple University Press, 1993), 177–211.

88. Audre Lorde, "The Master's Tools Will Never Dismantle the Master's House," in her *Sister Outsider: Essays and Speeches* (Berkeley: Crossing, 1984), 110–13, as cited and evaluated in Wei Hsien Wan, "Re-examining the Master's Tools: Considerations on Biblical Studies' Race Problem," in *Ethnicity, Race, Religion: Identities and Ideologies in Early Jewish and Christian Texts, and in Modern Biblical Interpretation*, ed. Katherine M. Hocky and David G. Horrell (New York: T&T Clark, 2018), 219–29 (here 227).

biblical traditions sketch a future scenario in which other nations will come to Israel in an act of political deference or even subordination. In Isa. 9, an expansive vision of "endless peace" is linked directly to military violence (v. 4) and the Davidic royal line (v. 7).[89] In Isa. 60, the nations are envisioned relocating to Jerusalem, bringing their silver and gold with them (vv. 9–11). Even though the term "peace" is not always used, this type of future scenario is one given multiple expressions in the Old Testament. Isaiah 60 further describes a subservient reversal in which "the descendants of those who oppressed you" will bend down low "at your feet" (v. 14).[90]

There is thus an apparent connection between the Old Testament's end-time vision and the political submission of other nations to Israel. Scholars debate just how literal or metaphorical such descriptions may be.[91] It is also quite possible that individual texts may have been heard in more than one way, especially over time. Psalm 72 describes how the king's enemies will bow before him, give him tribute, and "lick the dust" (v. 9). The psalm praises the king even as it also requests of God that the king rule with justice. In Zech. 9:10, Israel's king commands peace to the nations and establishes sovereignty "to the ends of the earth." One can easily imagine how such language might have once been heard in a realistic fashion, particularly if a text had existed in some form during the period of the monarchy, and how the same language could have naturally taken on a more symbolic valence in the postexilic period when there was no longer an actual Judean king in place. But there is no disguising how in the biblical tradition "peace" goes hand in hand with a notion of

---

89. J. J. M. Roberts, "The End of War in the Zion Tradition: The Imperialist Background of an Old Testament Vision of Worldwide Peace," in *Character Ethics and the Old Testament: Moral Dimensions of Scripture*, ed. M. Daniel Carroll R. and Jacqueline E. Lapsley (Louisville: Westminster John Knox, 2007), 119–28.

90. Cf. H. M. Orlinsky, "Nationalism-Universalism and Internationalism in Ancient Israel," in *Translating and Understanding the Old Testament: Essays in Honor of Herbert Gordon May*, ed. Harry Thomas Frank and William L. Reed (Nashville: Abingdon: 1970), 283–305.

91. Walter Harrelson, "Universalist and Particularist Perspectives on Zion (Jerusalem) in Biblical Texts," in *Christian Faith Seeking Historical Understanding: Essays in Honor of H. Jack Forstman*, ed. James O. Duke and Anthony L. Dunnavant (Macon, GA: Mercer University Press, 1997), 76–90.

political dominion. Moreover, this biblical association contributed in regrettable ways to the later history of global colonization by Western powers.[92]

Yet these traditions of political dominance also serve as a reminder that peace in the Bible is not only spiritual but "this worldly" and realistic. Peace is wrapped up in the messy affairs of nations and global politics. Peace is not somehow removed from that. There is also a desperate longing in the Bible for peace as the final state of all things, a restoration of creation. See, for instance, Isa. 9:2–7; 52:7; 54:10; 55:12; 66:12 (the NRSV substitutes "prosperity" for "peace"); Jer. 33:6 (the NRSV translates "peace and truth" as "prosperity and security"); Ezek. 37:26; Zech. 9:10.

Importantly, these texts do not underwrite the prospect of military invasion or a jingoistic foreign policy. In the Old Testament, the conception of Israel's relation to the other nations of the world tends in fact to be more of a centripetal one (e.g., Zech. 2:10–12), in which other nations are drawn to Israel, rather than the centrifugal notion of Israel going out into the nations (a conception that could be understood as a "missionary" or even a "crusader" paradigm). To be sure, there are scattered injunctions in the Old Testament with a centrifugal sense (e.g., "light to the nations" in Isa. 42:6; 49:6). While it also seems that a centrifugal understanding of the relationship between the nascent Christian church and other nations predominates in the New Testament, there are finally centripetal as well as centrifugal statements in both Testaments.[93] Although some Old Testament passages do appear to authorize armed engagement with other peoples,[94] such authorizations are largely limited to the period of Israel's entry into the land and the monarchic period. They

---

92. E.g., Andrew Mein, "Justice and Dominion: The Imperial Legacy of Psalm 72," *Bangalore Theological Forum* 41, no. 2 (2009): 143–66.

93. The older missiological distinction between a centripetal Old Testament and a centrifugal New Testament overdid it. See Richard Bauckham, *The Bible and Mission: Christian Witness in a Postmodern World* (Grand Rapids: Baker Academic, 2003), 72–80.

94. See Stephen B. Chapman, "Permanent War: The Case of Amalek," in *The Bible and Spirituality: Exploratory Essays in Reading Scripture Spiritually*, ed. Andrew T. Lincoln, J. Gordon McConville, and Lloyd K. Pietersen (Eugene, OR: Cascade Books, 2013), 1–19.

seem to have been treated in an increasingly symbolic fashion already within later biblical traditions.[95]

In whatever mode, the expansion of Israel's earthly dominion is consistently presented as for the benefit of the nations as well for Israel's benefit. The freedom of the nations to recognize this reality for themselves is characteristically preserved.[96] Prosperity, peace, and justice will be fully available to the nations in the coming new world order (Isa. 2:2–4//Mic. 4:1–4). Certainly, Israel is hardly neutral or objective in how it has conceived and transmitted these traditions. But just because Israel envisions itself at the center of God's plan for the world does not make that vision bad or unfair. The truth or falsity of the vision is not determined by the fact that it may be self-interested, since every political vision is inescapably self-interested. The truth or falsity of the vision will be determined by the effect it brings, by the actual nature of the situation that comes to pass (if it does come to pass): Does Israel's imagination encourage justice, or does it promote oppression? What *kind* of peace would occur in the biblical vision?

Peace is also at the heart of the New Testament's vision.[97] God is the "God of peace."[98] Christ is "our peace," according to Ephesians (Eph. 2:14). Colossians urges Christians to "let the peace of Christ rule in your hearts" (Col. 3:15a). Christians are to "pursue peace with everyone" (Heb. 12:14). The gospel message *is* peace (Acts 10:36). "Grace and peace" becomes the distinctive greeting of the New Testament's letters.[99]

---

95. Stephen B. Chapman, "Martial Memory, Peaceable Vision: Divine War," in *Holy War in the Bible: Christian Morality and an Old Testament Problem*, ed. Heath A. Thomas, Jeremy Evans, and Paul Copan (Downers Grove, IL: IVP Academic, 2013), 47–67.

96. In Joshua, e.g., the ability of Rahab and her family to choose Israel's God voluntarily is highlighted.

97. Willard M. Swartley, *Covenant of Peace: The Missing Peace in New Testament Theology and Ethics* (Grand Rapids: Eerdmans, 2006).

98. Rom. 15:33; 16:20; 1 Cor. 14:33; 2 Cor. 13:11; Phil. 4:9; 1 Thess. 5:23; 2 Thess. 3:16; Heb. 13:20.

99. E.g., Rom. 1:7; 1 Cor. 1:3; 2 Cor. 1:2; Gal. 1:3; Eph. 1:2; Phil. 1:2; Col. 1:2; 1 Thess. 1:1; 2 Thess. 1:2; 1 Tim. 1:2; 2 Tim. 1:2; Titus 1:4; Philem. 3; 1 Pet. 1:2; 2 John 3; Rev. 1:4. See Ashley, *Numbers*, 126n346.

Faced with this network of related biblical witnesses, some interpreters expand the notion of peace so much ("wholeness," "prosperity," "flourishing") that its proper concentration is eroded or lost. Peace means peace. While peace is finally about more than the absence of warfare in the biblical tradition, it is also not about less than that. Peace is first and foremost about overcoming violence (Lev. 26:6; Eccles. 3:8). Yet peace is about not only the prevention of injustice, hatred, coercion, and bloodshed but also the active pursuit and practice of behaviors that encourage communal harmony and social well-being (Isa. 59:1–8).[100] In his 1963 "Letter from a Birmingham Jail," Martin Luther King Jr. drew the same distinction by affirming that "a negative peace . . . is the absence of tension" while "a positive peace . . . is the presence of justice."[101] The biblical ideal is for justice and peace to "kiss each other" (Ps. 85:10).

It has become more difficult than ever to talk about peace as an individual and communal goal in this contemporary era of routine state violence and imperial power. Ever since the first Persian Gulf War in 1990–91, there has been a more or less "permanent war" waged by the US somewhere in the world.[102] I have been struck over these long years of death and destruction by how little any of it gets mentioned in church. In the congregation of which I am a member, and in the churches I visit, there are only rarely prayers for military personnel in active service or their families, or prayers for the victims of military engagements (including ongoing drone attacks), or prayers for enemies, or references to peace as part of the biblical vision for the world—and hardly any encouragements for congregants to live peaceable lives and forgo violence themselves, let alone at the cost of personal forbearance and self-sacrifice.

I do hear a lot about ethnic and racial diversity in church, and this topic is certainly not unrelated to the biblical vision of peace. Indeed, ethnic/racial diversity can be (and should be) urged as a living

---

100. Talmon, "Signification of [šlwm]," 102–15, describes "three concentric circles" of positive peace: for Israel internally, for Israel among the nations, and for an eschatological, cosmic peace.

101. Martin Luther King, Jr., *Why We Can't Wait* (Boston: Beacon, 1980), 96.

102. Phil Klay, *Uncertain Ground: Citizenship in an Age of Endless, Invisible War* (London: Penguin, 2022).

expression of God's peaceable kingdom. But usually such diversity is merely advocated on the basis of thin modernist notions of tolerance or "inclusivity." Yet as Walter Mignolo acutely observes:

> Inclusion is a one-way street and not a reciprocal right. In a world governed by the colonial matrix of power, he who includes and she who is welcomed to be included stand in codified power relations. The locus of enunciation from which inclusion is established is always a locus holding the control of knowledge and the power of decision across gender and racial lines, across political orientations and economic regulations.[103]

The Bible's understanding of peace is far richer than paternalistic inclusion, and the depth and breadth of its peaceable vision are particularly needed today in the face of corporate greed and nationalistic warmongering.

Today the Christian church seems to conspire in acknowledging its own insignificance, readily conceding power to the state and actively resisting opportunities to criticize the state's monopoly on power and meaning making. Fiscal benefit, political advantage, and national security regularly displace theological concerns. Instead of objecting, religious liberals and conservatives both seek instead to shelter in the power of the state. It is as if churchgoers and pastors have concluded that the contemporary church lacks genuine power, and that therefore the best thing they can do is to get on with their individual lives and attempt to leverage the state's power when and if possible. Church services are dominated by hospital announcements, expressions of psychological comfort, and moral advice. Genuine structural change for society is avoided in favor of the therapeutic, the sentimental, and the interpersonal. The function of worship is to provide an emotional high as a form of compensation for those whose lives have been ill-served by the neoliberal order.[104]

---

103. Walter Mignolo, *The Darker Side of Western Modernity: Global Futures, Decolonial Options* (Durham, NC: Duke University Press, 2011), xv.

104. For insightful analysis, see Matthew Guest, *Neoliberal Religion: Faith and Power in the Twenty-First Century* (London: Bloomsbury Academic, 2022). In neoliberalism, according to Guest, the exchange and consumption of goods and services are now "structuring social relations and defining hierarchies of status and

It is no wonder that many economically disadvantaged citizens have been abandoning Protestant churches.[105] One prominent exception seems to be those churches in which the message is, in effect, "beat the neoliberal order by joining it."[106] The modern political détente between church and state insists that religion is a private matter and that the state is entitled to hold all the real power. Yet it is disappointing to see how much Christians have bought into that compact. Christians may complain about government rules and restrictions, but they are generally supportive of the modern arrangement, which allows them to prioritize their personal lives and not be too politically responsible or, truth be told, too Christian either. I am not aware of any Christian denominations other than the Mennonite and Anabaptist "peace churches" in which peace is a frequent and explicit topic of theological reflection and discussion.[107] It remains their most important witness to the rest of us. Peace really does mean peace. It is not only a spiritual state but a social and political project.[108]

There is also a tendency for Christians to think that the problem of violence is "out there" in society somewhere rather than (also) internal to the church. But the horrific scandals of sexual abuse in Catholic and Protestant churches are only one indication (though

---

responsibility" (13). Religion is simultaneously privatized and commercialized. See also Rodney Clapp, *Naming Neoliberalism: Exposing the Spirit of Our Age* (Minneapolis: Fortress, 2021).

105. Ryan Burge, "Jesus Came to Proclaim Good News to the Poor. But Now They're Leaving Church," *CT* (November 27, 2019), http://christianitytoday.com/news/2019/november/income-inequality-church-attendance-gap-gss.html; W. Bradford Wilcox, Andrew J. Cherlin, Jeremy E. Uecker, and Matthew Messel, "No Money, No Honey, No Church: The Deinstitutionalization of Religious Life among the White Working Class," *Research in the Sociology of Work* 23 (2012): 227–50.

106. Cf. Jane Collier and Rafael Esteban, *From Complicity to Encounter: The Church and the Culture of Economism* (Harrisburg, PA: Trinity Press, 1998).

107. There are peace groups within other denominations (e.g., Anglican Pacifist Fellowship, Baptist Peace Fellowship of North America, Methodist Peace Fellowship, United Reformed Church Peace Fellowship), but on the whole they do not seem to exercise much influence.

108. On peace as a political challenge to modern assumptions about the nature of freedom and the proper roles of church and state, see Craig A. Carter, "Liberalism: The New Constantinianism," in *Peace Be with You: Christ's Benediction amid Violent Empires*, ed. Sharon L. Baker and Michael Hardin (Telford, PA: Cascadia, 2010), 28–54. Carter draws on the Augustinian tradition in an effort to chart the shape of freedom-for rather than freedom-from.

a very important one) that the problem of violence exists within the church as well: in its structures, its leaders, and its members.[109] Physical violence is sometimes excused or even promoted under the guise of spiritual authority and "traditional" gender roles purportedly mandated by the Bible. Verbal violence and a lack of charitable discourse have become urgent problems within contemporary church congregations, when Christians should instead be models of non-disparagement and "building up" others through their speech (Rom. 15:1–3), giving "grace to those who hear" (Eph. 4:29).[110] The New Testament already knows that "the tongue is a fire," because "from the same mouth come blessing and cursing" (James 3:6, 10).

In line with such New Testament admonitions, Stephen Fowl offers an insightful and valuable account of "interpretive charity."[111] This type of hermeneutical principle is not only needed in the interpretation of Scripture, but in church talk about the interpretation of Scripture, or just in church talk generally:

> Charity in interpretation is always directed toward maximizing agreement between interpreters. The point of this is not to reduce disagreement because disagreements are bad and upsetting. Rather charity assumes that if interpreters read each other's works in ways that maximize their agreements, then both the nature and the scope of their disagreements will be clearer and more capable of resolution. Such charity is particularly important when dealing with interpreters and interpretations that come from times, places, and cultures far different from our own. When we seek to maximize the agreements . . . we dismiss the temptation simply to reduce those interpreters to inferior versions of ourselves so that they can be easily dismissed. In this respect, when historical critics emphasize the temporal and cultural "strangeness" of the Bible, they are emphasizing a necessary, but not sufficient, aspect of interpretive charity.[112]

---

109. Here again the Mennonites have done important work. See Cameron Altaras and Carol Penner, eds., *Resistance: Confronting Violence, Power, and Abuse within Peace Churches* (Elkhart, IN: Institute of Mennonite Studies, 2022).

110. See Robert Jenson, "Violence as a Mode of Language," in *Essays in Theology of Culture* (Grand Rapids: Eerdmans, 1995), 40–49.

111. Stephen Fowl, "Theological Interpretation and Its Future," *AThR* 99, no. 4 (2017): 671–90.

112. Fowl, "Theological Interpretation," 680.

Charity in this sense is peaceable speech. It is speech that is not merely passively respectful but actively honoring, speech that patiently and kindly seeks common ground but is also unafraid to identify genuine differences (Eph. 4:25–32; James 4:11–12). The task given to Christians by Christ is not only to bless but to bless even enemies (Luke 6:27–28; cf. Rom. 12:14). Yet this basic Christian teaching is now openly viewed as unrealistic by otherwise faithful Christians in North America.[113]

The Priestly Blessing not only concludes with peace, it is also a prime example and model of *speaking peace*, of speaking peaceably. This is a practice and skill that God models (Ps. 85:8 [9H]) and that Christians need to reclaim and strive to sustain in their churches, as well as in the world. Peace should be a criterion for every Christian statement and action—and not only peace in the narrower sense of an absence of conflict but peace in its full sense as a communal existence in which all voices are heard and all views respectfully considered. Is what I intend to say or do conducive to *peace*? Or will my statement or action discourage peace? Peace is always a crucial question. And the first way to promote peace is to speak peaceably, which is also to bless. Blessing *is* peaceable speech, and speaking peace is blessing. Blessing and peace are linked, mutually implicating realities.[114] The act of blessing helps us understand what peace is, while the pursuit of peace reminds us of blessing's crucial importance.

A Threefold Blessing

The threefold character of the Priestly Blessing now comes fully into view.[115] Seen as a whole, the blessing highlights three divine gifts: protection (v. 24), promotion (v. 25), and peace (v. 26). Each one is a divine action *and* a divine attribute. Together they tell who God is

---

113. For sobering examples, see Russell D. Moore, *Losing Our Religion: An Altar Call for Evangelical America* (New York: Sentinel, 2023).

114. Pedersen, *Israel*, 1:311: "Peace and blessing are so closely united that they cannot be separated. Where there is blessing, there must be peace."

115. Cf. Klaus Seybold, *Der aaronitische Segen: Studien zu Numerii 6,22–27* (Neukirchen-Vluyn: Neukirchener, 1977), 43, who describes the blessing as detailing three modes of divine action, three types of divine gifts, and three spheres of divine responsiveness.

and what God does. God safeguards, God favors, and God reconciles. The structure of the blessing, with its main statement followed by two similar but expanding phrases, suggests that "the gifts of grace and peace are to be the foci in which blessing and protection materialize."[116] God's benedictory protection takes the form of God's gracious promotion and God's universal peace.

Because each of these gifts is presented as an elaboration of God's name, which itself appears prominently three times, the premodern Christian exegetes who treated the Priestly Blessing were being sensitive to the blessing's own idiom when they understood it in a trinitarian fashion.[117] This interpretation secured a place in the standard medieval annotated Bible, the *Glossa Ordinaria*, which reads: "Noting that the name of the Lord is introduced three times in this blessing. In this way the Holy Trinity is perceived, from whom and by whom and in whom are all good sought and achieved, because from him and by him and in him are all."[118] The trinitarian reading of the blessing was both followed and distinctively extended in a 1532 tract by Martin Luther.[119] Although he interprets the blessing throughout the bulk of his treatment as relating the worldly and spiritual gifts of the one God (without insisting on further specification), Luther suggests in his conclusion that worshipers might also hear the first phrase of the blessing as describing the gifts of the Father, the Creator, the second as naming the gifts of the Son, the Redeemer, and the third as about the gifts of the Spirit, the Sanctifier.

However, since the Priestly Blessing offers such a unified witness to YHWH, the God of Israel, the better type of trinitarian interpretation is not one that attempts to assign each phrase of the blessing to a

---

116. Rolf P. Knierim and George W. Coats, *Numbers*, FOTL 4 (Grand Rapids: Eerdmans, 2005), 94.

117. For background, see Nathan MacDonald, "A Trinatarian Palimpsest: Luther's Reading of the Priestly Blessing," *ProEccl* 21, no. 3 (2012): 299–313.

118. As translated in MacDonald, "Trinitarian Palimpsest," 307–8. For the Latin, see *Biblia Latina cum Glossa Ordinaria: Facsimile Reprint of the Editio Princeps; Adolph Rusch of Strassburg 1480/81*, 2 vols. (Turnhout: Brepols, 1992), 1:291.

119. WA 30/III, 574–82. For discussion, see Christopher Spehr, "Leiblicher und geistlicher Segen: Luthers Auslegung des Aaronitischen Segens aus dem Jahr 1532," *Luther* 87, no. 2 (2016): 68–74. The tract was based on an earlier sermon preached by Luther on December 8, 1527.

different person of the Trinity or a distinct trinitarian operation, but an interpretation that hears the blessing in its entirety as testifying to the threefold nature of the selfsame God, as Three in One.[120] The Father offers not only protection but also promotion and peace. The Son brings not only promotion (i.e., Christ is the one who is *for* us) but also protection and peace. The Spirit yields not only peace but also protection and promotion. The one true God, the God of Israel—Father, Son, and Spirit—blesses with protection, promotion, and peace. That is the full scope of the blessing's theological witness for Christians.

"Put My Name on Them"

After the words of the blessing, the biblical text resumes God's instructions for Aaron and his sons.[121] Especially interesting is how these instructions describe, and thus interpret, the words that have just been given. In pronouncing the blessing, God's name has not only been spoken but placed "on" (ʿ*al*) the people. There is a similar conception at work in Deut. 28:10, which tells of how "the LORD's name is proclaimed over you [ʿ*āleykā*]" (NJPS).[122] That is what the Priestly Blessing does. Three times in the blessing, God's personal name YHWH is proclaimed along with several chief characteristics of this deity. By pronouncing the blessing, the priests have, in effect, placed YHWH's *identity* on the people, a real presence that will reside with them and go with them as they depart from worship. And what will it mean for their lives now that God's name is "on" them? Because this expression is also similar to the formula for God's placing of God's holy name in the temple,[123] Robert Macina interprets the conclusion to

---

120. See Franz Delitzsch, "Der mosaische Priestersegen Num. VI, 22–27," *ZKWKL* 3 (1882): 127–30; cf. Dorothea Greiner, *Segen und Segnen: Eine systematisch-theologische Grundlegung* (Stuttgart: Kohlhammer, 1998), 266–355.

121. In the Greek Bible, v. 27 is repositioned just before the blessing, as if v. 23b. See John William Wevers, *Notes on the Greek Text of Numbers*, Septuagint and Cognate Studies 46 (Atlanta: Scholars Press, 1998), 105–6.

122. Milgrom, *Numbers*, 52. For *qr*ʾ + ʿ*al*, see also 2 Chron. 7:14; Jer. 14:9; Dan. 9:18–19; cf. Isa. 63:19.

123. Deut. 12:5; 1 Kings 9:3; 11:36; 14:21; 2 Kings 21:4, 7; 2 Chron. 6:20; 12:13; 33:7.

the Priestly Blessing as meaning that the worshipers' bodies "thereby become shrines of the LORD."[124] They carry God's name with them.[125]

Reinforcing the importance of the divine name in the Priestly Blessing is the blessing's liturgical placement at the conclusion of the main prayer service at the Jerusalem temple, when the priests would exit the temple and stand outside on the temple steps to proclaim the blessing to the people gathered in the inner courtyard (m. Tamid 7:2). Again, this occasion was apparently the only time—aside from the Day of Atonement—when the divine name was still spoken aloud in the later Second Temple period. As such, the spoken inclusion of the name in worship not only conveyed and powerfully confirmed God's blessing, it represented an actual manifestation of God's presence. The proclamation of the name constituted a culminating theophany for the assembled worshipers.[126]

The significance of this act of worship has been incorporated into the literary structure of the Pentateuch, as it has come down to us, so that the Priestly Blessing continues to have something of the same rhetorical effect through its position in the biblical text. The idea of a spatial correspondence between the biblical text and temple worship would be in keeping with what some other scholars have proposed. For Mary Douglas, the book of Leviticus offers, by virtue of its literary arrangement, an imaginative tour of the temple.[127] For Egbert Ballhorn, the book of Joshua provides a narrative topography or

---

124. Robert D. Macina, *The LORD's Service: A Ritual Analysis of the Order, Function, and Purpose of the Daily Divine Service in the Pentateuch* (Eugene, OR: Pickwick, 2019), 106n42.

125. Cf. Seybold, *Der aaronitische Segen*, 69, who describes those blessed as "newly named" (*neu benannt*) with the name of YHWH.

126. See Simeon Chavel, "The Face of God and the Etiquette of Eye-Contact: Visitation, Pilgrimage, and Prophetic Vision in Ancient Israel and Early Jewish Imagination," *JSQ* 19 (2012): 1–55; Jon D. Levenson, "The Jerusalem Temple in Devotional and Visionary Experience," in *Jewish Spirituality from the Bible through the Middle Ages*, ed. Arthur Green (New York: Crossroad, 1986), 32–61; Macina, *LORD's Service*, 106–7.

127. Mary Douglas, *Leviticus as Literature* (Oxford: Oxford University Press, 1999). See also Hannah Liss, "The Imagined Sanctuary: The Priestly Code as an Example of Fictional Literature in the Hebrew Bible," in *Judah and the Judeans in the Persian Period*, ed. Oded Lipschits and Manfred Oeming (Winona Like, IN: Eisenbrauns, 2006), 663–89.

"mental map" of the land of Israel.[128] Similarly, Jeremy Smoak argues that the location of the Priestly Blessing within Num. 5:1–10:10 draws on the memory of the temple courtyard, and that the blessing may once have been physically inscribed there.[129] In its biblical context, the Priestly Blessing, by appearing at the end of the tabernacle account in Exodus–Leviticus–Numbers and just before Israel begins its wilderness wanderings, completes God's self-revelation that began in Exodus 19 and initiates the transition to Israel's post-Sinai existence (Num. 7:1–10:10). Its narrative position reflects its observance at the conclusion of the Jerusalem temple liturgy even as it helps to construct a "narrative temple."

Although the Priestly Blessing does not appear at the very end of the traditional synagogue service, its placement just before the nineteenth concluding blessing of the main group of prayers or *Amidah* continues to mirror ancient temple practice.[130] The Priestly Blessing basically still concludes the Jewish community's prayers, just as it did at the temple.[131] Historically, worship elements probably only gradually entered synagogue practice, with synagogues initially being schools and study centers rather than worship sites per se.[132] Nonetheless, the Priestly Blessing in this way provides a direct link to the ancient past.

Rabbinic instructions and practices contain five traditional elements supporting an interpretation of the Priestly Blessing as an actual theophany or appearance of God.[133] First, the blessing continues to be delivered in Orthodox synagogues by priestly descendants,

---

128. Egbert Ballhorn, *Israel am Jordan: Narrative Topographie im Buch Josua*, BBB 162 (Göttingen: V&R Unipress, 2011).

129. Jeremy Smoak, "From Temple to Text: Text as Ritual Space and the Composition of Numbers 6:24–26," *JHS* 17 (2017), art. 2, https://doi.org/10.5508/jhs.2017.v17.a2.

130. Ron Isaacs, *Every Person's Guide to Jewish Blessings* (Brooklyn, NY: KTAV, 2021), 56.

131. Thus Paul F. Bradshaw, *The Search for the Origin of Christian Worship: Sources and Methods for the Study of Early Liturgy*, 2nd ed. (Oxford: Oxford University Press, 2002), 36n50.

132. See Heather A. McKay, *Sabbath and Synagogue: The Question of Sabbath Worship in Ancient Judaism*, RGRW 122 (Leiden: Brill, 1994).

133. For the following, a fascinating and essential resource is Avie Gold, *The Priestly Blessings: Background, Translation, and Commentary Anthologized from Talmudic, Midrashic, and Rabbinic Sources* (Brooklyn, NY: Mesorah, 1981).

who must first wash their hands and remove their shoes (b. Sotah 39a, 40a). Second, the Jewish worshipers who face them must avert their eyes, perhaps in reflection of how it is dangerous to behold God (cf. b. Hagigah 16a). Third, priestly descendants accompany their recitation of the blessing with a distinctive hand gesture in which both hands combine to make a shape like that of the Hebrew letter *šin*.

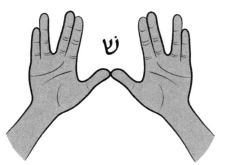

Figure 1 (dityazemli / Shutterstock)

There are multiple traditions in Judaism about the fine details of this hand gesture and how to interpret its symbolism. But the letter-sign is widely understood to refer to *'El Shaddai*, another of God's names in the Hebrew Bible, or to the *Shekinah*, an early rabbinic term referring to God's presence. The medieval Jewish scholar Rashi wrote movingly that when the priests pronounced the divine name, the Shekinah appeared on their fingertips.[134]

Excursus on *Star Trek*

Leonard Nimoy, who was of Jewish descent, adapted this traditional liturgical gesture to create the famous "Live long and prosper" Vulcan salute in *Star Trek*.[135] The Vulcan salute is essentially a one-handed version of the two-handed priestly hand sign. This remarkable cultural legacy is perhaps

---

134. Gold, *Priestly Blessings*, 41.
135. See Leonard Nimoy, *I Am Not Spock* (Millbrae, CA: Celestial Arts, 1975), 104–5.

the most influential way that the Priestly Blessing continues to affect the contemporary world outside of the Jewish and Christian worship traditions. Its popularity and recognizability pose in turn a critical question to those traditions: How is it that this characteristic gesture of blessing is no longer associated in popular culture with the worship of the God of Israel but with science fiction? The lingering power of the gesture even apart from its genuine liturgical context suggests a need for Jews and Christians to reclaim their traditional, distinctive gestures of blessing and to become more closely associated with them once more.

Fourth, the traditional congregational response to the blessing in the synagogue is: "Blessed is the Name, the Glory of His Kingship is forever and ever" (b. Sotah 40b), again identifying God's name with God's self. Fifth, rabbinic tradition reports that when the blessing was recited at the temple, the priests giving the blessing were supposed to elevate their hands above their heads. However, the high priest was only to raise his hands as high as the shiny frontlet on his turban, where the Tetragram appeared, thereby underscoring once more the centrality of the divine name to the ritual.[136]

Theophanic manifestation in the conferral of the name is mirrored in the biblical instructions for the blessing, especially the final directive from God for the priests to "put my name on the Israelites" (Num. 6:27). But what exactly is the force of "on" (*'al*)? The preposition remains odd. Why not "before" the Israelites or "toward" the Israelites? There is a curiously material quality to this expression in Num. 6:27, as if the name of God could be placed on the Israelites physically.

This idea becomes less strange if it is viewed against the backdrop of two ancient practices: the wearing of amulets and the branding or tattooing of the body. In this connection, it is worth recalling that the Ketef Hinnom texts containing the Priestly Blessing were from amulets worn around the wrist or neck. This appearance of the Priestly Blessing in the realm of personal or family religion (rather than, say, in the temple precinct) testifies to a wider range of uses for it, and its placement on amulets suggests that both the blessing and the divine name it contained were understood to have protective

---

136. Gold, *Priestly Blessings*, 36.

power (as do the references to protection from "evil" in the remainders of both inscriptions). There is a wealth of later evidence for the protective or apotropaic use of divine names in popular Judaism and Jewish magic.[137] Indeed, it is one of Jewish magic's most characteristic features.[138]

In light of these amulets, the idea of "putting on" the Priestly Blessing becomes less metaphorical. The blessing could actually be worn, and Num. 6:27 could even be understood as a divine injunction to bear God's name in some fashion on one's person. Such a practice would have an analogue in the Jewish traditions of the *mezuzah* (pl. *mezuzot*) and the *tefillin*. The *mezuzah* is the decorative holder traditionally affixed to the entryways of Jewish homes, containing a written copy of Deut. 6:4–9 and 11:13–21. The verses in Deut. 11 contain instructions about affixing God's commandments "as a sign on your hand . . . and as an emblem on your forehead" as well as on "the doorposts of your house and your gates." The verses in Deut. 6 are the words of the Shema, another identity statement about God containing the divine name: "Hear, O Israel: YHWH is our God, YHWH is one."[139] In Deut. 6 there are also instructions to "bind" (*q-š-r*) these words on one's hands and head, doorposts and gates (v. 8). *Tefillin* or phylacteries are small cases containing biblical verses too, but these are worn on the body.[140] Such customs of physically bearing God's word are aimed at the preservation of memory and the cultivation of faithful obedience, but some streams of Jewish

---

137. Josephus, *Ant.* 2.275–76; 8.42–49; Gideon Bohak, *Ancient Jewish Magic: A History* (Cambridge: Cambridge University Press, 2008).
138. Cf. Ephraim E. Urbach, *The Sages: Their Concepts and Beliefs*, trans. Israel Abrahams (Cambridge, MA: Harvard University Press, 1979), 130–31. The divine name YHWH was also used in curses, with supposedly deadly effect, and its effectiveness was thought to be the same whether uttered by Jews or non-Jews. Urbach, *Sages*, 132. This may have been one of the reasons why use of the name was restricted over time.
139. R. W. L. Moberly, *Old Testament Theology: Reading the Hebrew Bible as Christian Scripture* (Grand Rapids: Baker Academic, 2013), 24, nicely glosses the final phrase as "the one and only."
140. See Yehudah B. Cohn, *Tangled Up in Text: Tefillin and the Ancient World*, BJS 21 (Providence: Brown University, 2008); Mosheh Chanina Neiman, *Tefillin: An Illustrated Guide to Their Makeup and Use*, trans. Dovid Kratz (Jerusalem: Feldheim, 2995); David Rosenthal, "Tefillin Blessing in Eretz Israel and in Babylonia," *Tarbiz* 79, no. 1 (2010–11): 63–86.

tradition have additionally understood *mezuzot* and *tefillin* to possess apotropaic power (e.g., Numbers Rabbah 12:3).[141]

The idea of "bearing" God's name calls to mind the language in the Decalogue (Exod. 20:7; Deut. 5:11) about not "lifting up" or "bearing" (*n-ś-ʾ*) God's name "in vain" (*laššawʾ*). Although this commandment has most often been understood as relating to oaths and "swearing falsely," Carmen Imes has mounted a compelling argument that the scope of the commandment is broader than speech alone and—also gesturing toward ancient traditions of seal impressions, branding, and tattooing—she interprets the commandment as centered on the notion of belonging to YHWH.[142] Imes takes the Priestly tradition of the high priest's frontlet to be a prime example of "bearing" God's name.[143]

Even more concrete are body scarification practices. Leviticus 19 prohibits making "gashes in your flesh for the dead" or incising "a mark on yourselves" (v. 28). Although the precise sense of these admonitions is obscure, if "mark" (*qaʿăqaʿ*) is a tattoo, as is often thought (e.g., in the NRSV),[144] then here a link exists between body scarification and the honoring of the dead, who were traditionally conceived as divine or semi-divine entities in the ancient world.[145] In other words, Lev. 19:28 witnesses to an ancient connection between body art and religious identity. The potential danger is not the body art in and of itself, but the way it might undermine spiritual commitment to YHWH.

---

141. Cf. Angelika Berlejung, "Divine Presence and Absence," in *The Oxford Handbook of Ritual and Worship in the Hebrew Bible*, ed. Samuel E. Balentine (New York: Oxford University Press, 2020), 354: "The presence of a deity was believed to be real as soon as a priest (or any authorized person; e.g., the king) uttered or wrote down the divine name."

142. Carmen Joy Imes, *Bearing YHWH's Name at Sinai: A Reexamination of the Name Command of the Decalogue*, BBRSup 19 (University Park, PA: Eisenbrauns, 2017), 174, 180.

143. As this example indicates, Imes blends Priestly and non-Priestly traditions in the course of her argument. So the "original" meaning of the commandment remains in question. But in terms of the meaning of the commandment at the level of the Pentateuch as a whole, her proposal has much to commend it. On this point, see Jeremy Hutton's review in *JSS* 65, no. 1 (2020): 247–49.

144. For discussion, see Gilad J. Gevaryahu, "*Ketovet Kaʿaka* (Leviticus 19:28): Tattooing or Branding?," *JBQ* 38, no. 1 (2010): 13–20.

145. See Rachel Hachlili, *Jewish Funerary Customs, Practices and Rites in the Second Temple Period*, JSJSup 94 (Leiden: Brill, 2004); Kerry M. Sonia, *Caring for the Dead in Ancient Israel* (Atlanta: SBL Press, 2020).

One cannot claim to follow YHWH and yet bear the name of another deity on one's body.[146] The verse points to a fundamental association between one's body and the deity one honors. YHWH is not a deity who claims only a few pious thoughts now and then. YHWH wants worshipers' bodies too. YHWH wants everything.

So there is some uncertainty about whether the commandment in Num. 6:27 should be understood metaphorically or literally. Imes endorses a metaphorical understanding, which she suggestively describes as "oral branding."[147] She points to other instances of such a conception in the ancient Near East, such as a royal inscription from the time of Tiglath-pileser I (early 11th cent. BCE), which praises the deity Enlil as having his name "proclaimed over the princes." Another Akkadian text describes the deity Gibil as branding things by naming them: "Whatever is called by a name, you brand."[148] By contrast, Meir Bar-Ilan argues for an actual mark, going so far as to imagine that after reciting the Priestly Blessing Jewish priests would physically inscribe YHWH's name on the assembled worshipers' bodies.[149] This idea goes beyond the available evidence. Yet body marking did occur and was widely practiced throughout the ancient Near East.[150] Tattooed mummies have been discovered in Egypt, and tattooing, branding, and piercing were all known in Mesopotamia. Temple servants were customarily marked with physical symbols of the deity they served. The biblical tradition seems familiar with the practice (e.g., Isa. 44:5).[151]

---

146. Thus, the Jewish sage Ben Yehuda clarified that only tattooing the name of an idol on one's body was prohibited, not the name of God. See t. Makkhot 4:15, as cited in Catherine Hezser, *Jewish Literacy in Roman Palestine*, TSAJ 81 (Tübingen: Mohr Siebeck, 2001), 218.

147. Imes, *Bearing YHWH's Name at Sinai*, 76–77.

148. As noted by Imes, *Bearing YHWH's Name at Sinai*, 77, what is branded appears in this case to be the name of the thing instead of the name of the deity.

149. Meir Bar-Ilan, "Body Marks in Jewish Sources: From Biblical to Post-Talmudic Times," *Review of Rabbinic Judaism* 21 (2018): 57–81 (63).

150. See Fox, "Marked for Servitude," 267–70; Sandra Jacobs, "The Body Inscribed: A Priestly Initiative?," in *The Body in Biblical, Christian and Jewish Texts*, ed. Joan E. Taylor, LSTS 85 (London: Bloomsbury, 2014), 1–16.

151. R. W. L. Moberly, "Preaching Christ from the Old Testament," in *Reclaiming the Old Testament for Christian Preaching*, ed. Grenville J. R. Kent, Paul J. Kissling, and Laurence A. Turner (Grand Rapids: Baker Academic, 2010), 233–50 (244–46), further calls attention to how the city plan of Jerusalem is said to be inscribed on God's own hands in Isa. 49:14–16, perhaps like the statue of Gudea (the Sumerian king of

Body marking was still known in the third century CE, since Amoraic Jewish traditions refer to how the soldiers of Zedekiah inscribed the divine name on their hands, a practice which evidently took its scriptural warrant from Jer. 21:4, "Thus says the Lord, 'Behold, I will turn back the weapons of war that are *in your hands*'" (emphasis added).[152]

The Christian expression of the divine tattooing or branding tradition is the baptismal *sphragis* (or "seal"), the imposition of the sign of the cross with oil on the forehead of the Christian believer.[153] Although this rite was sometimes performed prior to baptism and sometimes after,[154] it is one of the most ancient Christian practices and is mentioned by Clement of Rome (2 Clem. 7:6), among other early authorities, and possibly even by Paul himself (2 Cor. 1:22; cf. Eph. 1:13).[155] The practice drew on multiple prior uses of the Greek term *sphragis* and therefore carried manifold connotations,[156] but the primary one was apparently that of ownership.[157]

As Jean Daniélou summarizes:

> The *sphragis* was the mark with which shepherds branded the beasts of their flock in order to distinguish them . . . [and] it was the custom

---

Lagash), which depicts him with a city plan in his lap. Moberly cites the eighteenth-century biblical scholar Robert Lowth's judgment that Isa. 49:16 is "certainly an allusion to some practice common among the Jews at the time, of making marks on their hands or arms by punctures on the skin, with some sort of sign or representation of the City or Temple, to shew their affection and zeal for it." Also interesting is how Lowth refers to similar practices among religious pilgrims in his own day.

152. Midrash Psalms 36:8. Cited in Hezser, *Jewish Literacy*, 218; Urbach, *Sages*, 132–33.

153. See Gottfried Fitzer, "*sphragis*," TDNT 7:939–52; Eldon Woodcock, "The Seal of the Holy Spirit," BSac 155 (1998): 139–63.

154. Postbaptismal anointing became standard in the Western church and was eventually its own rite. See Oskar Skarsaune, *In the Shadow of the Temple: Jewish Influences on Early Christianity* (Downers Grove, IL: InterVarsity, 2002), 368–71.

155. Jean Daniélou, *The Bible and the Liturgy* (Notre Dame, IN: University of Notre Dame Press, 1956), 54–55. The following discussion is beholden to his.

156. There was a close connection between documentary seals and the body in the ancient world because seals were carried and worn by individuals as markers of identity. See Alice Mandell, "Aaron's Body as a Ritual Vessel in the Exodus Tabernacle Building Narrative," in *New Perspectives on Ritual in the Biblical World*, ed. Laura Quick and Melissa Ramos, LHBOTS 702 (London: T&T Clark, 2022), 159–81 (esp. 166–68).

157. On the connection between body markings and ownership in ancient Israel, see Jacobs, *Body as Property*, 190–220.

in the Roman army to mark recruits as a sign of their enlistment; this mark was called the *signaculum* and consisted of a tattooing made on the hand or the forearm which represented an abbreviation of the name of the general.[158]

Related to this understanding of ownership was the practice of marking slaves. Cyril of Jerusalem (313–86 CE) encourages baptismal candidates to "come near and receive the sacramental seal (*mystike sphragis*) so that you may be recognized by the Master. Be numbered among the holy and recognized flock of Christ."[159] Here the pastoral and proprietary senses of the term merge.

Military associations with the practice funded Christian theological reflection as well. For example, Theodore of Mopsuestia (350–428 CE) similarly admonishes the newly baptized that they "are now marked as a sheep of Christ's, as a soldier of the King of heaven." Then he continues:

> The soldier chosen for service, found worthy, because of his physique and health, first receives on his hand a mark showing what king he is henceforth to serve; so now you, you have been chosen for the kingdom of heaven, and you can be recognized, when anyone examines you, as a soldier of the king of heaven.[160]

In this conception, baptism enrolls the Christian in a heavenly army and the baptismal seal is a mark of enlistment or active military duty. The association between the two practices appears similar to the Jewish tradition about the soldiers of Zedekiah.

Another stream of Christian tradition highlights the baptismal seal as a mark of protection rather than ownership or enlistment. Gregory of Nazianzus (329–90 CE) expresses this sense:

> If you fortify yourself with the *sphragis*, marking your souls and your body with the oil (*chrism*) and with the Spirit, what can happen to you? This is, even in this life, the greatest security you can have. The

---

158. Daniélou, *Bible and the Liturgy*, 55.
159. As quoted in Daniélou, *Bible and the Liturgy*, 56.
160. As quoted in Daniélou, *Bible and the Liturgy*, 58.

sheep that has been branded (*ephragismenon*) is not easily taken by a trick, but the sheep that bears no mark is the prey of thieves. And after this life, you can die in peace, without fear of being deprived by God of the helps that He has given you for your salvation.[161]

Building on such a view, Cyril of Jerusalem also writes of how the *sphragis* is "feared by the demons and recognized by the angels, so much so that the former flee and the latter accompany it as a friend."[162] This apotropaic sensibility draws on the ancient tradition of protective marks, as well as on the protective character of the divine name.

It is helpful to acknowledge these ideas and practices because they prevent modern believers from assuming too quickly that the *sphragis* was nonphysical and purely symbolic. Daniélou mentions a report by Prudentius (348–413? CE) describing how for an initiation into the cult of Dionysius "red-hot needles" were used to inscribe a *sphragis*, and how Herodotus (484–425 BCE) had much earlier related that a priest of Heracles bore physical stigmata to display his holiness and protect himself from anyone who might seek his harm.[163] According to Procopius of Gaza (465–528 CE), many Christians of his time "tattooed themselves on the hand or the arm with the name of Jesus or the cross."[164] This last comment also points to the close relationship between the sign of the cross and the name of Jesus, and how the tradition of the *sphragis* encompasses and reinforces the significance of both. The *sphragis* was understood to be physical and *indelible*, a permanent mark, whether it was invisible or visible—as it sometimes was.[165]

In biblical understanding as well, there is a personal knowledge of God that the believer carries bodily, like a wound. As Paul writes in 2 Cor. 4:7–11:

> But we have this treasure in clay jars, so that it may be made clear that this extraordinary power belongs to God and does not come from

---

161. As quoted in Daniélou, *Bible and the Liturgy*, 56–57.
162. As quoted in Daniélou, *Bible and the Liturgy*, 58.
163. Daniélou, *Bible and the Liturgy*, 60. Interestingly, Daniélou connects this kind of physical body marking with Gal. 6:17.
164. As quoted in Daniélou, *Bible and the Liturgy*, 60n11.
165. Cyril of Jerusalem can thus refer to "the holy and indelible *sphragis*." As Daniélou, *Bible and the Liturgy*, 68, notes, "this image is a very material one."

us. We are afflicted in every way, but not crushed; perplexed, but not driven to despair; persecuted, but not forsaken, struck down, but not destroyed; always carrying in the body the death of Jesus, so that the life of Jesus *may also be made visible in our bodies*. For while we live, we are always being given up to death for Jesus' sake, so that the life of Jesus may be made visible in our mortal flesh. (emphasis added)

In this passage, the human body is characterized as a crucial site not only for Christian identity but also for Christian witness (cf. Rom. 12:1–2; Phil. 1:20). The wider biblical tradition maintains an awareness that bodily knowledge of God, born in suffering, relates specifically to blessing and practices of naming, as in Gen. 32:22–32 (23–33H).[166] When Jacob wrestles with a mysterious man at the ford of the Jabbok, Jacob asks him, "Please tell me your name" (v. 29 [30H]). This name-knowledge now forms the conclusion to the story, and Jacob carries that knowledge with him from then on *in his body*. "So Jacob called the place Peniel, saying 'For I have seen God face to face, and yet my life is preserved.' The sun rose upon him as he passed Penuel, limping because of his hip" (vv. 30–31). The encounter remains visibly enshrined in his physical body, yet this weakness is his strength (cf. 2 Cor. 12:9).

Paul also reminds the Corinthians, "You were washed, you were ⸺fied, you were justified in the *name* of the Lord Jesus Christ and ⸺ Spirit of our God" (1 Cor. 6:11), witnessing to an early link ⸺en baptism and Jesus's name. "Repent and be baptized every one of you in the *name* of Jesus Christ," says Peter in Acts 2:38 (cf. Matt. 28:19; Acts 8:16; 10:48; 19:5).[167] Such references may not only

---

166. Cf. William R. Osborne, *Divine Blessing and the Fullness of Life in the Presence of God*, Short Studies in Biblical Theology (Wheaton, IL: Crossway, 2020), 69–70.

167. According to Lars Hartman, *"Into the Name of the Lord Jesus": Baptism in the Early Church*, SNTW (Edinburgh: T&T Clark, 1997), 37–50, the Greek form "*in* [*en*] the name" has arisen by imitation of similar Old Testament phrases relating to worship as "in [God's] name" (Deut. 10:8). However, "*into* [*eis*] the name," as in Matt. 28:19; Acts 8:16; 19:5, does not occur in the Septuagint and stands apart from normal Greek style. Hartman rejects previous scholarship identifying the expression as a banking metaphor indicating possession or ownership. He instead suggests that this form is based on Hebrew *ləšēm*. Hartman therefore concludes that the baptismal formula is "a literal translation of a Hebrew-Aramaic idiom" (43).

refer to an administration of baptism in which Jesus's name is invoked (Herm. Sim. 8.6.4; Justin, *Apol.* 1.61.10–13), but to an understanding of baptism as the *imposition* of Jesus's name on the baptized.

There is a fascinating interplay in the New Testament between Jesus's name and God's name.[168] Sometimes "name" references appear to embrace both the God of the Old Testament and Jesus simultaneously (e.g., Acts 2:21; 4:12; Rom. 10:13).[169] In other places, "name" references seem to refer to Jesus alone, and the power to heal and exorcise demons is attributed specifically to his name (Acts 3:16; 4:7, 10; 16:18; 19:13–17).[170] However, Charles Gieschen and others have argued that some name references, for instance in Phil. 2:9 ("the name that is above every name"; cf. Eph. 1:20–21), are not actually to the name "Jesus" but to the name that Jesus possesses or "YHWH"—in other words, that the genitive construction is subjective ("the name that Jesus has") rather than objective ("the name that is Jesus").[171] On this reading, the point of Phil. 2:5–11 is that Jesus bears the name YHWH, that Jesus is therefore a manifestation or hypostasis of YHWH, and that in this way Jesus *is* YHWH.[172] In classical trinitarian language, what is being affirmed is that the Person of the Son is the revelation of the Name of the Father (cf. Heb. 1:1–4; 2:11–12).[173]

---

168. See David B. Capes, *The Divine Christ: Paul, the Lord Jesus, and the Scriptures of Israel* (Grand Rapids: Baker Academic, 2018); C. Kavin Rowe, *Early Narrative Christology: The Lord in the Gospel of Luke*, BZNW 139 (Berlin: De Gruyter, 2006); B. Wilson, *Embodied God*, 127–29.

169. Richard N. Longenecker, *The Christology of Early Jewish Christianity*, SBT 2.17 (London: SCM, 1970), 44. This is especially clear because Acts 2:21 and Rom. 10:13 are citing Joel 2:32 (3:5H).

170. Longenecker, *Christology of Early Jewish Christianity*, 46.

171. Charles A. Gieschen, "The Divine Name in Ante-Nicene Christology," *VC* 57, no. 2 (2003): 128.

172. Intriguingly, Phil. 2:6 also appears to imply that God does have a form. See Markus Bockmuehl, "'The Form of God' (Phil. 2:6): Variations on a Theme of Jewish Mysticism," *JTS* 48, no. 1 (1997): 1–23.

173. Jean Daniélou, *The Theology of Jewish Christianity*, trans. and ed. John A. Baker (London: Darton, Longman & Todd, 1964), 150. Cf. Larry W. Hurtado, "'Jesus' as God's Name and Jesus as God's Embodied Name in Justin Martyr," in *Justin Martyr and His Worlds*, ed. Sara Parvis and Paul Foster (Minneapolis: Fortress, 2007), 128–44. See also Janet Soskice, *Naming God: Addressing the Divine in Philosophy, Theology, and Scripture* (Cambridge: Cambridge University Press, 2023), 216–17, for this same idea in Augustine and Aquinas.

The idea that Jesus possesses YHWH's name is memorably expressed in the account of the white rider in Rev. 19:1–16. Here Christ is depicted as having "a name inscribed that no one knows but himself" (Rev. 19:12). The book of Revelation also pictures the saints sealed with Christ's name *and* God's name on their foreheads (Rev. 14:1; 22:3–4; cf. 3:12). The Gospel of John makes the relationship between the names explicit by having Jesus say "I have come in my Father's name" (John 5:43; cf. 1:12), followed by similar statements in the Farewell Discourse (John 17:6, 11–12, 26).[174] The Johannine *egō eimi* statements (e.g., John 8:58, "Before Abraham was, I am") are also pertinent, as they mirror Old Testament discourse.[175] In 3 John 7, the word "name" is even used as a synonym for Jesus: "For they began their journey for the sake of the name" (although the NRSV changes "name" to "Christ").

The imposition of the sign of the cross in Christian baptism draws in typological fashion on Ezek. 9, in which God instructs a man clothed in linen with a writing case to put a *taw*-shaped mark on the foreheads of the faithful (v. 4) in order to protect them.[176] This is the tradition picked up in Rev. 14 (cf. Rev. 7:3–4, which speaks of the servants of God being "sealed" [*sphragisōmen*] on their foreheads, and Rev. 22:3–4). Whether there was a broader Jewish practice of forehead marking (Exod. 13:9, 16), which perhaps in time became a Christian practice, is an open question.[177] But Origen cites in his day a Jewish Christian who made the connection. According to Origen, the man said:

---

174. See Charles A. Gieschen, "The Divine Name That the Son Shares with the Father in the Gospel of John," in *Reading the Gospel of John's Christology as Jewish Messianism: Royal, Prophetic, and Divine Messiahs*, ed. Benjamin E. Reynolds and Gabriele Boccaccini, AJEC 106 (Boston: Brill, 2018), 405–8. See also Jarl E. Fossum, *The Image of the Invisible God: Essays on the Influence of Jewish Mysticism on Early Christianity*, NTOA 30 (Göttingen: Vandenhoeck & Ruprecht, 1995), 109–33.

175. Gieschen, "Divine Name That the Son Shares," 405–7; Longenecker, *Christology of Early Jewish Christianity*, 45. Cf. Catrin H. Williams, *I Am He: The Interpretation of 'Anî Hû' in Jewish and Early Christian Literature*, WUNT 2/113 (Tübingen: Mohr Siebeck, 2000), 255–303. I am grateful to Brittany Wilson for help with this literature.

176. In paleo Hebrew script a *taw* would have been designated with two crossed lines, like + or ×.

177. For evidence of a long tradition in the ancient Near East of forehead marking, see Othmar Keel, "Zeichen der Verbundenheit: Zur Vorgeschichte und Bedeutung der Forderung von Deuteronomium 6,8f. und Par.," in *Mélanges Dominique*

The old way of writing the Taw was in the form of the cross, so here [Ezek. 9:4] we have a prophecy of the sign that later was to be signed on the foreheads of Christians; and also of what believers now do, when they sign themselves whenever they begin a work, and especially before prayers and the holy readings.[178]

The Christian *sphragis* was also associated with Jewish circumcision as a bodily mark of identity (e.g., Rom. 4:11). A close connection between circumcision, the t-sign or cross, and the name of Jesus is fashioned in the Letter of Barnabas (70–132 CE) through a nifty numerological interpretation. Abraham's 318 "trained men" in Gen. 14:14 are understood to be circumcised servants, and 318 is read as *tau* (the numerical equivalent of 30 in Greek, used as a superlative for 300) plus *eta* (10) and *iota* (8). *Iota-eta* are the first two letters of the name Jesus in Greek.[179] Barnabas observes that in this fashion "Jesus [is signified] by two letters, and the cross by one" (9:8).[180]

The Odes of Solomon (first/second cent. CE?) may contain another reference to the link between the baptismal sign, whatever its precise form, and God's name: "For the Lord is a sign on/in them and the sign is the way of those who cross [rivers] in the name of the Lord. Put on, therefore, the name of the Most High and know him; then you shall cross without danger" (39:7–8).[181] The notion of threatening rivers is reminiscent of Isa. 43:2 and the language of "putting on the name" recalls Num. 6:27.

All of these witnesses testify to an almost forgotten tradition that not only closely linked the name of Christ and the sign of the cross but did so in a way implying a physical bearing of both by the believer.

Barthélemy: *Études bibliques offertes à l'occasion de son 60. anniversaire*, ed. Pierre Casetti, Othmar Keel, and Adrian Schenker, OBO 38 (Göttingen: Vandenhoeck & Ruprecht, 1981), 196–212.

178. As translated and discussed in Skarsaune, *In the Shadow of the Temple*, 371.

179. Earlier, 318 likely signified the value of the letters in the Hebrew form of the name Eliezer, Abraham's servant (Gen. 15:2). See Heckl, "Aaronic Blessing," 132.

180. See also Tomas Bokedal, "Scripture in the Second Century," in *The Sacred Text: Excavating the Texts, Exploring the Interpretations, and Engaging the Theologies of the Christian Scriptures*, ed. Michael Bird and Michael Pahl (Piscataway, NJ: Gorgias, 2010), 43–61 (54–56).

181. Michael Lattke, ed., *Odes of Solomon: A Commentary*, trans. Marianne Ehrhardt, Hermeneia (Minneapolis: Fortress, 2009), 539.

The Christian believer "puts on" the name of Christ. The *sphragis* tradition understands the imposition of the name/cross to occur at baptism. Modern Christians engage in a form of this tradition in making the sign of the cross, especially on Ash Wednesday when the mark of the cross is placed on their foreheads with ashes and they are enjoined to remember their baptism.

Baptism as the imposition of Jesus's name or name-sign (i.e., the cross) suggests the possibility of an additional nuance in the distinctive Pauline description of baptism as "putting on Christ" (Rom. 13:14; Gal. 3:27; cf. Col. 3:10). This language is usually interpreted as making metaphorical use of a literal expression meaning "to wear clothing" (e.g., Matt. 6:25; Mark 6:9; Acts 12:21; Rev. 19:14). The NRSV translates Gal. 3:27 on such an understanding: "As many of you as were baptized into Christ have clothed yourselves with Christ [*christon enedysasthe*]," and the Greek term *enedysasthe* can indeed have this sartorial sense.[182] But the idea of baptism as apparel may not communicate so well to modern Christians the ontological significance of baptism in Pauline theology.[183] Baptism involved being united with Christ in his death and resurrection, with physical, bodily consequences (Rom. 6:1–14; 1 Cor. 12:13).[184]

In critical scholarship, various soteriological connotations are attached to this terminology in order to amplify its adequacy.[185] Even if the expression "to put on Christ" is a clothing metaphor, it may have also expressed the existential "two ways" imagery of apocalypticism, with its urgent awareness of the new breaking in upon

---

182. Albrecht Oepke, "*enduō*," TDNT 2:319–20. The term often appears in LXX as a Greek translation for Hebrew *l-b-š* (wear). For a full study, see Jung Hoon Kim, *The Significance of Clothing Imagery in the Pauline Corpus*, JSNTSup 268 (London: T&T Clark 2004).

183. Hartman, *Into the Name*, 80–81.

184. Yu Chen, *The Ritual Dimension of Union with Christ in Paul's Thought*, WUNT 2/568 (Tübingen: Mohr Siebeck, 2022), 41–94.

185. E.g., for Hans Dieter Betz, *Galatians: A Commentary on Paul's Letter to the Churches in Galatia*, Hermeneia (Philadelphia: Fortress, 1979), 187n55, this terminology "presupposes the christological-soteriological concept of Christ as the heavenly garment by which the Christian is enwrapped and transformed into a new being.... It suggests an event of divine transformation."

the old, of a new way of life in opposition to the old way of death.[186] Yet the Testament of Levi (2nd cent. CE?) appears to describe the actual practice of baptism as involving the imposition of holy oil, washing with water, a eucharistic meal, and the donning of a new garment (8:4–5). As Daniélou notes, some early Christian writings actually use the term "garment" (*endyma*) as a synonym for baptism.[187] For instance, Hermas describes a white garment apparently used in baptism and accompanied by the *sphragis* (Herm. Sim. 8.2.4, "clothing and seals"). So the Pauline language of "putting on Christ" was likely a physically enacted understanding of how the Christian is transformed in baptism and ultimately conformed to Christ's glory (Rom. 8:29).[188]

Elsewhere Paul also describes baptism as having a close relation to the name of Christ. In 2 Thess. 1:12 Paul tells Christians to live out their calling "so that the name of our Lord Jesus may be glorified in you, and you in him." Other New Testament evidence suggests that the divine name YHWH was verbally pronounced in baptism (James 2:7, "the excellent name that was invoked over you"; cf. 5:14), perhaps in combination with the name of Christ and the mention of the Spirit (as in Justin Martyr, *Apol.* 1.61: "in the name of God, the Father and Lord of the universe, and of our Saviour Jesus Christ, and of the Holy Spirit, they then receive the washing with water").[189]

---

186. Michael Thompson, *Clothed with Christ: The Example and Teaching of Jesus in Romans 12:1–15:13*, JSNTSup 59 (Sheffield: JSOT Press, 1991), 149. There are multiple references in Second Temple sources to an apocalyptic restoration of a lost or damaged Adamic garment, and some scholars view this tradition as providing the background to Paul's rhetoric. For examples, see Crispin H. T. Fletcher-Louis, *All the Glory of Adam: Liturgical Anthropology in the Dead Sea Scrolls*, STDJ 42 (Leiden: Brill, 2002). However, Carey Newman has mounted a strong critique of this line of interpretation, insisting that the motif is decidedly absent in Paul's writings. See Carey C. Newman, "Paul on God and Glory," *PRSt* 47, no. 3 (2020): 299–316. According to Newman, the Greek term *doxa* typically meant "opinion" or "reputation." Its use to mean "glory" in the New Testament is distinctive and strikingly absent from Greco-Roman rhetoric about the gods. He believes the usage draws on the equation between *doxa* and *kābôd* first made in the LXX.

187. Daniélou, *Theology of Jewish Christianity*, 324.

188. See Teresa Kuo-Yu Tsui, "'Baptized into His Death' (Rom 6,3) and 'Clothed with Christ' (Gal 3,27): The Soteriological Meaning of Baptism in Light of Pauline Apocalyptic," *ETL* 88, no. 4 (2012): 395–417.

189. *ANF* 1:183.

There is thus an ancient association between baptism, naming, and use of a trinitarian formula.

A further suggestive parallel arises between the Christian notion of baptism as "putting on" Christ and the donning of the *tallit* or prayer shawl by a young Jewish man for the first time at his bar mitzvah, the ceremony marking his entrance into adulthood. After putting on the *tallit*, the young man recites a prayer and then also places the *tefillin* or phylacteries on his body.[190] Before donning the *tallit*, he checks the knotted cords or *tzitzit* that serve as its fringes while he prays in part:

> Bless the Lord, O my soul! Lord my God, thou art very great; thou art robed in glory and majesty. Thou wrappest thyself in light as in a garment; thou spreadest the heavens like a curtain [cf. Ps. 104:1–2].

Then as he dons the *tallit*, he prays:

> Blessed art thou, Lord our God, King of the universe, who has sanctified us with thy commandments, and commanded us to enwrap ourselves in the fringed garment.[191]

These and other prayers are repeated every morning in adult life with a daily donning of the *tallit*. Although it is difficult to trace the historical development of such rituals, the association between identity and clothing is similar to Christian baptism. Also, in both practices the clothing expresses not only a new personal identity but a freely chosen witness before God and neighbor. In both baptism and bar mitzvah, the point of the rite is not so much about being "owned" by God but "owning" the witness of one's tradition.

---

190. Some Jewish women wore *tefillin* in antiquity (see b. Eruvin 96a), and some do today; see Gabrielle Kaplan-Mayer, "Blessings in Boxes," in *Joining the Sisterhood: Young Jewish Women Write Their Lives*, ed. Tobin Belzer and Julie Pelc (Albany: State University of New York Press, 2003), 85–96. I thank Lauren Winner for this reference. The *tefillin* traditionally contain four biblical texts: Exod. 13:1–10; Exod. 13:11–16; Deut. 6:4–9; and Deut. 11:13–21. On a link between biblical name bearing and *tefillin*, cf. Imes, *Bearing YHWH's Name at Sinai*, 174–75.

191. Both translations are from the *Daily Prayer Book*, ed. and trans. Philip Birnbaum (New York: Hebrew Publishing Company, 1977), 3–6.

Whether as the assumption of a new garment and/or a new name, "putting on Christ" partakes of the same network of religious and cultural sensibilities recognizable in the motif of the divine name being "put on" the Israelites via the Priestly Blessing. The root understanding of bearing God's mark or name includes and incorporates aspects of ownership, protection, and commitment. It is somehow physical as well as spiritual. This type of "name theology" thus discloses a fuller, richer sense of God's presence, in which the manifestation of the divine embraces not only how God appears to human beings but how human beings transmit God's revealed glory to others. An influential biblical model is that of Moses's glowing face (Exod. 34:29–35), which is not only the afterglow of the Sinai theophany but also a continuation and extension of that theophany.[192]

Paul draws on this Mosaic tradition when he writes of how "all of us, with unveiled faces, seeing the glory of the Lord as though reflected in a mirror, are being transformed into the same image from one degree of glory to another; for this comes from the Lord, the Spirit" (2 Cor. 3:18).[193] Here "glory" becomes a transitive property of Christians, as represented by the divine name they bear. Or as Jesus says in the Gospel of Matthew: "In the same way, let your light shine before others, so that they may see your good works and give glory to your Father in heaven" (Matt. 5:16). Within the context of the Bible as a whole, Matt. 5 echoes Num. 6, even as Matthew further interprets divine blessing as a transformative reality in which God's light is not only received but shown (or "shone"!) by God's people to the world.

---

192. The Hebrew verb used to describe Moses's "shining" face is ostensibly from the root *q-r-n* but occurs in the *qal* only in Exod. 34:29–30, 35. The noun form of the root describes horns, leading to the medieval myth of a horned Moses. A better translation draws on the tradition of the radiance or *melammu* of ancient Near Eastern deities and kings. See Menahem Haran, "The Shining of Moses' Face: A Case Study in Biblical and Ancient Near Eastern Iconography," in *In the Shelter of Elyon: Essays on Ancient Palestinian Life and Literature in Honor of G. W. Ahlström*, ed. W. Boyd Barrick and John R. Spencer, JSOTSup 31 (Sheffield: JSOT Press, 1984), 159–73.

193. For reflections on how this aspect of Pauline theology coheres with its other aspects, see Carey C. Newman, "Paul on Christ and Glory," *PRSt* 47, no. 4 (2020): 309–413.

4

Putting the Blessing into Practice

Because of a shared emphasis on God's name and communal identity, the New Testament counterpart to the Old Testament's Priestly Blessing is the Lord's Prayer in Matt. 6:9–13/Luke 11:2–4.[1] Christians are likely to repeat this prayer in many worship services, as well as in personal and family devotions. Although its first petition is "hallowed be thy name," few Christians probably stop to wonder just what that means or what they are saying. As in the Priestly Blessing, the language is again subjunctive: "(May) your name be (made) holy." But is God's name not already holy? What sense does it make for (mere) human beings to express a desire for God's name to *become* holy or, even more, for them to participate somehow in making it holy?

Teasing out this logic requires an understanding of the Old Testament traditions about the divine name and blessing. According to Hans Urs von Balthasar, the New Testament preserves and reactivates the name discourse of the Old Testament:

> The mutual interpenetration of "holiness," "name" and "glory" [is] maintained in the New Testament, where Jesus' life's task is summarized as the glorification of the name of the Father (Jn 12.28; 17.4, 26),

---

1. For a theological exposition of the Lord's Prayer, see William M. Wright IV, *The Lord's Prayer: Matthew 6 and Luke 11 for the Life of the Church*, Touchstone Texts (Grand Rapids: Baker Academic, 2023).

and where he places the prayer for the hallowing of this same name on the lips of his disciples (Mt 6.9, *cf.* Isa 29.23), while Mary, hearkening back to Ps 119.9, praises the name of the Lord as holy (Lk 1.49).[2]

As von Balthasar recognizes, "name theology" is in fact central to the New Testament, as it is to the Old Testament. Just as Jesus can be understood as the revelation of God's name (John 17:6, 11–12, 26), so too the followers of Jesus are called to preserve the sanctity of God's name and convey that name to the world in imitation of Jesus (Col. 3:17). In other words, there is an onomastic analogy in place, even an onomastic ontology, binding Christ's followers to Christ and in turn to God.

This kind of name theology is not common in modern Christian consciousness, although it has been retained in traditional hymnody and contemporary praise choruses.[3] To reach for an illustration in popular culture, one might recall the "Brotherhood of the Cruciform Sword," which appears in Steven Spielberg's film *Indiana Jones and the Last Crusade*.[4] The brotherhood is a hereditary group whose members are devoted to preserving the location and security of the Holy Grail at all costs, even at the expense of their lives. They bear a special cross-shaped tattoo on their bodies to identify them. On both counts, they might be seen as a parable-like image for the Christian life. Christians come to bear not only a Christian identity in baptism but a special mark, God's own name. They therefore become embodiments of that name in the world, even as Christ embodied the name of God in the world. Within the context of the entire Christian Bible, God's name is thus a way of expressing God's incarnation in Christ, as well as the type of incarnational life to which Christians are called.

Another cultural vestige of this spiritual insight exists in the contemporary world. Wassim Razzouk's tattoo shop in Jerusalem is not only one of the oldest known of such establishments, operating now

---

2. Hans Urs von Balthasar, *The Glory of the Lord: A Theological Aesthetics*, 7 vols. (San Francisco: Ignatius, 1991), 6:66.
3. E.g., "Come Thou Almighty King, Help Us Thy Name to Sing" (anonymous, 18th cent.).
4. Paramount Pictures, 1989.

for perhaps seven centuries, it has become an increasingly frequent destination for Christian travelers (among others).[5] Tattooing has grown in popularity over the past few decades, which is a contributing factor. But a religious dimension to Razzouk's work is evident in the Holy Week pilgrims who opt for a tattoo from his shop as an unofficial "certificate of pilgrimage"—as well as in the religious identity of his own family (they are Coptic Christians).[6] Given the resistance to tattooing in some official Christian, Jewish, and Islamic teachings, the popularity of religiously oriented tattooing is striking and may well point to a deep logic of embodiment that has been minimized, overlooked, or flat out rejected by the modern forms of these religions. An accompanying danger is that tattooing, like other traditional customs, may become simply another capitalist commodity used to assume a faux identity, rather than constituting an authentic and meaningful practice.[7] On the other hand, part of the popularity of tattooing may arise precisely from a spirit of resistance to the way that modern life is increasingly dominated by the disembodied cyberspace of cellphones, internet sites, and virtual reality.[8]

Beginning with Descartes's identification of human existence with reason ("I think, therefore I am"), modernity has envisioned both reasoning and being in abstraction from the human body and the physical.[9] Contemporary neuroscience and philosophy have pushed

---

5. Isabel Kirshner, "Jerusalem Tattoo Artist Inks Pilgrims, Priests and Those Scarred by Conflict," *New York Times*, April 15, 2022, http://nytimes.com/2022/04/15/world/middleeast/jerusalem-tattoo-artist.html.

6. Coptic travelers to Jerusalem from Egypt have traditionally been expected to get tattoos as marks of their pilgrimage. See John Carswell, *Coptic Tattoo Designs*, 2nd ed. (Beirut: American University of Beirut, 1958), xii.

7. See Mike Featherstone, "The Body in Consumer Culture," in *The Body: Social Process and Cultural Theory*, ed. Mike Featherstone, Mike Hepworth, and Bryan S. Turner (London: Sage, 1991), 170–96; Scott Powell, Gary L. Welton, and Michael D. Wiese, "Religious Expression or Impression Management? Disparate Purchase Motivations for Products that Feature Christian Messages and Symbols," *Journal of Psychology and Christianity* 37, no. 4 (2018): 275–92.

8. See Charlene Spretnak, *The Resurgence of the Real: Body, Nature, and Place in the Hypermodern World* (New York: Routledge, 1999); P. Sweetman, "Anchoring the (Postmodern) Self? Body Mortification, Fashion and Identity," *Body and Society* 5, nos. 2–3 (1999): 51–76.

9. See Drew Leder, "Lived Body: A Tale of Two Bodies, the Cartesian Corpse and the Lived Body," in *Body and Flesh: A Philosophical Reader*, ed. Donn Welton

back against this reductionist move, advancing powerful arguments for "embodied knowledge."[10] But the most significant—and easiest to understand—criticism of modernist epistemology comes from the everyday knowledge that ordinary people regularly experience. People know that sometimes you learn things from the actions you perform and how you physically accomplish them.[11] It is not the case that ideas always come first and are then translated into action. Sometimes the actions come first and only gradually become ideas.[12] Rather than understanding actions as the bodily implementation of prior mental thoughts, it might be just as legitimate, or more so, to conceive of thoughts as the product of embodied actions.[13] Much biblical evidence points to a similar understanding of the human being and the relationship between ideas and actions.[14] Being and doing were not separate, disconnected states for early Jews and Christians.

The intrinsic relation between body and mind opens up a fresh vantage point for understanding worship, with its characteristic

---

(Oxford: Blackwell, 1998), 117–29. On the long shadow of Descartes in biblical studies, see Robert Lundin, "Interpreting Orphans: Hermeneutics in the Cartesian Tradition," in *The Promise of Hermeneutics*, ed. Robert Lundin, Clarence Walhout, and Anthony C. Thiselton (Grand Rapids: Eerdmans, 1999), 1–64.

10. Benjamin K. Bergen, *Louder than Words: The New Science of How the Mind Makes Meaning* (New York: Basic Books, 2012); George Lakoff and Mark Johnson, *Philosophy in the Flesh: The Embodied Mind and Its Challenge to Western Thought* (New York: Basic Books, 1999).

11. See Erin O'Connor, "Embodied Knowledge in Glassblowing: The Experience of Meaning and the Struggle towards Proficiency," *The Sociology Review* 55 (2007): 126–41.

12. Mark Johnson, *The Meaning of the Body: Aesthetics of Human Understanding* (Chicago: University of Chicago, 1997); Simon Roberts, *The Power of Not Thinking: How Our Bodies Learn and Why We Should Trust Them* (Lanham, MD: Rowman & Littlefield, 2022).

13. On how metaphorical and symbolic language arises from bodily awareness, see Ning Yu, "Metaphor from Body and Culture," in *The Cambridge Handbook of Metaphor and Thought*, ed. Raymond W. Gibbs Jr. (Cambridge: Cambridge University Press, 2010), 247–61. The most important figure in this regard is Edmund Husserl, especially his work *Ideas Pertaining to a Pure Phenomenology and to a Phenomenological Philosophy: Second Book, Studies in the Phenomenology of Constitution*, trans. Richard Rojcewicz and Andre Schuwer (Dordrecht: Kluwer Academic, 1989), in which Husserl describes a "kinaesthetic consciousness." This work is commonly known by the shorthand expression "Ideas 2."

14. See Klaus Berger, *Identity and Experience in the New Testament*, trans. Charles Muenchow (Minneapolis: Fortress, 2003).

combination of word and ritual. The significant point for the present discussion is that blessing is not only what is said but also what is done. Sometimes more weight is given to the words in the biblical tradition, sometimes more to the accompanying rite. But words of blessing have always been accompanied by actions. The actions without the words are insufficient.[15] The words without the actions are incomplete. Words and actions are twin aspects of blessing. Liturgical tradition holds them together.

Greater awareness of the prominent place of the Priestly Blessing within Jewish liturgical practice increases the likelihood that the conclusion of Luke's Gospel depicts a priestly act:

> Then he led them out as far as Bethany, and lifting up his hands, he blessed them. While he was blessing them, he withdrew from them and was carried up into heaven. And they worshiped him, and returned to Jerusalem with great joy; and they were continually in the temple blessing God. (Luke 24:50–53)

The narrative does not provide the actual wording of Jesus's blessing, but it does describe how he raises his hands just as the temple priests did. It also makes the point that the disciples worshiped him in response, even as they returned to the temple in Jerusalem to bless God. Jesus is thus a representative of God (as the priests also were), but also more than that. Jesus is a fitting object of veneration because he too is God.[16]

Luke's description is quite close to the description of Simon the high priest in Sir. 50:20–21, which likewise mentions a raising of the

---

15. For just this reason, normal Christian practice opposes the idea that a blessing may be imparted by a physical gesture alone, without it being accompanied by prayer or Scripture. See National Conference of Catholic Bishops, "General Introduction," *Book of Blessings* (Collegeville, MN: Liturgical Press, 1989), 4.27.

16. See Kelly M. Kapic, "Receiving Christ's Priestly Benediction: A Biblical, Historical and Theological Exploration of Luke 24:50–51," *WTJ* 67 (2005): 247–60. Claus Westermann, *Blessing in the Bible and the Life of the Church*, trans. Keith Crim, OBT (Philadelphia: Fortress, 1978), 87–88, resists this interpretation of Luke 24:50–53 because "the idea of a high priest who is taken away after he bestows his blessing is absurd." But Westermann's judgment stems from a worry that the priestly character of the blessing would undermine its Christological nature, and this does not need to be the case.

hands, a blessing, and worship. Sirach does not give the wording of this blessing either, but by focusing on a high priest the Priestly Blessing is clearly implied. For a priestly act to conclude Luke's Gospel furthermore forms a neat *inclusio* with its initial narrative scene, in which Zechariah the priest is burning incense at the Jerusalem temple (Luke 1:5–23).[17] Zechariah should perhaps proclaim the Priestly Blessing at the conclusion of this introductory account and yet is rendered mute by an angel. On this reading, the Priestly Blessing is then effectively postponed until the end of Luke's Gospel.[18]

A related interpretive possibility exists for Rev. 22:1–5, which presents a vision of "the throne of God and of the Lamb":

> And his servants will worship him; they will see his face, and his name will be on their foreheads. And there will be no more night; they need no light of lamp or sun, for the Lord God will be their light, and they will reign forever and ever. (3b–5)

The reference to God's name on the foreheads of the faithful recalls the high priestly diadem as well as the forehead marking of Ezek. 9:4, and the description of the light coming from God's face echoes the second phrase of the Priestly Blessing (cf. Rev. 7:3; 9:4).[19]

In these various ways, the Priestly Blessing's importance to the life of faith and the people of God is continued and emphasized in the

---

17. Thus Andrews George Mekkattukunnel, *The Priestly Blessing of the Risen Christ: An Exegetico-Theological Analysis of Luke 24,50–53* (Bern: Lang 2001), 196–97. A priestly interpretation of Luke 24:50–53 is also deemed "improbable" in Jean-Noël Aletti, *Without Typology—No Gospels: A Suffering Messiah; A Challenge for Matthew, Mark and Luke*, AnBib 17 (Rome: Pontifical Biblical Institute, 2022), 152–53, because (1) Jesus and the disciples are not in the temple; (2) the disciples worship Jesus rather than God; and (3) afterward the disciples return to the Jerusalem temple to worship God. But these differences are most likely part of a typology being established, in which the blessing both is and is not priestly, and Jesus both is and is not God. To be sure, as Aletti also points out, there are accounts of similar blessings elsewhere in the Old Testament that do not appear to involve the Priestly Blessing per se (e.g., Gen. 48:8–20; 1 Kings 8:14//2 Chron. 6:3).

18. Raymond E. Brown, *The Birth of the Messiah*, new updated ed. (New York: Doubleday, 1993), 263, 280. I thank Brittany Wilson for this reference.

19. David Mathewson, *A New Heaven and a New Earth: The Meaning and Function of the Old Testament in Revelation 21:1–22:5*, JSNTSup 238 (New York: Sheffield Academic, 2003), 206–14.

New Testament, even though it is not explicitly cited. At the end, no curse will remain in the New Jerusalem (Rev. 22:3a). Blessing triumphs. It is striking that a Christian vision of the final consummation of all things should rely on and use ancient Israel's tradition of blessing. What is new and climactic at the conclusion of Revelation is not something entirely unprecedented but rather the ultimate implementation of what has been in force and available all along: the blessing of God's name extended to the nations (Gen. 12:1–3; Amos 9:11–12).

More broadly, blessing is presented in the New Testament as a Christlike act (Acts 3:26) that all Christians should emulate. The injunction to "bless [*eulogeite*] those who curse you" in Luke's Sermon on the Plain (6:28) has echoes in Rom. 12:14; 1 Cor. 4:12; and 1 Pet. 3:9. This understanding of blessing relates it closely to the Christian virtues of humility, generosity, returning good for evil, and showing love toward enemies (Matt. 5:43–45; Luke 6:27; John 13:15–17; Acts 20:35).[20] At its most basic level, however, this emphasis flags a core Christian practice that has been discounted, misunderstood, or forgotten in many streams of contemporary Western Christianity: the activity of blessing. In the New Testament, it lies at the heart of Christian identity. "Repay evil with blessing, because to this you were called" (1 Pet. 3:9 NIV). In contrast to the largely secularized sensibilities of modern Christians, the New Testament highlights the responsibility of *every* Christian to bless.[21]

Today pastors might offer to pray with a hospital patient or a shut-in, but they rarely offer to bless. Most parents do not often, if ever, literally bless their children, and these and other acts of blessing do not commonly occur outside of worship—especially if blessing is understood as uttering out loud an explicit blessing statement (i.e.,

---

20. It should be observed that there are also Old Testament passages, particularly in the wisdom tradition, that lift up the importance of responding to enemies peaceably (e.g., Job 31:29–30; Prov. 24:17–18).

21. Cf. Reiner Kaczynski, "Blessings in Rome and the Non-Roman West," in *Handbook for Liturgical Studies IV: Sacraments and Sacramentals*, ed. Anscar J. Chupungco (Collegeville, MN: Liturgical Press, 2000), 393–410 (397): "All Christians, by reason of their participation, through baptism and confirmation, in the common priesthood and their having been personally blessed, are called to bless in their own sphere of life, which is always also part of the Church."

not just private thoughts or vague affirming words), perhaps even placing a hand on the one being blessed or anointing that person with oil. Certain practices of blessing do survive in highly liturgical as well as some conservative evangelical and Pentecostal streams of contemporary Christianity. But in these churches the emphasis is typically more on receiving a blessing than giving one. To hear the witness of the New Testament clearly is to realize that the true benefit of blessing comes from being an active blesser rather than a passive receiver of blessing.

When I was a young pastor serving in Hartford, Connecticut, I received a call one day from a family in my congregation. They had recently bought a house and wanted me to come over and bless it. I was nonplussed. What was I expected to do? Hartford has a large West Indian community, and the majority ethnic group in my highly diverse inner-city church was West Indian. These congregants were part of that group, and it occurred to me that different cultural expectations were in play. So I went over and started asking questions. What I heard in response was less about how such a blessing should be done and more just the firm conviction that it needed to happen. So we went together through the house, and in each room I offered a brief prayer and word of blessing for the home and its inhabitants.

Robert Elder offers this litany for blessing a Christian home:

> Remember not, Lord Christ, our offenses,
> nor the offenses of our ancestors.
> Spare us, good Lord.
> Spare your people whom you have redeemed with your blood.
> **Spare us, good Lord.**
>
> From spiritual blindness;
> from pride, envy, hatred, malice;
> from lack of loving-kindness—
> **Good Lord, deliver us.**
>
> From all deadly sin;
> and from the deceits of the world,
> the flesh and the devil;
> from all spirits, past or present, who harass us—
> **Good Lord, deliver us.**

> Bless this house, O Lord, we pray,
> as a haven for those who live here;
> as a refuge from the evil one who taunts us;
> as a hospitable place where strangers may find welcome.
> **Make this house your own, Good Lord.**[22]

As this litany demonstrates, any worries about whether this practice might be too "superstitious" can be disarmed by employing rich, authentically Christian language.[23]

Kevin Adams similarly reports a tradition of home visitation in his congregation during the church season of Epiphany. He offers to bless the home of anyone who attends his church and then prays through each house room by room. He also sometimes writes the letters C, M, and B on the door of the home. They stand both for the initials of the traditional names of the magi (Casper, Melchior, and Balthasar) and *Christus mansionem benedicat* (Latin for "May Christ bless the dwelling").[24] Doorpost marking is not only a traditional Jewish practice but in fact a traditional Christian one as well.[25] Annual home visitations featuring blessings by the pastor would be an excellent practice to institute within a congregation.

My own experience has remained with me as an example of how immigrants are sometimes re-evangelizing the West by reminding bourgeois, disenchanted moderns that religious faith is not merely a matter of a few core ideas or mental goodwill on the part of isolated individuals, but a way of life involving habitual practices and faith communities.[26] A similar realization came to me when an undergraduate

---

22. Robert J. Elder, "Bless This House: The Idea of Angry Spirits in a Member's Home Was a New One to Our Congregation," *RW* 40 (1996): 38–39. The boldface lines are to be spoken by the congregants. Elder also provides a prayer of consecration and other liturgical elements for such a service.

23. For further recommendations about such practices, see Elaine Ramshaw, "Bringing the Blessing Home: The Many Occasions for House Blessings," *Liturgy* 21, no. 4 (2006): 19–27.

24. Kevin Adams, "Living Epiphany: Framing Worship and Blessing Homes," *RW* 137 (2020): 37–39.

25. See R. W. L. Moberly, *Old Testament Theology: Reading the Hebrew Bible as Christian Scripture* (Grand Rapids: Baker Academic, 2013), 29.

26. See George Rupp, *Beyond Individualism: The Challenge of Inclusive Communities* (New York: Columbia University Press, 2015); Larry Siedentop, *Inventing*

Christian student at Duke once told me how his Muslim roommate had asked when he in fact prayed—because the Muslim student had never *seen* him do it.[27] In modern Western Christianity, religious practices have often become weak metaphors, honored in theory but unpracticed and unobserved, replaced by more vital "cultural liturgies."[28]

In this light, it is crucial to see that in a biblical understanding, blessing is not just thinking uplifting thoughts or mouthing encouraging words.[29] The biblical view of blessing is much more robust. Blessing is a physical act as well as a verbal one. It invites God's action and asserts an alignment between the circumstances of the present and the purposes of God. To bless in the Christian sense is to affirm God's identity as Creator and Ruler of the world, despite all appearances to the contrary. To bless is to reaffirm the Christian commitment to let God be God, because God's will for Christians and all people is human flourishing and indeed the flourishing of all creation.

The struggle of the church in North America arises in no small part because Christians are no longer disposed to engage in religious practices much at all within their highly affluent society. Reviving Christian practices like blessing (alongside prayer and Bible reading) in homes and families, rather than only in church, would do much to strengthen Christian commitment in the present and ensure the continued formation of Christians in the future.[30]

---

the Individual: The Origins of Western Liberalism (Cambridge, MA: Harvard University Press, 2014).

27. For reflections on how the recovery of traditional Christian practices might promote, rather than hinder, interreligious conversation and understanding, see Cynthia M. Campbell, *A Multitude of Blessings: A Christian Approach to Religious Diversity* (Louisville: Westminster John Knox, 2007), 91–93.

28. See Phil Davignon, *Practicing Christians, Practical Atheists: How Cultural Liturgies and Everyday Social Practices Shape Christian Life* (Eugene, OR: Cascade Books, 2023); James K. A. Smith, *Desiring the Kingdom: Worship, Worldview, and Cultural Formation* (Grand Rapids: Baker Academic, 2009).

29. Emily R. Brink, "Make Me a Blessing: Benedictions Are More Than Pious Wishes," *RW* 19 (1991): 2–3.

30. See Tony Jones, *The Sacred Way: Spiritual Practices for Everyday Life* (Grand Rapids: Zondervan, 2005). A potential pitfall for any program of family devotions lies in only reinscribing the cultural norms of middle-class society within the home. Christian devotions should be rooted in Scripture and tradition and focused on God, rather than offering profiles of stereotypical gender roles or stressing a perverse notion of "submission" to the husband-father.

With this in mind, Barbara Brown Taylor offers an appropriate challenge:

> The next time you are at the airport, try blessing the people sitting at the departure gate with you. Every one of them is dealing with something significant. See that mother trying to contain her explosive two-year-old? See that pock-faced boy with the huge belly? Even if you cannot know for sure what is going on with them, you can still give a care. They are on their way somewhere, the same way you are. They are between places too, with no more certainty than you about what will happen at the other end. Pronounce a silent blessing and pay attention to what happens in the air between you and that other person, all those other people.[31]

Blessing can be as simple, straightforward, and unassuming as that. However, it can also be, and deserves to be, much more than that: audible, visible, public, ceremonial, and beautiful. Brown Taylor's proposal is welcome but lacks discernible words and physical gestures. The power of blessing only increases with the boldness of its expression.

Blessing versus Benediction

Most often today, blessing is thought to occur in the form of a closing benediction in Christian worship, and the benediction itself will therefore consist of some nice words at the end of the service—but not necessarily a blessing per se. Congregants often awkwardly bow their heads for it, as if they are not quite sure what to do. Is it a prayer? Is it not a prayer? Better to close one's eyes and hope for the best. In Catholic churches, the benediction will often conclude with a trinitarian formula, and the priest and the worshipers will make the sign of the cross. But in this type of practice the trinitarian emphasis threatens to displace the genuine character of blessing, which loses its own proper meaning and significance.[32] A blessing is not a prayer

---

31. Barbara Brown Taylor, *An Altar in the World: A Geography of Faith* (New York: HarperOne, 2009), 202.
32. Antonio Donghi, *Words and Gestures in the Liturgy*, trans. William McDonough, Dominic Serra, and Ted Bartagni (Collegeville, MN: Liturgical Press,

or a trinitarian formula; it is a *pronouncement* of God's benevolent will.[33] The practice of blessing should furthermore not be limited to the end of the service or to the narrower notion of "benediction," as if a blessing is merely a religious way of saying goodbye.

Neither should blessing be used as a less committed substitute for the partaking of communion. In this type of eucharistic practice, Christian congregants come to the front of the sanctuary but request a blessing instead of receiving the communion elements. Sometimes they will cross their arms over their chest to signal such a request. In traditions where congregants are familiar with Paul's stern words about the need for self-examination prior to the Lord's Supper (1 Cor. 11:27–32) or hear pastoral strictures about their need to be in "a state of grace," certain worshipers may feel unworthy of participating in the rite fully. So it is understandable that an alternative liturgical possibility would be offered, and the introduction of another opportunity for blessing within Christian worship is always salutary.[34] Some churches will also bless children rather than distributing the communion elements to them.

In such cases, however, blessing effectively becomes a replacement for something else considered weightier or more important, and that diminishes the character and power of blessing.[35] Practices of blessing as "lesser than" illustrate the need to reclaim the distinctive form of blessing in Christian worship. Tellingly, even when worshipers opt to receive a blessing rather than the communion elements, what they often receive is in fact a brief prayer, which

---

2009), 58, insists that "the sign of the cross makes evident how the benevolence of the Father shows itself by means of the cross." But most worshipers will not connect those dots, and the concluding benediction will remain more of an affirmation of the Trinity than a blessing.

33. Contra Donghi, *Words and Gestures in the Liturgy*, 58: "Prayer is the true expression of blessing." For blessing as "pronouncement," see Michael R. Emlet, "Benediction: Living under God's Good Word," *Journal of Pastoral Counseling* 35, no. 3 (2021): 2–12 (5), drawing on Terry Johnson, *Leading in Worship* (Oak Ridge, TN: Covenant Foundation, 1996), 36.

34. Heidi Haverkamp, "Take and Eat? When Church Members Prefer Just a Blessing," *ChrCent* 133, no. 16 (Aug. 2, 2016): 20–22.

35. Helen Oppenheimer, "Blessing," in *The Weight of Glory: A Vision and Practice for Christian Faith; The Future of Liberal Theology*, ed. D. W. Hardy and P. H. Sedgwick (Edinburgh: T&T Clark, 1991), 221–30 (221): "So blessing is treated as a second best, a substitute for something else seen as the 'real thing.'"

underscores the "blessing forgetfulness" of many contemporary Christian clergy.[36]

There has historically been a close connection in the Christian tradition between the priestly or ministerial role and the act of blessing.[37] Still, it is sometimes easier, even for an ordained clergyperson, to offer nice (nonperformative) words at the conclusion of a worship service or on pastoral visits rather than taking the risk of venturing performative speech. In order to bless, a pastor needs a sense of the pastoral vocation up to the task.[38] The performative language of blessing creates new expectations and introduces heightened accountability. What if the lived reality of those who are blessed does not afterward show evidence of what the blessing was supposed to bestow? Or what if it does? The act of blessing requires a combination of commitment and courage, which is probably why in some ecclesial traditions it has been restricted to clergy along with the celebration of the Eucharist. Blessing also unfortunately came to be associated with absolution of sin, which was traditionally a priestly prerogative.[39] However, even clergy cannot bless adequately without having a firm conviction in their own calling and standing before God. Although they should not be the only people in the church to bless, they certainly should bless, early and often, as an embodied expression of their ministerial vocation.

To pronounce a genuine blessing is a strange, countercultural act.[40] As in preaching, in blessing as well clergy members audaciously claim to speak for God.[41] Yet the performance of blessing can also be a means of *recovering* a more robust sense of vocation, which is another reason why clergy should seek every opportunity to do it.[42] For

36. If churches continue this eucharistic practice, clergy should at least provide actual blessings (e.g., "I bless you in the name of the Father, Son, and Holy Spirit").

37. Charles Sherlock, "Who May Bless in God's Name? Bless What? And How?," *Australian Journal of Liturgy* 17, no. 2 (2020): 97–107.

38. Will Willimon, *Worship as Pastoral Care* (Nashville: Abingdon, 1979), 210–13.

39. Sherlock, "Who May Bless in God's Name?," 99.

40. Cf. Irma Fast Dueck, "Worship Made Strange," in *The Church Made Strange for the Nations: Essays in Ecclesiology and Political Theology*, ed. Paul G. Doerksen and Karl Koop (Eugene, OR: Pickwick, 2011), 112–22.

41. Will Willimon, *Preachers Dare: Speaking for God* (Nashville: Abingdon, 2020).

42. On this point, see Paul Pruyser, "The Master Hand: Psychological Notes on Pastoral Blessing," in *The New Shape of Pastoral Theology: Essays in Honor of Seward Hiltner*, ed. William B. Oglesby (Nashville: Abingdon, 1969), 352–65.

instance, clergy might offer not only prayers on pastoral visits but also blessings.[43] The variety and frequency of blessings could beneficially be expanded, both within worship and outside of worship. Blessings are powerful. They have a real effect. Used appropriately, the power of human touch can also add to the act of blessing, as can the use of anointing oil.[44]

Regular acts of blessing in the home and other arenas of daily life can be reintroduced. Blessing has always had a place in Christian care for the sick and the dying (James 5:14–16).[45] Blessing children (cf. Matt. 19:13–15; Mark 10:13–16; Luke 18:15–17) can be a transformative act for both children and parents alike.[46] On the Jewish sabbath in the home, the father of the household blesses his children using the Priestly Blessing.[47] Blessings might also be used in worship to mark important transitions that often go unacknowledged for congregants—for example, for departing or returning soldiers, wedding anniversaries, or newly divorced Christians. Some churches now sponsor an annual Blessing of the Animals, in which congregants (and sometimes non-congregants) bring their creaturely companions for a blessing. This kind of rite is a way to honor how nonhuman friends are partners in God's covenant alongside human beings (see Gen. 9:8–10; Ps. 36:6 [7H]), as well as yet another means of expanding the role of blessing in the life of a church. Some churches maintain the tradition of Rogation Days, in which the fields and woods are blessed and the sacramental character of God's creation is reaffirmed.

---

43. Pruyser, "Master Hand," 361–62.

44. On the pastoral challenge of using touch appropriately, see Donna Giver Johnston, "Touch of Grace: The Laying On of Hands," *Call to Worship* 45, no. 4 (2012): 17–26; Christopher J. Monaghan, "Wrestling for a Blessing: Is There a Place for Touch in the Church Today?," *The Furrow* 71, no. 1 (2020): 3–9.

45. Aimé Georges Martimort, "Prayer for the Sick and Sacramental Anointing," in *The Church at Prayer: An Introduction to the Liturgy*, ed. Aimé Georges Martimort, 4 vols. (Collegeville, MN: Liturgical Press, 1986–87), 3:117–37.

46. For reflections on blessing in the home in a way that avoids reinscribing a patriarchal mentality, see Steve Thorngate, "Blest and Kept: Why and How I Bless My Children," *ChrCent* 133, no. 16 (Aug. 2, 2016): 22–24. A valuable resource is *Catholic Household Blessings and Prayers* (Washington, DC: National Conference of Catholic Bishops, 1989).

47. William P. Simpson, *Jewish Prayer and Worship: An Introduction for Christians* (London: SCM, 1965), 35.

Blessing is a way to restore diminished aspects of lived Christianity within the modern world.

Such blessing practices also move a congregation from viewing its neighbors with suspicion and defensiveness to a stance of generosity and hospitality. As Graham Tomlin has written:

> A church that gets wrapped up in its own internal ordering is a church that has lost its way. It has forgotten its identity as a priestly people called to bless the world. Instead, a healthy church is one that is constantly looking for ways to bless the community around it, meeting whatever human need it is able to address out of its own resources, whether that means providing food, or comfort for the bereaved. The Church is most itself when it is enacting the priestly blessing of Jesus on the poor, the hungry, those who weep and those who are despised (Luke 6:20–22).[48]

Blessing is not only part of the basic "job description" for clergy and individual Christians, it is also the proper stance of the church toward the world.

There are numerous print publications containing blessings that are recommended within various ecclesial traditions and denominations. Even for ministers and congregations outside of these traditions, the publications offer helpful guidance and sample blessings that can be used and adapted to other circumstances. So, for instance, the official *Book of Blessings* (part of the Roman Missal) approved by the National Council of Catholic Bishops contains *eight hundred pages* of blessings covering many situations in which a blessing might be performed, although they are mostly ecclesial in character.[49] The United Methodist Church has *Blessings and Consecrations: A Book of Occasional Services*.[50] Lutheran blessings may be found in

---

48. Graham Tomlin, *The Widening Circle: Priesthood as God's Way of Blessing in the World* (London: SPCK, 2014), 105. On blessing as a missional strategy, also see David M. Shaw, "Called to Bless: Considering an Under-Appreciated Aspect of 'Doing Good' in 1 Peter 3:8–17," *BTB* 50, no. 1 (2020): 161–73.

49. National Conference of Catholic Bishops, *Book of Blessings* (Collegeville, MN: Liturgical Press, 1989).

50. The United Methodist Church, *Blessings and Consecrations: A Book of Occasional Services* (Nashville: Abingdon, 1984).

Evangelical Lutheran Worship: Occasional Services for the Assembly.[51] Episcopalians have a *Book of Occasional Services*.[52] Many other unofficial blessing collections appear in print and online.[53] Blessing is particularly emphasized in Celtic Christianity, which is one of the main reasons for its current popularity. Some of the better blessing collections come out of this tradition.[54] However, all such collections should of course be used with appropriate discernment.

Jewish blessings are in a different category, but they have grown out of the same blessing tradition that Christians hold in common. The Jewish blessings used in synagogue worship may be found in the *Siddur* or *Daily Prayer Book*.[55] There are many more in the Talmud. Jewish blessing practices offer an instructive, inspiring example of a lived piety with a focus on blessing. There is a blessing for almost everything. And if one does not already exist, perhaps it can be devised. I am fond of the scene in the movie *Fiddler on the Roof*[56] in which the local rabbi is asked, "Is there a blessing for the tsar?" He responds, "God bless and keep the tsar . . . far, far away from us!" But would a contemporary North American Christian ever think to seek out a clergyperson for a blessing? Why or why not?

Liturgical innovation would also be helpful. Reserving blessing for the conclusion of the service reduces the prominence of blessing in worship and limits a congregation's sense of what blessing is. Blessing is an overlooked resource for church renewal.[57] One liturgical

---

51. The Evangelical Lutheran Church of America, *Evangelical Lutheran Worship: Occasional Services for the Assembly* (Minneapolis: Augsburg, 2009).

52. The Episcopal Church, *The Book of Occasional Services*, authorized by the 2003 General Convention (New York: Church Publishing, 2003).

53. A couple of standouts are Kate Bowler and Jessica Richie, *The Lives We Actually Have: 100 Blessings for Imperfect Days* (New York: Convergent Books, 2023); and John O'Donohue, *To Bless the Space Between Us: A Book of Blessings* (New York: Convergent Books, 2008).

54. E.g., Northumbria Community, *Celtic Daily Prayer: Inspirational Prayers and Readings from the Northumbria Community* (London: HarperCollins, 2005).

55. *Daily Prayer Book*, trans. Philip Birnbaum (New York: Hebrew Publication Company, 1977). See also Marcia Falk, *The Book of Blessings: New Jewish Prayers for Daily Life, the Sabbath, and the New Moon Festival* (San Francisco: Harper, 1996).

56. Norman Jewison, dir., United Artists, 1971.

57. See N. Graham Standish, *Becoming a Blessed Church: Forming a Church of Spiritual Purpose, Presence, and Power*, 2nd ed. (Lanham, MD: Rowman & Littlefield, 2016). The activity of blessing awakens a generative spirit within a local

possibility is to reclaim the ancient Christian practice of singing or reciting the *Benedictus* as a regular part of Sunday worship.[58] The *Benedictus* consists of the words of Zechariah, father of John Baptist, in Luke 1:68–79, which begin "Blessed be the Lord God of Israel" (cf. Pss. 41:13; 72:18).

Here is the version in the *United Methodist Hymnal*, designed to be recited or sung responsively:

> Blessed be the Lord, the God of Israel,
>> who has come to set the chosen people free.
>
> **The Lord has raised up for us**
>> **a mighty Savior from the house of David.**
>
> Through the holy prophets, God promised of old
>> to save us from our enemies,
>> from the hands of all who hate us;
>
> **to show mercy to our forebears**
>> **and to remember the holy covenant.**
>
> This was the oath God swore to our father Abraham
>> **to set us free from the hands of our enemies,**
>> **free to worship without fear,**
>> **holy and righteous in the Lord's sight,**
>> **all the days of our life,**
>
> and you, child, shall be called the prophet of the Most High,
>> for you will go before the Lord to prepare the way,
>
> **to give God's people knowledge of salvation**
>> **by the forgiveness of their sins.**
>
> In the tender compassion of our God
>> the dawn from on high shall break upon us,
>
> **to shine on those who dwell in the darkness and the shadow**
>> **of death,**
>> **and to guide our feet into the way of peace.**[59]

---

congregation and shifts its posture toward the community around it from detachment to engagement.

58. Indeed, it has been argued that the *Benedictus* is a Christian rewriting of the Priestly Blessing. See Meir Gertner, "Midrashim in the New Testament," *JSS* 7 (1962): 267–92.

59. *United Methodist Hymnal* (Nashville: United Methodist Publishing House, 1989), no. 208. Boldface lines are intended to be spoken by the congregants.

This canticle has traditionally been part of early morning worship, either at Lauds or Matins. It is also sometimes used today during the penitential seasons of Advent and Lent instead of the *Te Deum*, another ancient hymn of praise.[60] The language of the *Benedictus* draws closely on Old Testament worship traditions and concludes, as the Priestly Blessing does, with an appeal to God's shining light and the hope of peace.

More fundamentally, John Kleinig calls attention to how six acts of blessing provide the underlying structure for the eucharistic service within his own (Lutheran) tradition: (1) the introductory dominical greeting ("The Lord bless you"); (2) the apostolic greeting before the sermon ("Grace and peace to you from God our Father and the Lord Jesus Christ"); (3) the word concluding the sermon ("The peace of God, which passes all understanding, keep your hearts and minds in Christ Jesus"); (4) the word after the consecration of the elements ("The peace of the Lord be with you always"); (5) the dismissal after communion ("The body of our Lord Jesus Christ and his precious blood strengthen and preserve you in body and soul to life eternal. Go in peace"); and (6) the Priestly Blessing at the end of the service.[61] Such blessings are also used in other services like baptisms, weddings, and funerals.

Thinking of blessings as not just liturgical add-ons or segues but as actually forming the basic grammar of worship could reinvigorate Christian liturgy for celebrants and congregants. Greater use of blessings would help Christian worship regain its proper function and character. What if the "benediction" was regarded as the true culmination of Christian worship, as it was in the worship of ancient Israel, rather than only an afterthought?

The Priority of Gratitude

Lament has become fashionable nowadays among some biblical exegetes and theologians, and one can understand why. Not only is

---

60. See Tyler C. Arnold, "The Benedictus: A Liturgical Framework for Extraordinary Pastoral Care," *Logia* 29, no. 2 (2020): 7–14.
61. John W. Kleinig, "Pastoring by Blessing," *LTJ* 43, no. 1 (2009): 28–38.

lament an important biblical theme, a recognition of the need for the spiritual practices associated with lament is almost entirely absent from contemporary Christian worship—even funerals! (Compare the character of Lent and other Christian penitential observances, including Advent, in earlier eras.[62]) Contemporary worship services routinely fail to address the realities of suffering, death, and mourning. Moreover, they often convey an attitude that to do so would amount to a lack of faith. Much contemporary Christian worship today is almost pathologically upbeat and superficially cheerful, as if only this affective mode is permitted.

At their best, these worship services rightly offer to God praise that is due and encourage people who are in need of encouragement. But such services can also reinforce what Anthony Giddens has called "the sequestration of experience" in modern life, the reduced quality of contemporary existence in which only a limited range of emotions and experiences is possible and/or desirable.[63] In reaction, many people seek out more extreme activities, or they read and watch about intense situations secondhand (e.g., action movies, horror films, true crime television shows, and so on). In the words of Aldous Huxley's everyman figure Savage, "But I don't want comfort. I want God, I want poetry, I want real danger, I want freedom, I want goodness. I want sin."[64] From this vantage point, the desire to include lament in corporate Christian worship is entirely understandable and salutary.[65]

62. William Stringfellow, "Advent as a Penitential Season," *The Witness* 64, no. 12 (Dec. 1961): 10–12.

63. Anthony Giddens, *Modernity and Self-Identity: Self, Society in the Late Modern Age* (Stanford, CA: Stanford University Press, 1991), 144–80. In Giddens's analysis, a (largely unintended) effect of modern institutions is to "repress a cluster of basic moral and existential components of human life," which are thereby "squeezed to the sidelines" (167). Cf. Christopher Lasch, *The Minimal Self* (London: Picador, 1985). The response to this reduction of the self often involves the overcompensations represented by narcissism and self-promotion.

64. Aldous Huxley, *Brave New World* (New York: Harper Collins, 2017), 240.

65. See Scott Harrower and Sean M. McDonough, eds., *A Time for Sorrow: Recovering the Practice of Lament in the Life of the Church* (Peabody, MA: Hendrickson, 2019); Henry L. Novello, *Setting Our Hearts upon the Deep: Acknowledging Lament in Christian Life, Worship, and Thought* (Eugene, OR: Pickwick, 2023). On lament as a needed response to damage caused by Christian practices themselves, see Lauren F. Winner, *The Dangers of Christian Practice: On Wayward Gifts, Characteristic Damage, and Sin* (New Haven: Yale University Press, 2018).

However, a preoccupation with lament may occlude the practices of praise and gratitude, which are also central to the Christian life. "And whatever you do, in word or deed, do everything in the name of the Lord Jesus, giving thanks to God the Father through him" (Col. 3:17). While there is certainly more of praise than lament in contemporary Christian worship, this "praise" is in fact often far from the biblical variety. It has a reduced, safe, sentimental quality about it—praise as an emotional high and individual good feeling. Biblical praise is just as much corporate as personal, as much thoughtful as emotional. To praise God is to employ political speech.[66] To praise God is to make the claim that one's allegiance to God is uppermost (Matt. 6:33, "Seek first the kingdom of God") and to renounce the pretension of any other claimant to that number one spot. Genuine praise is risky and not necessarily reassuring or comfortable at all. It has an objective quality about it. Like blessing, praise names the way things really are, and it is not especially concerned with the subjective experience of those doing the praising. Praise is not about happiness but honesty. Praise grows out of wonder, and wonder is crucial to resisting the reduction of contemporary life to making and having.[67]

James Wilhoit reminds Christians that thankfulness is a Christian virtue and gratitude an essential spiritual practice.[68] The deeper problem with lament is that it can all too easily be co-opted by the spirit of cynicism and complaint that seems pervasive in contemporary Western culture. The present-day temper prefers critique to edification, pessimism to hope, and anti-heroes to heroes. Lament can play into that spirit by undermining or displacing hope. Lament is finally too convenient for people who want to resist giving thanks and beg off from engaging in the tough spiritual work of living a life of genuine appreciation. Intriguingly, Wilhoit also points to a close connection between the practice of gratitude and naming.[69] Knowing

---

66. Rolf Jacobson, "The Costly Loss of Praise," *ThTo* 57, no. 3 (2000): 375–85.
67. Cf. Dietrich von Hildebrand and Balduin Schwarz, with Joseph Ratzinger and Romano Guardini, *Gratitude* (Steubenville, OH: Hildebrand Press, 2023), 8: "The person who is filled with gratitude toward God, whose whole life is permeated by this primary attitude of gratitude, is also the only person who is truly awake."
68. James C. Wilhoit, *Spiritual Formation as if the Church Mattered: Growing in Christ through Community*, 2nd ed. (Grand Rapids: Baker Academic, 2022), 223–24.
69. Wilhoit, *Spiritual Formation*, 224–25.

and using the names for things is one of the basic ways to be thankful for them and to cultivate a spirit of gratitude.

I can testify to this connection. I have observed how learning the names of the flowers and trees outdoors makes me slow down, see them with fresh eyes, and become more grateful for their distinctive features and respective locations. If I know the name of a plant, it then becomes more real to me and I appreciate it more keenly. As I have tried to grow various flowers and shrubs in my yard, I have learned about their preferred soil cultures, their respective needs for light and water, and their annual growing cycles. There is an aged oak at the back of my property that I can only think of as "wise."[70] Knowing their names is often the first step in paying attention and developing a form of relational understanding: this is foxglove, that is campion, and over there osmanthus. The same is of course true with people. To learn a person's name is to develop greater respect and compassion for that person, and by extension other people as well. Knowing the names for things encourages a certain way of being in the world, just as "anonymous" living promotes another type of existence.[71] Not to know and use people's names conveys disrespect, and even more it encourages me to think less of others and too much of myself. What I am calling anonymous living is finally another term for selfishness. Deuteronomy 29:18–20 [17–19H] instructively contrasts divine blessing with "blessing oneself"—turning away from God and indulging in untruthful self-regard. The opposite of blessing is not actually cursing but vanity.

So too with God's name. To know and use God's name is to be schooled in the practice of recognizing God and giving thanks to God. A close relationship exists between blessing and praise in the Bible, so much so that at times they are treated as synonyms (e.g., Pss. 34:1 [2H]; 145:2; Neh. 9:5; 1 Chron. 16:35–36). The Priestly Blessing, as

---

70. For fascinating accounts of how modern science is revealing the sentient nature of plants and woodlands, see Zoë Schlanger, *The Light Eaters: How the Unseen World of Plant Intelligence Offers a New Understanding of Life on Earth* (New York: Harper, 2024); Peter Wohlleben, *The Hidden Life of Trees: What They Feel, How They Communicate—Discoveries from a Secret World* (Glasgow: William Collins, 2016).

71. The close relationship between attentiveness and prayer is brilliantly unfolded in Simone Weil, "Reflections on the Right Use of School Studies with a View to the Love of God," in *Waiting for God* (New York: Perennial, 2001), 57–65.

a liturgical pronouncement of God's name and identity, reflects and models this all-important spiritual dynamic. Lament continues to have value, and there does need to be more room in Christian worship for sorrow and suffering, loneliness and loss. But praise and blessing cannot be displaced by lament either. To give and receive a blessing is precisely to put gratitude and hope into practice.

Blessing as truth-telling in turn raises the challenging question of inappropriate blessings. Can a blessing be inadvisable because the thing to be blessed is not something for which we are truly grateful or even should be grateful? There are moral conditions for worship in the Bible (e.g., Pss. 15; 24; 1 Cor. 11:27–32).[72] These are difficult to acknowledge and affirm in modern society, in part because they have been horribly abused. Yet most Christians would be uncomfortable with the prospect of blessing things that are immoral, unjust, or violent. To bless such things could itself become sinful or abusive, just as all liturgical acts can be perverted and put to false purposes. God blesses the righteous (Ps. 5:12 [13H]).

Moreover, there is the reality of biblical curses to consider. Cursing is also on display in the Bible,[73] which at the very least should signal that not everything is to be blessed. Here again, modern liberals have largely ignored biblical curses and some modern conservatives have abused them, especially by co-opting such curses for use in contemporary politics.[74] As hard as it is to acknowledge, cursing is a prominent biblical practice, mostly employed in the context of covenantal unfaithfulness.[75] A covenantal relationship with God entails the possibility of curse

---

72. See Blessing Onoriode Boloje and Alphonso Gruenewald, "Accessing Yahweh's Presence: Ethical Implications of the Entrance Liturgy of Psalm 15," *Stellenbosch Theological Journal* 2, no. 2 (2016): 131–52.

73. On biblical curses, see Brian Britt, *Biblical Curses and the Displacement of Tradition* (Sheffield: Sheffield Phoenix, 2011); Anne Mare Kitz, *Cursed Are You! The Phenomenology of Cursing in Cuneiform and Hebrew Texts* (Winona Lake, IN: Eisenbrauns, 2014).

74. See Joseph L. Conn, "A Taxing Situation: IRS Investigates 'Imprecatory Prayer' Pastor Wiley Drake for Church Electioneering," *Church & State* 61, no. 3 (2008): 55–56.

75. E.g., Deut. 27–28; Rom. 2:1–11; 1 Cor. 16:22; Gal. 3:10–14; Heb. 12:14–17. See Delbert R. Hillers, *Treaty-Curses and the Old Testament Prophets*, BibOr 16 (Rome: Pontifical Biblical Institute, 1964); Laura Quick, *Deuteronomy 28 and the Aramaic Curse Tradition* (Oxford: Oxford University Press, 2018).

as well as blessing.[76] God is even sometimes depicted as the agent of cursing (e.g., Gen. 3:14–19; Jer. 11:1–5; Mal. 2:2).[77] Nor is this only an Old Testament tradition, as New Testament examples of cursing bear witness.[78] The Lukan Beatitudes contain "woes" too (Luke 6:24–26).[79] Peter curses Simon Magus (Acts 8:20–22). Paul curses Bar-Jesus (Acts 13:6–12). There is even at least one example of Jesus cursing.[80]

So to bless anything and everything would be to abandon the integrity of blessing and court the danger of indiscriminate approval.[81] But how to discriminate? How is one to tell when something should be blessed and when it should not? Gordon Lathrop frames the issue like this:

> Do our blessings tell the truth? Do they genuinely celebrate the comfort of the afflicted, the death of Christ as the source of life, the giving away of whatever is blessed for the sake of a hungry world, the end of the boundaries of "mine" and "thine," the care of a wounded earth, the welcome of the rejected?[82]

In other words, the content and context of a blessing need to fit authentically within the theological framework of Christian understanding. A blessing must not betray the gospel if it is to be a Christian blessing. Blessing is about truth-telling.

---

76. E.g., Gen. 12:1–3; Deut. 11:26–28; 30:19–20; Matt. 25:31–46.

77. Kit Barker, *Imprecation as Divine Discourse: Speech Act Theory, Dual Authorship, and Theological Interpretation*, JTISup 16 (Winona Lake, IN: Eisenbrauns, 2016).

78. Luke 10:11; Acts 23:3; 1 Cor. 5:4–5; 16:22; Gal. 1:8–9; 5:12; 1 Tim. 1:20; James 3:9–10.

79. See Julia Van Den Brink, "Luke's Beatitudes and Woes: Are They Covenant Blessings and Curses?," *Stimulus* 23, no. 3 (2016): 12–17.

80. Matt. 11:20–24//Luke 10:13–15; Matt. 21:18–22//Mark 11:12–14; cf. Matt. 23:13–36. See Peter M. Scott, "Seasons of Grace? Christ's Cursing of a Fig Tree," in *Christology and Scripture: Interdisciplinary Perspectives*, ed. Andrew Lincoln and A. Paddison (New York: Bloomsbury, 2008), 188–206.

81. National Conference of Catholic Bishops, *Book of Blessings*, 841: "It is not fitting to turn every object or situation into an occasion for celebrating a blessing (for example, every monument erected no matter what its theme, the installation of military weapons, frivolous events)."

82. Gordon W. Lathrop, *Saving Images: The Presence of the Bible in Christian Liturgy* (Minneapolis: Fortress, 2017), 160.

At the root of the confusion is a tendency to understand blessing as purely an expression of approval or affirmation, a phenomenon occurring even in some recent translations of the Bible.

Excursus on Reductionism

The CEV translation of 1 Pet. 3:9 waters down and secularizes its words: "Don't be hateful and insult people just because they are hateful and insult you. Instead, treat everyone with kindness. You are God's." Here "repay with a blessing [*eulogountes*]" becomes "treat with kindness." Kind words are never a bad thing, but they are not identical to blessing. In many contemporary books about blessing, blessing is similarly reduced to psychological encouragement and interpersonal affirmation.[83] But blessing is more than that. Blessing is an act of God. By focusing primarily on human actions and feelings, such works neglect God's role and substitute psychology for theology. On the other hand, they do tend to stress how blessing, even though watered down, is something to be given and not merely received, which is a welcome emphasis.

Blessing can be just as much an admonition as an affirmation, a reminder to live out, and live up to, God's wishes for the well-being of creation and its creatures. For this reason, I suggest that it is better to think of blessing as *commendation* rather than affirmation. In an act of blessing, the blesser commends something or someone to God. People being blessed are likewise signaling their readiness to be commended, to allow God's ways to take precedence in their lives, their actions, and their relationships. On this understanding, the hackneyed phrase "God bless America," if used, should not be considered an assertion that God favors America in comparison with other nations, but that the speaker wishes for God to extend benevolence and protection to America, even as America is given the strength

---

83. For examples of reductionistic accounts of blessing, see John Trent, Gary Smalley, and Kari Trent Stageburg, *The Blessing: Giving the Gift of Unconditional Love and Acceptance* (Nashville: Thomas Nelson, 2019); Alan Wright, *The Power to Bless: How to Speak Life and Empower the People You Love* (Grand Rapids: Baker Books, 2021).

and courage to live up to God's insistent demand for justice and compassion. This understanding would preserve the biblical tradition's conviction that genuine blessing always ultimately comes from God and that blessing is about more than approval.

The ultimate criterion in deciding whether or not to bless should be, in the best judgment of the blesser and the blessing community, whether the thing or person to be blessed is already, or potentially, or willing to be in line with the purposes of God. This approach follows the practice and teaching of Jesus himself. At one point, he tells his disciples:

> Whatever town or village you enter, find out who in it is worthy, and stay there until you leave. As you enter the house, greet it. If the house is worthy, let your peace [*eirēnē*] come upon it; but if it is not worthy, let your peace return to you. If anyone will not welcome you or listen to your words, shake off the dust from your feet as you leave that house or town. (Matt. 10:11–14)

Not every household is to receive the disciples' blessing; it must demonstrate its worthiness by being welcoming and willing to listen. Paul can also refrain from apostolic approval: "Now in the following instructions I do not commend you," he tells the Corinthians (1 Cor. 11:17).

On the one hand, the New Testament instructs all Christians to bless. So there is a great opportunity today to expand blessing practices considerably. Even if Jesus did not apparently think everything was worthy of blessing, he nevertheless stretched blessing radically—particularly by encouraging the blessing of enemies, which is a good reason to consider blessing as transformative or *sanctifying* (to use Christian theological language) rather than justifying. Blessing does not instantly turn enemies into friends. Blessing does not get people right with God or make people Christians. It encourages and empowers them to live holier lives.[84]

---

84. Cf. Stephen J. Rossetti, *The Priestly Blessing: Rediscovering the Gift* (Notre Dame, IN: Ave Maria, 2018), 48: "[Blessings] can offer graced spiritual effects to help us live out our baptismal calling." Here the traditional Catholic distinction between "sacraments" and "sacramentals" points in the same direction.

On the other hand, it remains a real problem if blessing is detached from justice, if blessing is a premature response to sin, or if blessing becomes a substitute and replacement for repentance.[85] Some contemporary Christian practices can unintentionally create this misunderstanding—for example, the practice of providing a blessing instead of the eucharistic elements at the Lord's Supper. When the act of blessing is severed from any apparent connection to morality, it becomes not only a less imposing act but also a less ethical one. Why should people think that unforgiven sin might make it inadvisable for them to receive the elements but not to receive a blessing? Blessings in the Bible sometimes occur in agonistic contexts, generating fear rather than reassurance (e.g., Gen. 27:33; 32:26; 1 Sam. 25:14 [here the NRSV translates "salute" instead of "bless"]).

So blessing must not be immoral or amoral, but it cannot become a hostage to moralism either. A blesser's reach should exceed a blesser's grasp. Blessing remains at its core a type of verbal over-acceptance. It is transforming and gratuitous. Blessing seeks to inspire greater faithfulness and should never be conceived as something only given in response to demonstrated achievement, like a merit badge. Not everything should be blessed, but the burden of deciding when to bless should not lie with whether to *extend* a blessing but whether to *withhold* one. Blessing does represent and affirm some degree of sanction by the blesser and the blessing community. But because blessing is fundamentally related to and an expression of the goodness of God's creation, and because Jesus's practice of blessing went beyond the conventional understanding of blessing in his day, there is more reason to increase contemporary Christian practices of blessing than to restrict them. So when in doubt, Christians should bless. But they should not bless thoughtlessly or carelessly, as if the act of blessing is an inconsequential nicety. A blessing matters. A blessing upholds and encourages the very goodness that it expresses and on which it is premised.[86]

One of the ways these issues have recently crystallized within church practice relates to the question of church blessings for same-sex

---

85. Cf. Garrett Galvin, "Curses: Psalms, Deuteronomy, and Protection against Evil," *TBT* 58, no. 4 (2020): 223–30 (225): "Curses take the justice of God seriously."

86. Cf. John Koenig, *Rediscovering New Testament Prayer: Boldness and Blessing in the Name of Jesus* (San Francisco: Harper, 1992).

couples. Toward the end of 2023 both the Church of England and the Roman Catholic Church controversially announced that they would permit such blessings under narrow sets of circumstances. The Church of England released the texts of "Prayers of Love and Faith" for use in private devotions and public worship, with the caution that *marriage* was still held to be a "life-long, faithful and exclusive covenant between one man and one woman."[87] For the Catholic Church likewise, the blessings could not create an impression that the union was a marriage or even be "formal liturgical blessings." In providing a rationale for this change, one statement describes how "when people ask for a blessing, an exhaustive moral analysis should not be placed as a precondition for conferring it. For, those seeking a blessing should not be required to have prior moral perfection."[88] By contrast, opponents like Cardinal Gerhard Müller characterized the move as "self-contradictory" because the church was continuing to hold that marriage was properly between a man and a woman: "The church cannot celebrate one thing and teach another," he writes.[89]

This debate again illustrates the confusion over the relationship between blessing and morality within contemporary Christianity. A more transformational view of blessing has also been expressed in the debate. The South African Catholic Bishops Conference welcomed the pope's new policy by saying that "the blessing is done with the hope of conversion."[90] This type of perspective retains, rather than surrendering, the link between blessing and morality but does not

---

87. As posted December 12, 2023, at https://www.churchofengland.org/media/press-releases/prayers-love-and-faith-be-made-available-use-sunday.

88. In the instructions provided by the US Conference of Catholic Bishops, posted December 18, 2023, at https://www.usccb.org/news/2023/doctrinal-dicastery-explains-how-when-gay-couples-can-be-blessed.

89. Gerhard Ludwig Müller, "The Only Blessing of Mother Church Is the Truth That Will Set Us Free: Note on the Declaration *Fiducia supplicans*," as reproduced in *The Pillar* (December 21, 2023), https://www.pillarcatholic.com/p/muller-fiducia-supplicans-is-self.

90. As cited in Gerald Imray, "Some Catholic Bishops Reject Pope's Stance on Blessings for Same-Sex Couples. Others Are Confused," *Associated Press* (December 22, 2023), https://apnews.com/article/vatican-pope-francis-samesex-blessings-baabeaf96ad180aa20e1df9fb4b4657e. However, it is also not entirely clear what is meant by "conversion" in this statement—whether, e.g., it refers to becoming a Christian or whether it refers to so-called gender conversion.

make sinlessness a condition for being blessed. Yet "conversion" is too strong. Blessing does not convert or prepare the way for conversion. Still, a notion of blessing as sanctifying is in line with the biblical tradition. Blessing is not a divine pat on the head for living virtuously. It is an undeserved sign of God's favor in the midst of human brokenness and confusion.

Mark Jordan has thoughtfully explored the question of same-sex marriage and blessing from a theological perspective.[91] An important aspect of his treatment is his insistence that same-sex marriage needs to be considered within the context of the church's overall approach to marriage. He is devastating on the debased theological nature of the typical Christian wedding.[92] He poses the key question: When a church marries people, just what does it imagine it is doing? This question becomes especially acute when church history is reviewed and the relatively late emergence of marriage vows is acknowledged.[93] For the first several centuries of the Christian tradition, marriage was for the most part a civil rather than a sacred act, and there was no standard liturgy for it.[94] What followed was a gradual christianization of marriage, extending well into the medieval period. As late as the Reformation, Luther could still write: "Since marriage and the married estate are worldly matters, it behooves us pastors or ministers of the church not to attempt to order or govern anything connected with it, but to permit every city and land to continue its

---

91. Mark D. Jordan, *Blessing Same-Sex Unions: The Perils of Queer Romance and the Confusions of Christian Marriage* (Chicago: University of Chicago Press, 2005).

92. Jordan, *Blessing Same-Sex Unions*, 3: "The challenge for the churches is not to justify blessing same-sex unions. The challenge is justifying any blessings of unions at all." Cf. p. 4: "At most church weddings, the chief ritual specialist is not the pastor or priest, but the wedding planner, followed closely by the photographer, the florist, and the caterer."

93. Lathrop, *Saving Images*, 160, notes that Christian marriage was formerly constituted by a blessing prayer, and that marriage vows were not introduced until the fourteenth century. He further suggests that such vows were modeled on monastic vows and intended to make marriage more like a Christian vocation. He cites Kenneth Stevenson, "Marriage: 3, Medieval and Western," in *The New SCM Dictionary of Liturgy and Worship*, ed. Paul Bradshaw (London: SCM, 2002), 300.

94. See Stevenson, "Marriage: Early Christianity," and M. Daniel Findikyan, "Marriage: Eastern Churches," in *The New SCM Dictionary of Liturgy and Worship*, ed. Paul Bradshaw (London: SCM, 2002), 297–98, 298–300 (respectively).

own use and custom."[95] For Luther, the marriage ceremony is more a matter of prayer and blessing than vows, which are conspicuously absent in his order of service.

In continuity with ancient Jewish practice, Christian marriage had traditionally consisted of two parts: a betrothal and a confirmation. The betrothal, like engagements today, required an indication by both parties of a desire to wed. It typically occurred at the door of the church rather than in the sanctuary so that it would be public. Rings would be exchanged, and the officiating priest would declare the couple married. The physical consummation of the marriage often occurred after the betrothal and before what is today considered the actual wedding. The later church service consisted of a pastoral blessing before the altar.[96] Only in the seventeenth century did the church service become the "constitutive act" in which the marriage occurred, and the consent statements of the betrothal were shifted to the church service as vows. In the eighteenth century, church marriage became a legal act performed by the church as an agent of the state.[97]

There is thus a strong argument to be made from history that the Christian tradition has always largely followed cultural practices and norms in relation to marriage. In response, some might simply say "so be it" and advocate that the church continue to follow cultural expectations about marriage today. But the danger of such a course is that the church's view of marriage would be driven too much by cultural values rather than a proper Christian understanding of it. I would want to retain an appropriate theological basis for how Christians marry. Such a line of reflection would need to include consideration of singleness and divorce.[98] Based on the ambivalent statements

---

95. Martin Luther, "The Order of Marriage for Common Pastors (1529)," *Luther's Works (American Edition)*, vol. 53, ed. Ulrich S. Leupold (Philadelphia: Fortress, 1965), 110–15 (here 111).

96. Philip Lyndon Reynolds, *Marriage in the Western Church: The Christianization of Marriage during the Patristic and Early Medieval Periods*, VCSup 24 (Leiden: Brill, 1994), 362–85. Cf. John Witte Jr., *From Sacrament to Contract: Marriage, Religion, and Law in the Western Tradition*, 2nd ed. (Louisville: Westminster John Knox, 2012).

97. Philip H. Pfatteicher, "Marriage: Lutheran," in *The New SCM Dictionary of Liturgy and Worship*, ed. Paul Bradshaw (London: SCM, 2002), 304–5.

98. Jordan, *Blessing Same-Sex Unions*, 160–78, eventually argues for the acceptability of multiple partner relationships. While there are a few examples in the Bible

about marriage and family in the Gospels (e.g., Matt. 10:37; 22:29–30; Luke 12:51–53; 14:26; 18:29–30; 20:34–35), it is hard not to feel that some contemporary Christians possess inflated, romanticized views of these things—as well as an unchristian suspicion of singleness.[99]

However, the main point in the present context is to underscore how an uncertainty about the character of blessing is a contributing factor to debates in the church and wider society about the nature of Christian marriage and the appropriateness of blessing same-sex partnerships. Christians will not be able to decide about the appropriateness of blessing same-sex unions without clarifying their understanding of what blessing means.

Blessing and Prosperity

Prosperity religion does score a point by repudiating the modern separation of the spiritual from the material. But it can also be extremely damaging, both in terms of the theology it advocates and the way that it affects people's lives. By implying that Christians have a right and a duty to *claim* blessings, there is a persistent tendency in this part of the contemporary church to blame those who lack prosperity as possessing insufficient faith. Moreover, the emphasis on prosperity takes center stage, edging out biblical teachings about the value of self-sacrifice, the dangers of riches, and the spiritual benefits of poverty (e.g., Ps. 37:16; Prov. 19:1; 28:6; Isa. 25:4; Luke 6:20; James 2:5).

Brent Sandy has compiled a useful list of the individual blessings and curses occurring in the Old Testament.[100] They are remark-

---

(of one man with multiple wives), biblical tradition and historic church practice predominantly oppose such a possibility (Prov. 2:17; 1 Cor. 6:18; 7:2–7; Heb. 13:4).

99. In response, see Jana Marguerite Bennett, *Singleness and the Church: A New Theology of the Single Life* (New York: Oxford University Press, 2017); Lina Toth, *Singleness and Marriage after Christendom: Being and Doing Family* (Eugene, OR: Cascade Books, 2021); Danielle Treweek, *The Meaning of Singleness: Retrieving an Eschatological Vision for the Contemporary Church* (Downers Grove, IL: IVP Academic, 2023).

100. D. Brent Sandy, *Plowshares & Pruning Hooks: Rethinking the Language of Biblical Prophecy and Apocalyptic* (Downers Grove, IL: InterVarsity, 2002), 214–23.

ably concrete, with clusters referring to agriculture, livestock, food, children, and even roads. There is a long history in Christianity of interpreting such biblical blessings in a more abstract, metaphorical way—and the biblical language itself already moves in that direction. It is frequently believed that it is inappropriately "materialistic" to validate concrete, physical blessings (and curses), as the Old Testament does. But with regard to any tension between materialism and metaphor, the biblical tradition happily operates with a both/and rather than an either/or. Biblical blessings, in both Testaments, are simultaneously both physical and spiritual.[101]

A crucial part of the excitement once generated by Bruce Wilkinson's *The Prayer of Jabez* was precisely its rejection of the modernist spirituality that disdains miracle on the one hand and material well-being on the other.[102] Modern Christian believers often feel that it is *unseemly* to ask or expect worldly things from God.[103] Prosperity advocates are right that such an attitude not only silences important elements of the biblical tradition, it corrupts biblical teaching by promoting a spiritualizing, docetic gospel. The problem with prosperity teaching is not that it advances a focus on material blessings but that such blessings are often emphasized beyond other essential aspects of Christian living, such as holiness, suffering, and witness.[104]

Reviving a more frequent practice of blessing in contemporary churches could go a long way toward recovering from a failure of nerve on the part of many Christians, for whom the modernist divorce between the "natural" and the "supernatural" has become accepted and internalized.[105] Despite sustained critiques of metaphysical

---

101. William R. Osborne, *Divine Blessing and the Fullness of Life in the Presence of God*, Shorter Studies in Biblical Theology (Wheaton, IL: Crossway, 2020), 17.

102. Bruce Wilkinson, with David Kopp, *Prayer of Jabez: Breaking Through to the Blessed Life* (Sisters, OR: Multnomah, 2000).

103. Wilkinson, *Prayer of Jabez*, 23: "Blessing gets watered down to something vague and innocuous like 'Have a nice day.' . . . To bless in the biblical sense means to ask for or to impart supernatural favor." Wilkinson also rejects the modern view that to ask for a blessing for oneself is somehow "selfish" (19).

104. Carol Zaleski, "The Prayer of Jabez," *ChrCent* 118, no. 17 (May 23–30, 2001): 42.

105. For a robust defense of contemporary miracles, see Craig S. Keener, *Miracles Today: The Supernatural Work of God in the Modern World* (Grand Rapids: Baker Academic, 2021). For discussion of how the modernist stance arose and its abiding

naturalism from important Western thinkers, including natural scientists and physicists, the greatest pressure for a different outlook is at present being felt from other voices in the global church, especially in Africa and East Asia.[106]

The line between blessing and magic continues to be a thin one. Some of the criticism of Wilkinson's treatment, at least in how it sometimes came to be implemented, had to do with the prayer's repeated recitation, almost like an incantation or spell.[107] Blessings in the Bible are indeed like a kind of magic, understood to help bring about material changes in the lives of individuals and communities. But in the Bible these changes have God as their ultimate source. Blessings do not so much harness divine power as they confess God's power and express confidence in God's sovereign ability to bring to pass that which is in accord with God's nature and will. For this reason only, the agents and objects of blessing may be said to participate in God's power. Blessing is indeed about power, real power, but the power always comes from God.

Blessings in the Bible are not only cognitive but physical. The act of blessing includes a bodily gesture as well as a verbal sentiment. The gesture incarnates the words, and in doing so communicates something crucial about the nature of blessing. The point of blessing is not only to experience God's favor and to be protected from harm, but to embody and extend God's favor into the world. Whether or not blessing involves actual touch, as a bodily gesture it points to the physicality of God's way within the world. The form of blessing is itself incarnational.

One way to underscore the physicality of blessing—and at the same time reorient inadequate understandings of benediction—is to invite congregants to open their hands while a blessing is spoken

---

contours in the philosophy of religion, see, further, D. Z. Phillips and Timothy Tessin, eds., *Religion and Hume's Legacy* (New York: St. Martin's Press, 1999).

106. However, see the careful distinguishing between African thought and pure supernaturalism in Polycarp Ikuenobe, "Modernity and African Moral Thought," in *Inculturation and Postcolonial Discourse in African Theology*, ed. Edward P. Antonio, Society and Politics in Africa 14 (New York: Lang, 2006), 267–90.

107. Richard Schultz, "Praying Jabez's Prayer: Turning an Obscure Biblical Narrative into a Miracle-Working Mantra," *TJ* 42, no. 1 (2003): 113–19.

(see Ps. 134:2; Matt. 14:19//Mark 6:41//Luke 9:16).[108] A concluding benediction is not a prayer: "The congregation should not have bowed heads and closed eyes, but should look up into the heavens from which the Lord, the maker of heaven and earth sends our help."[109] An open-handed posture expresses an experiential stance of receptivity and involves worshipers bodily in worship. David Taylor resorts to punning to draw out this aspect of liturgical practice: "When Christians repeatedly open their hands to receive the pastor's benediction, it is a way for them to get a *handle* on a life that remains always open to God's blessing.... We gain a body knowledge of our identity as the true Body of Christ."[110] The open-handed posture is then the mirror image of the hand gestures traditionally used by Christian clergy when blessing: they raise one or two hands, either fully open or configured into a specific liturgical shape.[111] When blessing is accompanied with a "laying on of hands" (cf. Gen. 48:14), the physicality of blessing is even stronger.[112] Antonio Donghi comments: "The hand in its vitality expresses a person's heat and energy, his or her state of soul and expectations. The hand is never only a little expressive. It expresses the heart of the human being as it says to another, 'You are not alone; I am with you.'"[113] Churches could do more with hand gestures in worship, not only on the part of clergy but the laity as well.

In contrast to the typically passive, prayer-like stance most Christians adopt during a benediction, an open-handed posture on the part of worshipers encourages a more active sense of involvement. If it is the case that some contemporary Christian worship emphasizes

---

108. It might also be a more appropriate stance for prayer (1 Tim. 2:8) than a submissive folding of the hands in one's lap. See Jürgen Moltmann, *The Living God and the Fullness of Life*, trans. Margaret Kohl (Louisville: Westminster John Knox, 2015), 202–3, on prayer postures.
109. Ryan M. McGaw, "The Benediction in Corporate Worship," *The Confessional Presbyterian* 7 (2011): 111–22 (here 120).
110. W. David O. Taylor, *A Body of Praise: Understanding the Role of Our Physical Bodies in Worship* (Grand Rapids: Baker Academic, 2023), 22 (emphasis original).
111. In Roman Catholicism, the blessing hand is open, with the fingers fully extended and conjoined. In Orthodoxy, the blessing hand is partly open, with only the first two fingers extended and the fourth finger bent and joined with the thumb. This gesture is also sometimes used by Catholic bishops and popes.
112. Pruyser, "Master Hand," 362.
113. Donghi, *Words and Gestures in the Liturgy*, 49.

physical involvement too much (worship is not Jazzercize), it is also the case that many Christian churches continue to be overly suspicious of and antagonistic to the worshiping body, the neglect of which encourages a reduced, disembodied understanding of spirituality and even a resistance to the incarnational truth at the heart of the gospel.[114]

James Smith writes confessionally about this aspect of his own worship experience:

> I remember how *physically* difficult it was to get my body to participate in worship. I remember the utter awkwardness of raising a hand in praise, almost as if it were cemented to my side. But then I also remember the remarkable sense of release—the almost sacramental dispensation of grace and liberation and renewal that seemed to flow down through upstretched arms, as if the very positioning of my body opened channels for grace to flow where it couldn't otherwise. I remember the remarkable charge of grace that would come with a hand laid on my shoulder in prayer—the very embodied, material connection that was solidified by touch.[115]

This tactile, haptic dimension of worship has been yet another casualty of modernity, although the Pentecostal tradition has helped to reintroduce it to the global church.

The problem sometimes arising from this new bodily awareness is that physical expression in worship can become viewed as an exclusively good thing and even worship's goal, with the lack of such expression seen only as unfaithful inhibition. Physical gestures need to have a rationale and purpose beyond themselves in worship. Moreover, quieter and more sedentary forms of worship are not for that reason alone somehow lacking or suspect. There is a danger in equating physical expression too neatly with the movement of the Holy Spirit, as well as in interpreting the lack of such expression as the absence of the Spirit. Just as ritual characteristically combines word and action, physical expression in worship must be combined with the Word and only finds its legitimacy and proper rationale in relation to the Word.

---

114. Cf. W. Taylor, *Body of Praise*, 40. As he points out, Christian suspicion of the body has also often been unfairly gendered and directed toward women.
115. James K. A. Smith, *Thinking in Tongues: Pentecostal Contributions to Christian Philosophy* (Grand Rapids: Eerdmans, 2010), 61 (emphasis original).

Modernity has struggled with other material aspects of the blessing tradition in the Bible. Blessings for long life, wellness, family, fertility, professional success, financial security—Christian exegetes and theologians have been skittish about such things in the modern era because they have seemed too worldly, too liable to lead away from the spiritual core of the faith. Schleiermacher's account of piety as a religious state of "mind and heart," especially when combined with a developmental approach to "religion" in history, led to a view of Judaism and the Old Testament as particularistic and insufficiently spiritual.[116] The modern privatization of religion has colored even how exegetes and theologians think, encouraging them to imagine that biblical faith is more "spiritual" than it is.[117] Contemporary Protestantism is especially prone to underestimate, discount, and simply ignore the material aspects of religious devotion, in everything from art and architecture to religious practices themselves.

For this reason, I think it is appropriate not to dismiss out of hand the notion that objects as well as people might be blessed.[118] There has traditionally been more of an emphasis on this aspect of blessing in Catholicism than Protestantism.[119] Indeed, some Protestant theologians have been quick to rule it out on principle.[120] On the one hand, there are not many examples of objects being blessed in the Bible, and the ones that are blessed are things that directly sustain human life. But on the other hand, these things *are* nonhuman creatures and objects: livestock, fields, crops, barns, baskets, wine, oil, land, rain

---

116. Friedrich Schleiermacher, *Christian Faith: A New Translation and Critical Edition*, ed. Terrence N. Tice, Catherine L. Kelsey, and Edwina Lawler, 2 vols. (Louisville: Westminster John Knox, 2016), 1:49–55.

117. Cf. Matthew Guest, *Neoliberal Religion: Faith and Power in the Twenty-First Century* (London: Bloomsbury Academic, 2022), 16.

118. For an overview, see David Power, "On Blessing Things," in *Blessing and Power*, ed. Mary Collins and David Power, Concilium 178 (Edinburgh: T&T Clark, 1985), 24–39.

119. See Kaczynski, "Blessings in Rome"; Thomas G. Simons, *Blessings: A Reappraisal of Their Nature, Purpose and Celebration* (Saratoga, CA: Resource, 1981), 33–59. Medieval Catholicism knew a great diversity of blessings for various objects.

120. E.g., Ephraim Radner, "Blessing: A Scriptural and Theological Reflection," *ProEccl* 19, no. 1 (2010): 1–27, proposes a distinction between blessing and the "consecration" of religious objects, which sets them apart for a religious purpose but does not infuse them with additional holiness.

(e.g., Gen. 1:22; Exod. 23:25; Deut. 7:13; 26:15; 28:1–14; Isa. 65:8; Ezek. 34:26).[121]

At a time in which humans are threatening to bring the natural world to a devastating collapse through the instrumentalization of creation and the profligate consumption of its resources, anything that might reinvest material objects with spiritual significance seems like a helpful corrective. I too am inclined to resist the view that blessing an object adds extra sanctity to it. But it seems to me there is still room to bless an object on the understanding that it is being brought to particular attention within a Christian community, so that its "native" holiness can be celebrated and it can be designated for protection.[122] On this view, blessed water would not become water with additional capabilities, but water that is drawn into a Christian community's purview in a special manner.[123]

As Reiner Kaczynski summarizes,

> Things do not thereby undergo any change in their nature; rather their nature is more deeply understood and better acknowledged, namely, that they have their origin in the blessing given by the Creator and are meant to be pointers to the new blessing that redemption has brought to the world. In this way, the concrete reality in which human beings live becomes transparent to the realities of salvation.[124]

I choose to take this middle way, because the modernists are not entirely wrong. There is a tension to be observed between the materiality of blessing in the Old Testament broadly and Jesus's stricture not to "worry about your life, what you will eat or what you will drink, or about your body, what you will wear" because life is "more than food

---

121. In this context, Paul's "cup of blessing that we bless" (1 Cor. 10:16) is always mentioned as well.

122. Oppenheimer, "Blessing," 226, stresses how the blessing of objects might be viewed as an expression of sacramental theology. The blessed object is not infused with an extra quality but rather offered up to God by the community, on analogy with the eucharistic Anaphora, in which the bread and wine are lifted up in the expectation that God will accept and use them.

123. Keith Grüneberg, *Blessing: Biblical Meaning and Pastoral Practice* (Ridley Hall, Cambridge: Grove, 2003), 21–22, suggests that blessing food at meals and other objects is not so much to make them "special" but to ask God to bless us through them.

124. Kaczynski, "Blessings in Rome," 396.

and the body more than clothing" (Matt. 6:25). The New Testament does not disparage the body (contrary to what some Christians continue to think), but neither does it elevate it above spiritual things (as other Christians now do in reaction). In the Old Testament too there is a sense of a noumenal realm accompanying and finally exceeding the phenomenal (e.g., Deut. 4:12; 8:3; 1 Kings 8:27; Jer. 23:23–24).[125]

In both Testaments, there exists a sense of a mysterious connection between the material and spiritual worlds. When God chooses to appear and act, God characteristically does so in and through creation. When God liberates Israel out of Egypt, the biblical narrative attributes the miracle at the sea simultaneously to God *and* a "big wind" (Exod. 14:21). They operate together; God works *through* the natural world. Indeed, the modern distinction between the natural and the supernatural is just that, a modern distinction. The distinction did not exist in the same way in the ancient world. This is what, at the most basic level, the physical gestures of blessing express and reinforce: that God appears and acts in and through the material. To the eyes of faith, the created world can therefore become something like a parable of God. The gestures of blessing not only alert worshipers to this cosmic reality, they also enlist and embolden worshipers to do the same, to go forth from worship as a living *embodiment* of God's presence in the world.[126]

Such an understanding of lived faith is urged in the New Testament as well as the Old. Paul writes, "Bless those who persecute you; bless and do not curse them. . . . Do not repay anyone evil for evil, but take thought for what is noble in the sight of all. If it is possible, so far as it depends on you, live peaceably with all" (Rom. 12:14, 17–18). Peter writes, "Do not repay evil for evil or abuse for abuse; but, on the contrary, repay with a blessing. It is for this that you were called—that you might inherit a blessing" (1 Pet. 3:9). In such New Testament witnesses, blessing describes an embodied way of life. The

---

125. This point is treated in a sustained fashion in John Calvin, *Institutes of the Christian Religion*, ed. John T. McNeill, trans. Ford Lewis Battles, 2 vols., LCC 20–21 (Philadelphia: Westminster, 1960), 1:428–49.

126. Cf. Kaczynski, "Blessings in Rome," 397: "Blessings awaken and deepen faith, unite believers more closely to God, and enable the believing community (family, priest) to experience their union in faith."

embodiment of blessing is also described in the Epistle to Diognetus (155–225 CE?), one of the earliest accounts of the ancient Christian community and its distinctive response to bigotry and persecution:

> For Christians are not distinguished from the rest of humanity by country, language, or custom. For nowhere do they live in cities of their own, nor do they speak some unusual dialect, nor do they practice an eccentric way of life. . . . They live in their own countries, but only as nonresidents; they participate in everything as citizens, and endure everything as foreigners. . . . They love everyone, and by everyone they are persecuted. . . . They are cursed, yet they bless; they are insulted, yet they offer respect. (5:1–2, 5, 11, 15; cf. 1 Cor. 4:10–13)[127]

Blessing those who curse you is more than tolerance or forbearance or non-retaliation. It entails constructive engagement, honoring the other, and restorative rather than retributive justice.

Identity and Witness

"Remember your baptism." This familiar admonition in the church remains valuable but is finally too weak and distancing. Baptism is "historicized" in such a formulation, characterized as a past event that at best can only be dimly remembered (if at all). Lost is a vital sense of ongoing identity, especially in any bodily way—although the imposition of ashes at the beginning of Lent along with the admonition does gesture powerfully to the physical claim of God on the believer. Yet "live out your baptism" would be better! Christians are given a new identity in baptism when they "put on" Christ. Christian baptism is not simply a rite of initiation. It is the imposition of a name.[128]

Biblically and liturgically, Christians are not baptized into Christ but into the *name* of Christ ("I baptize you in the name of . . .").[129]

---

127. As translated in Michael W. Holmes, *The Apostolic Fathers in English*, 3rd ed. (Grand Rapids: Baker Academic, 2006), 288–301 (here 295–96).

128. As detailed in Lars Hartman, *"Into the Name of the Lord Jesus": Baptism in the Early Church*, SNTW (Edinburgh: T&T Clark, 1997).

129. Frank Crüsemann, "Von der Bedeutung des Namens Gottes für den christlichen Glauben: Eine Predigt über Ex 20,1–7," in *Alttestamentliche Wissenschaft und*

For just this reason, there is a long tradition of "Christian names" associated with christening and/or baptism. On analogy with being baptized into Christ's name, some Christian believers take a new name for themselves at baptism to signal their new identity (cf. Isa. 65:15, "To his servants he will give a different name"). Even more, however, all baptized Christians should understand themselves as now bearing Jesus's name. This conception has both positive and negative consequences. Positively, Christians are called to honor the One whose name they bear. Negatively, they must avoid dishonoring that name. Much constructive pastoral work can be done along these lines.[130]

For Christians, the *ongoing practice* of baptism is the key to Christian living. Baptism should be not only a past event but also a present claim on the life of the Christian believer, a way of thinking and acting now and in the future. The Priestly Blessing can be understood as a call to do just that, as a charge to live in the world as a witness to God. It reminds Christians that blessing is a primary means of expressing their baptismal identity. All Christians, and not only clergy, are instructed to bless.

The Priestly Blessing is already interpreted in its immediate scriptural context as something to be "placed on" individual worshipers (Num. 6:27), a metaphor that I have suggested is actually less metaphorical and more literal than ordinarily thought. I have proposed that this notion of "wearing" God's protective name can profitably be linked to New Testament baptismal texts, which present a similar understanding of name bearing. While Pauline baptismal texts characteristically employ sartorial imagery, such imagery can falsely suggest a view of baptismal identity as superficial rather than ontological, and baptism is certainly an ontological change in status for Paul.[131] The misunderstanding would seem to arise in part from

---

kirchliche Praxis: Festschrift Jürgen Kegler, ed. Manfred Oeming and Walther Boës, BVB 18 (Berlin: LIT, 2009), 331–36.

130. As a Baptist, I am particularly saddened to see so little liturgical recognition of baptism by Baptist churches after the initial act. If ever congregants are to be challenged and encouraged to remember and live out their baptisms, it should be in Baptist churches. After all, Baptists can actually remember their baptisms!

131. Jung Hoon Kim, *The Significance of Clothing Imagery in the Pauline Corpus*, JSNTSup 268 (London: T&T Clark, 2004), 2.

a view of clothing as only an outer reality and one not intrinsically related to the inner or whole person. The traditional (and unfortunately gendered) saying "Clothes make the man" is a helpful pointer in a different direction.

As Lauren Winner engagingly describes, clothing can be understood as a much more robust metaphor for the life of faith.[132] As with virtues, there is an aspirational dimension to clothing. We wear what we want to be and become. But as Winner notes, "Clothing doesn't just shape identity. It also communicates something about our identity to the people we meet."[133] By communicating identity, clothing can reinforce and sustain communities of affiliation.[134] While it is certainly also true that clothing can, and has, exacerbated social difference, Winner asserts:

> Jesus is not the kind of clothing that creates social divisions but the kind of clothing that undoes them. Jesus is not a Vineyard Vines dress or a Barbour jacket; He is the school uniform that erases boundaries between people. Or at least that is the kind of clothing that Jesus wants to be. When those of us clothed in Him trespass boundaries in His Name, we allow Him to be that school uniform; when we put up walls in the name of Jesus, we are turning the Lord into an expensive designer dress.[135]

I am less comfortable with the school uniform analogy, since it might be understood to inhibit difference and enforce sameness. I again prefer the image of a salad bowl in which social differences can be preserved and celebrated, rather than a melting pot in which everyone has to be identical. But more fundamental, it seems to me, is the accompanying notion of a school outfit as reflecting and expressing an institutional identity. Here is where the analogy usefully underscores how clothing is not merely external but conveys an identity in the form of a public witness. "As many of you as were baptized

---

132. Lauren F. Winner, *Wearing God: Clothing, Laughter, Fire, and Other Overlooked Ways of Meeting God* (New York: HarperOne, 2015).
133. Winner, *Wearing God*, 41. See also Alison Lurie, *The Language of Clothes* (New York: Random House, 1981).
134. Winner, *Wearing God*, 46.
135. Winner, *Wearing God*, 50.

into Christ have clothed yourselves with Christ" (Gal. 3:27; cf. Col. 3:13–14; 1 Pet. 5:5).

A contemporary example comes from theologian Ellen Charry, who describes her encounter with Luther and the Augsburg Confession when she began to study theology. As she read, she thought:

> *Justification by grace through faith . . . justification by grace through faith*—what are they talking about? So I decided to try it on. I lifted my arms up and I put it over me like a dress, the doctrine. I tried it on myself. I tried it out. It wasn't just words; I tried it. And I fell off the chair. It was in July, it was very hot; I was on the third floor in my study. . . . I tried it on like a dress, and I just fell over.[136]

This experience was a crucial episode in Charry's journey toward becoming a Christian. In her recounting of it, the accent in this type of "wearing" is not exclusively on the outer person but also on adopting, embracing, and integrating—on the external as a means of bringing an altered way of life into the inner person. A change of clothing is about not only a new appearance but also a new possibility for a provisional self. Clothing seems especially "secondary" when the self becomes essentialized, homogenized, and inflated. But as a good deal of twentieth-century philosophical work has emphasized, the self is not a given but a project, always under construction in relation to events, experiences, and other people.[137] Clothing is therefore not only a matter of personal expression but also one of the means by which people go about determining who they are. In what we wear—as in other activities and relationships—we try *ourselves* on for size.

So too in the Priestly Blessing, which offers worshipers the opportunity to "try on" God's name and identity as a constitutive reality for their lives, to "wear" God's name and protective blessing. Winner writes, "I become professional or hip, depending on what I am wearing. I feel different when I am wearing different clothes. I act different. I let my Talbots suits and my vintage shirts remake me

---

136. As quoted in Tim Stafford, "The New Theologians," *CT* 43, no. 2 (February 8, 1999), 30–49 (47, emphasis original).

137. Jerrold Seigel, *The Idea of the Self: Thought and Experience in Western Europe since the Seventeenth Century* (New York: Cambridge University Press, 2005).

in their image. I want to let Jesus do the same."[138] For Christians, "wearing" the Priestly Blessing is also about being conformed to the body of Christ. As Kendall Soulen perceives, the Priestly Blessing "*claims and transforms* those who receive it, so that they are suited for the service of God's name before the eyes of the world."[139] The Priestly Blessing is finally about witness.

In Judaism, one ideal for the life of faith is known as *kiddush ha-Shem* or "sanctifying the Name." Particularly striking is the way that the reputation of God's name among the other peoples of the world is understood to be a matter of Jewish responsibility. Jews are to live in a fashion that brings honor to God's name among non-Jews. The roots of this view lie in the Bible. God's name is to be "hallowed" or sanctified (Neh. 1:11; Isa. 29:23; Ezek. 36:23; 39:7; Mal. 1:11). The phrase "sanctify God" appears as something that human beings are expected—and able—to do (e.g., Lev. 22:32; cf. 18:21; 21:6; 22:2). The early Christian apostles are likewise said to "rejoice that they were considered worthy to suffer dishonor for the sake of the *name*" (Acts 5:41, emphasis added; cf. John 15:21; Acts 9:16; 21:13; 1 Pet. 4:13–14). Paul encourages Christians to live in such a manner that "the *name* of our Lord Jesus may be glorified in you" (2 Thess. 1:12, emphasis added).

In fact, *kiddush ha-Shem* embraces an even wider field of behavior and action within Jewish tradition. It is one of the cornerstones of Jewish ethics and used as a basic principle in moral reasoning (e.g., b. Sotah 10b). The opposite principle, adduced as a way to understand unethical behavior, is *ḥillul ha-Shem* or "profaning the Name" (e.g., Lev. 18:21; 19:12; 20:3; 21:6; 22:2, 32; Isa. 48:9–11; Jer. 34:16; Ezek. 36:20–23; Amos 2:7). Faced with the prospect of idolatry, unchastity, or murder, which would profane God's name, a faithful Jew must instead accept martyrdom in order to "sanctify the Name" (b. Sanhedrin 74a). *Kiddush ha-Shem* and martyrdom can even be treated as synonyms in some rabbinic writings (e.g., b. Berakhot 20a).

---

138. Winner, *Wearing God*, 41.
139. R. Kendall Soulen, "The Third Word: The Blessing of God's Name," in *The Ten Commandments for Jews, Christians, and Others*, ed. Rogert E. Van Harn (Grand Rapids: Eerdmans, 2009), 47–61 (here 55, emphasis original).

Christians have much to (re)learn from this network of ideas and associations—particularly the close connections between God's name, God's reputation, and what it means to live faithfully in the world. From this perspective, the Priestly Blessing can be understood as being about not only "wearing" but "bearing," as about sanctification, sacrifice, and witness. Christians who have received God's name during worship in the form of the Priestly Blessing should not only think in the coming week about how God's blessing will protect them (and it will), but also about how their choices and actions may bring honor or dishonor to the name of God they embody.[140] Exodus 20:24 promises, "In every place where I cause my name to be remembered I will come to you and bless you." Christians bear the name of God and the name of Christ (Rev. 14:1). Their sins not only bring them into disrepute but undermine God's esteem and enterprises. This is a point with too many negative (and depressing) contemporary examples to catalogue. The stature of the Christian church, religious faith, and God have been greatly damaged by the unethical, selfish, and self-righteous behavior of many Christians, especially well-known Christian figures in the public eye. As Nietzsche's Zarathustra said of Christians, "Better songs they will have to sing for me before I learn to believe in their redeemer, more redeemed his disciples would have to look!"[141]

Rather than hearing the Priestly Blessing only as a comforting word of individual encouragement, Christians need to hear it as a basic statement of God's identity and their own identity before God, a dual identity that they are now charged to bear and display before the world, and an identity to which God is holding them accountable.[142] Blessing is the *vocation* of every Christian and Christian

---

140. For discerning reflections along these lines, see Daniel I. Block, "Bearing the Name of the LORD with Honor," in *How I Love Your Torah, O LORD! Studies in the Book of Deuteronomy* (Eugene, OR: Cascade Books, 2011), 61–71; Carmen Joy Imes, *Bearing God's Name: Why Sinai Still Matters* (Downers Grove, IL: IVP Academic, 2019).

141. Friedrich Nietzsche, *Thus Spoke Zarathustra: A Book for All and None*, ed. Adrian del Caro and Robert B. Pippin (Cambridge: Cambridge University Press, 2006), 71.

142. See Stanley Szczapa, "Go! You Are Sent with God's Blessing to Bring the Good News of God's Love to All You Meet," *Liturgical Ministry* 12 (2003): 156–59.

community.[143] This vocational identity is not finally constituted by a certain history or doctrine or institutional membership, but by a name. Colossians 3:17 once again: "Whatever you do, in word or deed, do *everything* in the name of the Lord Jesus" (emphasis added).

In a radio address prepared shortly before his death, Karl Barth said, "The last word which I have to say as a theologian and also as a politician is not a term like 'grace,' but a name, 'Jesus Christ.' *He* is grace, and he *is* the last, beyond the world and the church and even theology."[144] Barth's strikingly onomastic focus is the native language of Christian discipleship (cf. John 20:31). Its roots lie in Israel's Priestly Blessing, which—in Christian understanding—speaks to the selfsame reality. Christians bear a name. It is the name of blessing. It is finally all they have and all they need.

Writing more recently, David Ford emphasizes how the blessing or hallowing of God's name has traditionally lain at the core of both the Jewish and Christian walks of faith.[145] For Ford, the act of blessing God and the provision of God's name in turn reinforce the fundamental reality of God's blessedness: that there is in God "a certain completeness which is yet full of life and goodness, and free to overflow abundantly. It indicates the abundant God who is the creator of abundant life."[146] The *abundance* of God is a notion ripe for reintroduction within Christian churches (John 10:10b).[147] In the

---

143. For additional exegetical grounding, see Siegbert Rieckert, *Ein Priestervolk für alle Völker: Der Segensauftrag Israels für alle Nationen in der Tora und den Vorderen Propheten*, SBB 59 (Stuttgart: Katholisches Bibelwerk, 2007).

144. As cited in Eberhard Busch, *Karl Barth: His Life from Letters and Autobiographical Texts*, trans. John Bowden (Grand Rapids: Eerdmans, 1994), 496 (Barth's emphases).

145. David F. Ford, *Shaping Theology: Engagements in a Religious and Secular World* (Malden, MA: Blackwell, 2007), 208.

146. Ford, *Shaping Theology*, 208.

147. See also Jeremy Begbie, *Abundantly More: The Theological Promise of the Arts in a Reductionist World* (Grand Rapids: Baker Academic, 2023); Moltmann, *Living God*, 196: "Life must not be misused as if it were a means to an end. . . . If a life is led in the light of Christ's resurrection, we can recognize that there the power of death has been broken, and the powers of death have lost their rights over us. In the wonder of the resurrection, a life becomes new. It is no longer a life leading to death, it is a life leading to the fullness that God has promised. The radiance of the resurrection makes it a life that is buoyant."

contemporary West, social existence is often framed in terms of scarcity.[148] Such scarcity is both real and imagined. Yet even the acquisitive materialism of modern Western society grows out of a deep anxiety about not having enough. People worry that "there aren't enough good things to go around,"[149] and they obsess about what they may be missing. In responding, much contemporary Christian preaching and teaching combines the worst aspects of sentimentality and moralism—each one damaging on its own but even more devastating in tandem. The true gospel message is that the emptiness of scarcity is filled by giving rather than receiving.

In this vein, Ford instructively sketches a précis for an entire Christian theology oriented toward blessing:

> Creation, with humanity, being blessed by a generous God, but going wrong; the challenge of receiving and being transformed by blessings that are always more than we can believe possible or want to receive; Jesus Christ as the one who is blessing incarnate, and in his ascension blesses with pierced hands (that might be the key event and image for a Christology of blessing that looks back to his life, death, and resurrection under the sign of blessing, and forward to Pentecost and his ultimate recapitulation of all things under the same sign); the Holy Spirit as an anticipation of that eschatological blessing of God; and the need daily to discern in specific ways the blessings of God in creation, in fellow human beings and in our own lives—and at the same time be alert to the many ways in which God's blessings are rejected, distorted, misunderstood, turned into curses.[150]

Sustained use of the Priestly Blessing in the church will preserve and embolden exactly this type of theological vision.

From within a contemporary culture obsessed with scarcity, finitude, and death, the biblical tradition of blessing offers a profound

---

148. Walter Brueggemann, "Liturgy of Abundance, and the Myth of Scarcity," *ChrCent* 116, no. 10 (Mar. 24–31, 1999): 342–47; Fredrik Albritton Jonsson and Carl Wennerlind, *Scarcity: A History of the Origins of Capitalism to the Climate Crisis* (Cambridge, MA: Harvard University Press, 2023).

149. Brueggemann, "Liturgy of Abundance," 342.

150. Ford, *Shaping Theology*, 208.

alternative. There is *more*. God is the source of ever-surprising newness, generosity, and abundant living. Blessing is the origin, sign, and seal of that bounty. Blessed be God, who "by the power at work within us is able to accomplish abundantly far more than all we can ask or imagine" (Eph. 3:20).

Appendix: Translation

> The Lord bless you and protect you;
> The Lord's face shine upon you and be gracious to you;
> The Lord's face look with favor upon you and give you peace.
> —Numbers 6:24–26

This translation incorporates the word choices made in this volume, seeking a good balance between the sense of the source language (Hebrew) and the conventions and rhythms of the target language (English). It foregrounds the name of God at the beginning of each phrase, just as the Hebrew text does—although it uses the traditional substitution Lord for YHWH. The second and third phrases shift the subject slightly to God's face in an effort to highlight the blessing's "face" language. While the substitution Lord might be viewed by some as possessing male, authoritarian connotations, the translation reworks the second ("make his face shine") and third ("lift up his countenance") phrases to avoid using the male pronoun. Furthermore, the first phrase of the blessing is noticeably set apart as the basic summary statement of the blessing as a whole.

This translation thus emphasizes more clearly than the traditional version ("face"—"countenance") how the second and third phrases both highlight the same Hebrew word (*pānîm*). This common feature unites them even as it underscores their shared difference from the blessing's first phrase, which remains distinct from them and primary. I have opted for "upon" rather than "on" because I think it scans better and slightly elevates the register of the blessing. (It bears reminding that blessings are poetic speech. Blessings should not only be interpreted but *delivered* as poetic speech.)

A shortcoming of this translation is that it does not draw out the parallelism in Hebrew between "putting on" peace and "putting on" God's name, which is established by the use of the same verb (ś-y-m) in the blessing's final phrase (Num. 6:26) and the closing word of divine instruction (Num. 6:27). Preachers and teachers can, and should, still make this connection plain when discussing the Priestly Blessing. What recipients of the blessing are to "put on," and thus *bear* is both God's peace and God's name. Homiletically, hearers might be invited to imagine God's peace and God's name as twin garments—the shirt and jacket of the Christian believer.

Here is an alternative inclusive language version:

> God bless you and protect you;
> God's face shine upon you and be gracious to you;
> God's face look with favor upon you and give you peace.

This translation substitutes "God" for LORD, which some congregations may prefer as a means of avoiding any possible authoritarian overtones to LORD. Like the primary translation, it also avoids the male pronoun. I have otherwise sought to keep this alternative version as close as possible to the first.

Selected Bibliography

Commentaries and Exegetical Treatments

Ashley, Timothy R. *The Book of Numbers*. 2nd ed. NICOT. Grand Rapids: Eerdmans, 2022.

Awabdy, Mark A. "The Holiness Composition of the Priestly Blessing." *Biblica* 99, no. 1 (2018): 29–49.

Berlejung, Angelika. "Der gesegnete Mensch: Text und Kontext von Num 6,22–27 und den Silberamuletten von Ketef Hinnom." In *Mensch und König: Studien zur Anthropologie des Alten Testaments; Rüdiger Lux zum 60. Geburtstag*, edited by Angelika Berlejung and Raik Heckl, 37–62. Freiburg: Herder, 2008.

———. "Ein Programm fürs Leben: Theologisches Wort und anthropologischer Ort der Silberamulette von Ketef Hinnom." *ZAW* 120, no. 2 (2008): 204–30.

Briggs, Richard S. *Theological Hermeneutics and the Book of Numbers as Christian Scripture*. Notre Dame, IN: University of Notre Dame Press, 2018.

Davies, Eryl W. *Numbers*. NCBC. Grand Rapids: Eerdmans, 1995.

De Boer, P. A. H. "Numbers VI 27." *VT* 32, no. 1 (1982): 3–13.

Delitzsch, Franz. "Der mosaische Priestersegen Num. VI,22–27." *ZKWKL* 3 (1882): 113–36.

Dozeman, Thomas. "The Book of Numbers: Introduction, Commentary, and Reflections." In *The New Interpreter's Bible*, edited by Leander E. Keck, 2:3–268. Nashville: Abingdon, 1998.

Fishbane, Michael. "Form and Reformulation of the Biblical Priestly Blessing." *JAOS* 103, no. 1 (1983): 115–21.

Forsling, Josef. *The Theology of the Book of Numbers*. OTT. Cambridge: Cambridge University Press, forthcoming.

Freedman, David Noel. "The Aaronic Benediction (Numbers 6:24–26)." In *No Famine in the Land: Studies in Honor of John L. McKenzie*, edited by James W. Flanagan and Anita Weisbrod Robinson, 35–48. Missoula, MT: Scholars Press, 1975.

Gane, Roy. *Leviticus, Numbers*. NIVAC. Grand Rapids: Zondervan, 2004.

Geiger, Michaela. "Synergie zwischen priestlichem und göttlichem Handeln im Aaronitischen Segen (Num 6,22–27)." *VT* 68, no. 1 (2018): 51–72.

Glodo, Michael J. *The Lord Bless You and Keep You: The Promise of the Gospel in the Aaronic Blessing*. Wheaton, IL: Crossway, 2023.

Gold, Avie. *Bircas Kohanim/The Priestly Blessings: Background, Translation, and Commentary Anthologized from Talmudic, Midrashic, and Rabbinic Sources*. Brooklyn, NY: Mesorah Publications, 1981.

Heckl, Raik. "The Aaronic Blessing (Numbers 6): Its Intention and Place in the Concept of the Pentateuch." In *On Dating Biblical Texts to the Persian Period*, edited by Richard J. Bautsch and Mark Lackowski, 119–38. FAT 2/101 Tübingen: Mohr Siebeck, 2019.

Knierim, Rolf P., and George W. Coats. *Numbers*. FOTL 4. Grand Rapids: Eerdmans, 2005.

Korpel, Marjo C. A. "The Priestly Blessing Revisited (Num. 6:22–27)." In *Unit Delimitation in Biblical Hebrew and Northwest Semitic Literature*, edited by Marjo C. A. Korpel and Josef M. Oesch, 61–81. Pericope. Assen: Van Gorcum, 2003.

Levine, Baruch A. *Numbers: 1–20: A New Translation with Introduction and Commentary*. AB 4A. New York: Doubleday, 1993.

Milgrom, Jacob. *Numbers*. JPS Torah Commentary. Philadelphia: Jewish Publication Society, 1990.

Miller, Patrick D. "The Blessing of God." *Int* 29, no. 3 (1975): 240–51.

Noth, Martin. *Numbers: A Commentary*. Translated by James D. Martin. OTL. Philadelphia: Westminster, 1968.

Rossetti, Stephen J. *The Priestly Blessing: Rediscovering the Gift.* Notre Dame, IN: Ave Maria, 2018.

Seebass, Horst. "YHWH's Name in the Aaronic Blessing (Num 6:22–27)." In *The Revelation of the Name YHWH to Moses: Perspectives from Judaism, the Pagan Graeco-Roman World and Early Christianity*, edited by George H. van Kooten, 37–65. Leiden: Brill, 2006.

Seybold, Klaus. *Der aaronitische Segen: Studien zu Numeri 6,22–27.* Neukirchen-Vluyn: Neukirchener, 1977.

Spehr, Christopher. "Leiblicher und geistlicher Segen: Luthers Auslegung des Aaronitischen Segens aus dem Jahr 1532." *Luther* 87, no. 2 (2016): 68–74.

Spieckermann, Hermann. "'YHWH Bless You and Keep You': The Relation of History of Israelite Religion and Theology Reconsidered." *SJOT* 23, no. 2 (2009): 166–82.

Additional Secondary Literature

Adams, Kevin. "Living Epiphany: Framing Worship and Blessing Homes." *RW* 137 (2020): 37–39.

Aitken, J. K. *The Semantics of Blessing and Cursing in Ancient Hebrew.* ANESSup 23. Leiden: Peeters, 2007.

Anderson, Gary A. "The Tabernacle Narrative as Christian Scripture." In *The Identity of Israel's God in Christian Scripture*, edited by Don Collett, Mark Elliott, Mark Gignilliat, and Ephraim Radner, 81–95. Resources for Bible Study 96. Atlanta: SBL Press, 2020.

———. *That I May Dwell among Them: Incarnation and Atonement in the Tabernacle Narrative.* Grand Rapids: Eerdmans, 2023.

Artus, Olivier. "The Pentateuch: Five Books, One Canon." In *The Oxford Handbook of the Pentateuch*, edited by Joel S. Baden and Jeffrey Stackert, 23–40. New York: Oxford University Press, 2021.

Aster, Shawn Zelig. *The Unbeatable Light: Melammu and Its Biblical Parallels.* AOAT 384. Munster: Ugarit-Verlag, 2012.

Aune, David E. *Apocalypticism, Prophecy and Magic in Early Christianity: Collected Essays.* WUNT 199. Tübingen: Mohr Siebeck, 2006.

Bar-Ilan, Meir. "Body Marks in Jewish Sources: From Biblical to Post-Talmudic Times." *Review of Rabbinic Judaism* 21 (2018): 57–81.

Berlejung, Angelika. "Divine Presence and Absence." In *The Oxford Handbook of Ritual and Worship in the Herew Bible*, edited by Samuel E. Balentine, 345–61. New York: Oxford University Press, 2020.

———. "Divine Presence for Everybody: Presence Theology in Everyday Life." In *Divine Presence and Absence in Exilic and Post-Exilic Judaism*, edited by Nathan MacDonald and Izaak J. de Hulster, 67–93. FAT 2/61. Tübingen: Mohr Siebeck, 2013.

Berlin, Adele, and Marc Zvi Brettler, eds. *The Jewish Study Bible*. 2nd ed. New York: Oxford University Press, 2014.

Block, Daniel I. "Bearing the Name of the LORD with Honor." In *How I Love Your Torah, O LORD! Studies in the Book of Deuteronomy*, 61–71. Eugene, OR: Cascade Books, 2011.

Boersma, Hans. *Seeing God: The Beatific Vision in Christian Tradition*. Grand Rapids: Eerdmans, 2018.

Bohak, Gideon. *Ancient Jewish Magic: A History*. Cambridge: Cambridge University Press, 2008.

Bowler, Kate. *Blessed: A History of the American Prosperity Gospel*. New York: Oxford University Press, 2013.

Bradshaw, Paul, ed. *The New SCM Dictionary of Liturgy and Worship*. London: SCM, 2002.

Brink, Emily R. "Make Me a Blessing: Benedictions Are More Than Pious Wishes." *RW* 19 (1991): 2–3.

Brueggemann, Walter. "Liturgy of Abundance, and the Myth of Scarcity." *ChrCent* 116, no. 10 (Mar. 24–31, 1999): 342–47.

Brunner, Emil. *The Christian Doctrine of God: Dogmatics, Vol. 1*. Translated by Olive Wyon. London: Lutterworth, 1949.

———. *Revelation and Reason: The Christian Doctrine of Faith and Knowledge*. Translated by Olive Wyon. Philadelphia: Westminster, 1946.

Caputo, John D. "The Subjunctive Power of God." *Concilium* 3 (2020): 12–21.

Chapman, Stephen B. "Historical Criticism, Moral Judgment, and the Future of the Past." In *A Sage in New Haven: Essays on the Prophets, the Writings, and the Ancient World in Honor of Robert R. Wilson*, edited by Alison Acker Gruseke and Carolyn J. Sharp, 297–307. Munster: Zaphon, 2023.

———. "Pentateuch and Blessing." In *T&T Clark Handbook of the Doctrine of Creation*, edited by Jason Goroncy, 44–55. London: Bloomsbury Academic, 2024.

———. "The Pentateuch as Canon." In *Canon Formation: Tracing the Role of Sub-Collections in the Biblical Canon*, edited by W. Edward Glenny and Darian R. Lockett, 101–19. London: Bloomsbury T&T Clark, 2023.

———. "Psalm 115 and the Logic of Blessing." *HBT* 44, no. 1 (2022): 47–63.

Chen, Yu. *The Ritual Dimension of Union with Christ in Paul's Thought*. WUNT 2/568. Tübingen: Mohr Siebeck, 2022.

Cohn, Yehudah B. *Tangled Up in Text:* Tefillin *and the Ancient World*. BJS 21. Providence: Brown University, 2008.

Dalferth, Ingolf U., and Philipp Stoellger, eds. *Gott Nennen: Gottes Namen und Gott als Name*. Religion in Philosophy and Theology 35. Tübingen: Mohr Siebeck, 2008.

Daniélou, Jean. *The Bible and the Liturgy*. Notre Dame, IN: University of Notre Dame Press, 1956.

———. *The Theology of Jewish Christianity*. Translated and edited by John A. Baker. London: Darton, Longman & Todd, 1964.

Davignon, Phil. *Practicing Christians, Practical Atheists: How Cultural Liturgies and Everyday Social Practices Shape Christian Life*. Eugene, OR; Cascade Books, 2023.

Davison, Andrew. *Blessing*. Faith Going Deeper. Norwich: Canterbury, 2014.

Dawes, Stephen B. "'Bless the Lord': An Invitation to Affirm the Living God." *ExpTim* 106, no. 10 (July 1995): 293–96.

Elbogen, Ismar. *Jewish Liturgy: A Comprehensive History*. Translated by Raymond P. Scheindlin. Philadelphia: Jewish Publication Society, 1993.

Elder, Robert J. "Bless This House: The Idea of Angry Spirits in a Member's Home Was a New One to Our Congregation." *RW* 40 (1996): 38–39.

Emlet, Michael R. "Benediction: Living under God's Good Word." *Journal of Pastoral Counseling* 35, no. 3 (2021): 2–12.

Ford, David F. *Self and Salvation: Being Transformed*. Cambridge: Cambridge University Press, 1999.

———. *Shaping Theology: Engagements in a Religious and Secular World*. Malden, MA: Blackwell, 2007.

Fowl, Stephen. "Theological Interpretation and Its Future." *AThR* 99, no. 4 (2017): 671–90.

Fox, Nili. "Marked for Servitude: Mesopotamia and the Bible." In *A Common Cultural Heritage: Studies on Mesopotamia and the Biblical World in Honor of Barry L. Eichler*, edited by Grant Frame et al., 267–78. Bethesda, MD: CDL, 2011.

Fretheim, Terence E. "Salvation in the Bible vs. Salvation in the Church." *WW* 13, no. 4 (1993): 363–72.

Gieschen, Charles A. "The Divine Name in Ante-Nicene Christology." *VC* 57, no. 2 (2003): 115–58.

———. "The Divine Name That the Son Shares with the Father in the Gospel of John." In *Reading the Gospel of John's Christology as Jewish Messianism: Royal, Prophetic, and Divine Messiahs*, edited by Benjamin E. Reynolds and Gabriele Boccaccini, 387–410. AJEC 106. Boston: Brill, 2018.

Greiner, Dorothea. *Segen und Segnen: Eine systematisch-theologische Grundlegung*. Stuttgart: Kohlhammer, 1998.

Gruber, Mayer I. *Aspects of Nonverbal Communication in the Ancient Near East*. StPohl 121.I–II. Rome: Biblical Institute Press, 1982.

———. "The Many Faces of Hebrew *nāśāʾ pānîm* 'lift up the face.'" *ZAW* 95, no. 2 (1983): 252–60.

Grüneberg, Keith. *Blessing: Biblical Meaning and Pastoral Practice*. Ridley Hall, Cambridge: Grove, 2003.

Guelich, Robert. *The Sermon on the Mount: A Foundation for Understanding*. Waco: Word Books, 1982.

Guest, Matthew. *Neoliberal Religion: Faith and Power in the Twenty-First Century*. London: Bloomsbury Academic, 2022.

Hartman, Lars. *"Into the Name of the Lord Jesus": Baptism in the Early Church*. SNTW. Edinburgh: T&T Clark, 1997.

Haverkamp, Heidi. "Take and Eat? When Church Members Prefer Just a Blessing." *ChrCent* 133, no. 16 (Aug. 2, 2016): 20–22.

Heckel, Ulrich. *Der Segen im Neuen Testament: Begriff, Formeln, Gesten; mit einem praktisch-theologischen Ausblick*. WUNT 150. Tübingen: Mohr Siebeck, 2002.

Hezser, Catherine. *Jewish Literacy in Roman Palestine*. TSAJ 81. Tübingen: Mohr Siebeck, 2001.

Hundley, Michael. *Gods in Dwellings: Temples and Divine Presence in the Ancient Near East*. Atlanta: SBL Press, 2013.

———. "To Be or Not to Be: A Reexamination of Name Language in Deuteronomy and the Deuteronomistic History." *VT* 59 (2009): 533–55.

Imes, Carmen Joy. *Bearing God's Name: Why Sinai Still Matters*. Downers Grove, IL: IVP Academic, 2019.

---. *Bearing YHWH's Name at Sinai: A Reexamination of the Name Command of the Decalogue*. BBRSup 19. University Park, PA: Eisenbrauns, 2017.

Isaacs, Ron. *Every Person's Guide to Jewish Blessings*. Brooklyn, NY: KTAV, 2021.

Jacobs, Sandra. *The Body as Property: Physical Disfigurement in Biblical Law*. LHBOTS 582. London: Bloomsbury T&T Clark, 2014.

---. "The Body Inscribed: A Priestly Initiative?" In *The Body in Biblical, Christian and Jewish Texts*, edited by Joan E. Taylor, 1–16. LSTS 85. London: Bloomsbury, 2014.

Jarvis, Cynthia A. "Ministry in the Subjunctive Mood." *ThTo* 66 (2010): 445–58.

Johnston, Donna Giver. "Touch of Grace: The Laying On of Hands." *Call to Worship* 45, no. 4 (2012): 17–26.

Johnston, Sarah Iles. "Magic." In *Religions of the Ancient World: A Guide*, edited by Sarah Iles Johnston, 139–52. Cambridge, MA: Belknap, 2004.

Jonsson, Fredrik Albritton, and Carl Wennerlind. *Scarcity: A History of the Origins of Capitalism to the Climate Crisis*. Cambridge, MA: Harvard University Press, 2023.

Jordan, Mark D. *Blessing Same-Sex Unions: The Perils of Queer Romance and the Confusions of Christian Marriage*. Chicago: University of Chicago Press, 2005.

Kaczynski, Reiner. "Blessings in Rome and the Non-Roman West." In *Handbook for Liturgical Studies IV: Sacraments and Sacramentals*, edited by Anscar J. Chupungco, 393–410. Collegeville, MN: Liturgical Press, 2000.

Keel, Othmar. "Zeichen der Verbundenheit: Zur Vorgeschichte und Bedeutung der Forderung von Deuteronomium 6,8f. und Par." In *Mélanges Dominique Barthélemy: Études bibliques offertes à l'occasion de son 60. anniversaire*, edited by Pierre Casetti, Othmar Keel, and Adrian Schenker, 196–212. OBO 38. Göttingen: Vandenhoeck & Ruprecht, 1981.

Kim, Jung Hoon. *The Significance of Clothing Imagery in the Pauline Corpus*. JSNTSup 268. London: T&T Clark, 2004.

Kleinig, John W. "Pastoring by Blessing." *LTJ* 43, no. 1 (2009): 28–38.

Knohl, Israel. *The Sanctuary of Silence: The Priestly Torah and the Holiness School*. Minneapolis: Augsburg Fortress, 1995.

Koenig, John. *Rediscovering New Testament Prayer: Boldness and Blessing in the Name of Jesus*. San Francisco: Harper, 1992.

Kugel, James. "The Irreconcilability of Judaism and Modern Biblical Scholarship." *Studies in the Bible and Late Antiquity* 8 (2016): 12–31.

Lathrop, Gordon W. *Holy Ground: A Liturgical Cosmology.* Minneapolis: Fortress, 2003.

———. *Saving Images: The Presence of the Bible in Christian Liturgy.* Minneapolis: Fortress, 2017.

Levine, Amy-Jill. *The Misunderstood Jew: The Church and the Scandal of the Jewish Jesus.* San Francisco: Harper, 2006.

Longenecker, Richard N. *The Christology of Early Jewish Christianity.* SBT 2.17. London: SCM, 1970.

MacDonald, Nathan. "A Trinitarian Palimpsest: Luther's Reading of the Priestly Blessing (Numbers 6.24–26)." *ProEccl* 21, no. 3 (2012): 299–313.

Macina, Robert D. *The LORD's Service: A Ritual Analysis of the Order, Function, and Purpose of the Daily Divine Service in the Pentateuch.* Eugene, OR: Pickwick, 2019.

Mandell, Alice. "Aaron's Body as a Ritual Vessel in the Exodus Tabernacle Building Narrative." In *New Perspectives on Ritual in the Biblical World*, edited by Laura Quick and Melissa Ramos, 159–81. LHBOTS 702. London: T&T Clark, 2022.

———. "Writing as a Source of Ritual Authority: The High Priest's Body as a Priestly Text in the Tabernacle-Building Story." *JBL* 141, no. 1 (2022): 43–64.

Mekkattukunnel, Andrews George. *The Priestly Blessing of the Risen Christ: An Exegetico-Theological Analysis of Luke 24,50–53.* Bern: Lang, 2001.

Miller, Robert D., II. *Yahweh: Origin of a Desert God.* FRLANT 284. Göttingen: Vandenhoeck & Ruprecht, 2018.

Mitchell, Christopher Wright. *The Meaning of BRK "to Bless" in the Old Testament.* SBLDS 95. Atlanta: Scholars Press, 1987.

Moberly, R. W. L. *Old Testament Theology: Reading the Hebrew Bible as Christian Scripture.* Grand Rapids: Baker Academic, 2013.

———. "Salvation in the Old Testament." *JTI* 15, no. 2 (2021): 189–202.

Moltmann, Jürgen. *The Living God and the Fullness of Life.* Translated by Margaret Kohl. Louisville: Westminster John Knox, 2015.

Monaghan, Christopher J. "Wrestling for a Blessing: Is There a Place for Touch in the Church Today?" *The Furrow* 71, no. 1 (2020): 3–9.

Oorshot, Jürgen, and Markus Witte, eds. *The Origins of Yahwism.* BZAW 484. Berlin: De Gruyter, 2017.

Oppenheimer, Helen. "Blessing." In *The Weight of Glory: A Vision and Practice for Christian Faith*, edited by D. W. Hardy and P. H. Sedgwick, 221–30. Edinburgh: T&T Clark, 1991.

Osborne, William R. *Divine Blessing and the Fullness of Life in the Presence of God*. Shorter Studies in Biblical Theology. Wheaton, IL: Crossway, 2020.

Peterman, Gerald W. "Plural You: On the Use and Abuse of the Second Person." *BBR* 20, no. 2 (2010): 201–14.

Power, David Noel. "On Blessing Things." In *Blessing and Power*, edited by Mary Collins and David Noel Power, 24–39. Concilium 178. Edinburgh: T&T Clark, 1985.

Pruyser, Paul. "The Master Hand: Psychological Notes on Pastoral Blessing." In *The New Shape of Pastoral Theology: Essays in Honor of Seward Hiltner*, edited by William B. Oglesby, 352–65. Nashville: Abingdon, 1969.

Radner, Ephraim. "Blessing: A Scriptural and Theological Reflection." *ProEccl* 191 (2010): 1–27.

Ramshaw, Elaine. "Bringing the Blessing Home: The Many Occasions for House Blessings." *Liturgy* 21, no. 4 (2006): 19–27.

Reynolds, Philip Lyndon. *Marriage in the Western Church: The Christianization of Marriage during the Patristic and Early Medieval Periods*. VCSup 24. Leiden: Brill, 1994.

Riecker, Siegbert. *Ein Priestervolk für alle Völker: Der Segensauftrag Israels für alle Nationen in der Tora und den Vorderen Propheten*. SBB 59. Stuttgart: Katholisches Bibelwerk, 2007.

Rosenthal, David. "Tefillin Blessing in Eretz Isrrael and in Babylonia." *Tarbiz* 791 (2010): 63–86.

Seebass, Horst. "Moses' Preparation of the March to the Holy Land: A Dialogue with Rolf P. Knierim on Numbers 1:1–10:10." In *Land of Israel in the Bible, History, and Theology: Studies in Honor of Ed Noort*, edited by Jacques van Ruiten and Jacobus C. de Vos, 99–110. VTSup 124. Leiden: Brill, 2009.

Shaw, David M. "Called to Bless: Considering an Under-Appreciated Aspect of 'Doing Good' in 1 Peter 3:8–17." *BTB* 50, no. 1 (2020): 161–73.

Sherlock, Charles. "Who May Bless in God's Name? Bless What? And How?" *Australian Journal of Liturgy* 17, no. 2 (2020): 97–107.

Simons, Thomas G. *Blessings: A Reappraisal of Their Nature, Purpose and Celebration*. Saratoga, CA: Resource, 1981.

Simpson, William W. *Jewish Prayer and Worship: An Introduction for Christians.* London: SCM, 1965.

Skemer, Don C. *Binding Words: Textual Amulets in the Middle Ages.* University Park: Pennsylvania State University Press, 2006.

Smith, James K. A. *Thinking in Tongues: Pentecostal Contributions to Christian Philosophy.* Grand Rapids: Eerdmans, 2010.

Smith, Mark S. "'Seeing God' in the Psalms: The Background to the Beatific Vision in the Hebrew Bible." *CBQ* 50, no. 2 (1988): 171–83.

Smoak, Jeffrey D. "From Temple to Text: Text as Ritual Space and the Composition of Numbers 6:24–26." *JHS* 17 (2017), art. 2, https://doi.org/10.5508/jhs.2017.v17.a2.

———. *The Priestly Blessing in Inscription and Scripture: The Early History of Numbers 6:24–26.* New York: Oxford University Press, 2016.

———. "Silver Scripts: The Ritual Function of Purified Metal in Ancient Judah." In *New Perspectives on Ritual in the Biblical World*, edited by Laura Quick and Melissa Ramos, 237–53. LHBOTS 702. London: T&T Clark, 2022.

———. "Wearing Divine Words: In Life and Death." *Material Religion* 15, no. 4 (2019): 433–55.

———. "'You Have Refined Us Like Silver Is Refined' (Ps. 66:10): Yahweh's Metallurgical Powers in Ancient Judah." *Advances in Ancient, Biblical, and Near Eastern Research* 1, no. 3 (2021): 81–115.

Soulen, R. Kendall. *The Divine Name(s) and the Holy Trinity: Distinguishing the Voices.* Louisville: Westminster John Knox, 2011.

———. "'Hallowed Be Thy Name!': The Theological Significance of the Avoidance of God's Name in the New Testament." In *Strangers in a Strange Land: A Festschrift in Honor of Bruce C. Birch upon His Retirement as Academic Dean of Wesley Theological Seminary*, edited by Lucy Lind Hogan and D. William Faupel, 145–59. Lexington: Emeth, 2009.

———. "The Third Word: The Blessing of God's Name." In *The Ten Commandments for Jews, Christians, and Others*, edited by Roger E. Van Harn, 47–61. Grand Rapids: Eerdmans, 2009.

Standish, N. Graham. *Becoming a Blessed Church: Forming a Church of Spiritual Purpose, Presence, and Power.* 2nd ed. Lanham, MD: Rowman & Littlefield, 2016.

Szczapa, Stanley. "Go! You Are Sent with God's Blessing to Bring the Good News of God's Love to All You Meet." *Liturgical Ministry* 12 (2003): 156–59.

Taylor, Barbara Brown. *An Altar in the World: A Geography of Faith*. New York: HarperOne, 2009.

Taylor, W. David O. *A Body of Praise: Understanding the Role of Our Physical Bodies in Worship*. Grand Rapids: Baker Academic, 2023.

Thiselton, Anthony C. *Promise and Prayer: The Biblical Writings in the Light of Speech-Act Theory*. Eugene, OR: Cascade Books, 2020.

———. "The Supposed Power of Words in the Biblical Writings." *JTS* 25 (1974): 283–99.

Thorngate, Steve. "Blest and Kept: Why and How I Bless My Children." *ChrCent* 133, no. 16 (Aug. 2, 2016): 22–24.

Tomlin, Graham. *The Widening Circle: Priesthood as God's Way of Blessing in the World*. London: SPCK, 2014.

Urbach, Ephraim E. *The Sages: Their Concepts and Beliefs*. Translated by Israel Abrahams. Cambridge, MA: Harvard University Press, 1979.

Van Den Brink, Julia. "Luke's Beatitudes and Woes: Are They Covenant Blessings and Curses?" *Stimulus* 23, no. 3 (2016): 12–17.

Van den Doel, Anthonie. "Blessing and Cursing in the New Testament and Related Literature." PhD diss., Northwestern University, 1968.

Van Slyke, Daniel G. "Toward a Theology of Blessings: Agents and Recipients of Benedictions." *Antiphon* 15, no. 1 (2011): 47–60.

Westermann, Claus. *Blessing in the Bible and the Life of the Church*. Translated by Keith Crim. OBT. Philadelphia: Fortress, 1978.

Wijk-Bos, Johanna van. "Writing on Water: The Ineffable Name of God." In *Jews, Christians, and the Theology of the Hebrew Scriptures*, edited by Alice Ogden Bellis and Joel Kaminsky, 45–59. SymS 8. Atlanta: Society of Biblical Literature, 2000.

Wilhoit, James C. *Spiritual Formation as if the Church Mattered: Growing in Christ through Community*. 2nd ed. Grand Rapids: Baker Academic, 2022.

Williamson, Clark M. *Way of Blessing, Way of Life: A Christian Theology*. St. Louis: Chalice, 1999.

Wilson, Brittany E. *The Embodied God: Seeing the Divine in Luke-Acts and the Early Church*. Oxford: Oxford University Press, 2021.

Wilson, Ian. *Out of the Midst of the Fire: Divine Presence in Deuteronomy.* SBLDS 151. Atlanta: Scholars Press, 1995.

Winner, Lauren F. *Wearing God: Clothing, Laughter, Fire, and Other Overlooked Ways of Meeting God.* New York: HarperOne, 2015.

Witvliet, John D. "On Ordination and Worship Leadership." *RW* 69 (2003): 42–43.

Woodcock, Eldon. "The Seal of the Holy Spirit." *BSac* 155 (1998): 139–63.

Scripture and Ancient Sources Index

Old Testament

Genesis
1–3 28
1:1 52
1:1–2:3 61
1:3 33, 77, 79
1:22 94, 162
1:26 33
2:6 80
2:15 72
3:14–19 149
4:5–6 91
4:9 72
4:15 94n71
4:26 41
5:2 20
6:8 88
8:13 80
9:8–10 140
9:27 30
12:1–3 133, 149n76
12:3 4
12:10–20 28
14:14 122
15:2 122n179
15:12–16 28
17:2 30
17:9–10 71
19:21 89
24:48 62
24:48–49 16n61
27 36
27:33 152
27:35–37 36
30:27 37
30:31 71
30:37–43 37
32:21 89
32:22–32 119
32:26 152
32:29 119
32:30 83, 85
32:30–31 119
33:1–11 87
33:10 80
37:28 46
39:21 87
44:5 37
48:8–20 132n17
48:14 159
49 28
49:25 28n30
49:26 28n30
50:24 28

Exodus
2:16 46
3–4 43, 54
3:1 46
3:1–6 79
3:1–4:17 42
3:6 42, 91
3:13 42–43
3:13–15 47
3:14 43, 54
3:15 42
3:16–18 43
6:2–3 41
7:8–12 37
10:28–29 80
13:1–10 125n190
13:9 121
13:11–16 125n190
13:16 121
14:21 163
15:3 83
15:6 83
15:8 83
18:1 46
18:8–12 46
19 110
19–20 54
19:5 71
19:25 66
20:1–17 66, 69
20:2 54
20:3 48
20:5 48
20:6 71
20:7 59, 114
20:8 71
20:17b 69
20:24 169
23:15 81
23:17 81
23:20–24 53
23:25 162
23:27 78

24:9–11 51, 83
25 29n33
25–31 11
28:36–38 13, 54
29:38–42 13
33–34 54
33:11 85, 85n35
33:12–17 87
33:14 82
33:14–16 81
33:19 54, 88
33:20 83
34:5–7 54
34:6 88
34:6–7 77n5
34:14 48, 53n122
34:24 81
34:29–30 126n192
34:29–35 79, 126
34:35 126n192
35–40 11
40 29n33

Leviticus

8:9 54
9 29, 29n33
9:22 29
9:22–23 13n52
9:23 29n33
9:24 29n33
17–26 25n15
18:4–5 72
18:21 168
18:26–30 72
19 114
19:12 168
19:15 90
19:28 114
19:37 72
20:3 168
20:22–24 72
21:6 168
22:2 168
22:32 168
24:11 42

24:16 42
26:6 102

Numbers

1:53 72
3:28 72
3:32 72
5 26
5–6 26–27
5:1–4 26
5:1–10:10 110
5:5–10 26
5:9 26
5:11–31 26
5:15 26
5:19–22 24n14
6 24, 26–27, 29–30, 90, 126
6:1–21 26
6:10 26
6:13 26
6:22 24–25
6:22–23 75
6:22–24 21
6:22–27 xviii, 29
6:23 24, 38
6:23b 25–26
6:24–26 1, 11, 17, 29, 34n46, 57, 91, 173
6:25 11, 76–77, 89
6:25–27 75
6:26 90, 174
6:27 24–26, 50, 70, 75, 95, 112–13, 115, 122, 165, 174
7:1 29
7:1–10:10 110
10:11–12 29
10:29 46
12:8 51
22–24 36
23:20 36
28:1–8 13

Deuteronomy

1:1–5 28
4 49, 51
4:11 79
4:12 49, 163
4:15–19 50
4:24 79
4:36 51–52
4:44–49 28
5:1 72
5:1–5 66
5:4 85
5:6–21 66
5:7 48
5:9 48
5:10 71
5:11 114
5:32 72
6 113
6:3 72
6:4–9 113, 125n190
6:25 72
7:9 71
7:11 72
7:13 162
8:1 72
8:3 163
8:18 36n56
9:3 49, 79
10:1–2 49
10:8 13n52, 119n167
11 113
11:13–21 113, 125n190
11:26–28 149n76
12 48
12–26 48
12:5 50, 108n123
12:11 50
14:23 50
16:2 50
16:6 50
16:11 50

16:16 81
21:5 13n52
26:2 50
26:15 51, 162
27–28 28, 148n75
28:1–2 37
28:1–14 162
28:10 108
28:11 36n56
28:50 89
28:58 53n122, 55
29:18–20 147
30:1–5 28
30:19–20 149n76
31:11 81
32:8–9 45n87, 48
33 28
33:2 46, 76
33:13 28n30
33:15–16 28n30
34:10 85

Judges

1:16 46
4:11 46
5:4–5 46–47
6:22 85
6:22–23 83

Ruth

1:8–9 55
2:4 26, 55
2:20 55

1 Samuel

1:18 81
5:2 19n75
15:13 26, 55
25:14 152
27:10 46n94
28 38
30:29 46n94

2 Samuel

2:22 89, 93
11:7 95

15:16 71
16:21 71
17:11 80
19:38 30
20:3 71
22 79

1 Kings
8 50n110
8:14 132n17
8:22 52, 52n116
8:27 163
8:30 52
8:32 52
8:34 52
8:36 52
8:39 52
8:43 52
8:45 52
8:49 52
8:54 52, 52n116
8:54–56 59n146
9:3 35n49, 50, 51n115, 108n123
11:36 108n123
14:21 108n123
14:27 71
18:41 30
22:19 51

2 Kings
3:14 90
4:29 26
5:1 90
9:32 89
11:5–6 71–72
12:9 72
16:10–14 19n75
17:30 53
21:4 108n123
21:4–7 50
21:7 108n123
22–23 48
23:4 72
25:18 72

1 Chronicles
16:29 53n122, 54
16:35–36 62, 147
23:13 13n52

2 Chronicles
6:3 132n17
6:20 108n123
7:13–14 92
7:14 108n122
12:13 108n123
32:2 80
33:7 108n123

Ezra
6:12 53

Nehemiah
1:9 53
1:11 168
9:5 62, 147

Job
9:27 93n66
10:20 93n66
11:15 89, 93
13:8 90
13:10 90
22:26 89, 93
29:24 76, 91
31:29–30 133n20
32:21 89
42:8–9 89

Psalms
1:1 68
4:6 77, 90
4:6–7 76
5:12 148
11:7 82
12:6 11
13:1 81, 92
15 148
17:15 51, 82
18 79
18:6–15 47
18:28 77
20:1 55
22:27 81
23:5 87
24 148
24:6 81
27:1 76
27:1–4 90
27:4 82
27:8 81–82
29:2 53n122, 54
31 76, 83
31:16 76
34:1 62, 68, 147
34:14 95
34:16 81
36:6 140
36:9 79
37:1–6 90
37:4 36n56
37:16 156
39:14 93n66
40:4 68
41:13 143
42:2 82
43:3 76
44:3 76
44:24 92
63:2 81
66:2 54
66:4 53n122
67 18, 76
67:1 76
67:4 76
67:6–7 17
68 56
68:4 56, 81
68:7–8 46–47
69:17 92
69:30 56
72 99
72:9 99
72:18 143
80 76
80:3 76
80:7 76
80:16 81
80:19 76
82:2 90
84:4–5 68
84:11 77
84:12 68, 88
85:8 95, 106
85:10 102
86:9 53n122, 56
88:14 92
89:15 77
90:8 77
96:8 54
97:3 49
102:2 81
103:1 56
104:1–2 78, 125
104:2 77
105:4 81
112:4 88
118:26b 26
119:1 68
119:9 128
119:58 86
119:105 77
119:135 76
121:5 72
124:8 54
129:8 55
134:2 159
143:7 81
145:2 62, 147
145:5 78

Proverbs
2:17 156n98
3:1–4 12
6:23 77
6:35 89–90, 93
7:1–3 12
16:15 76, 78
18:5 90
18:10 54
19:1 156

24:17–18 133n20
28:6 156

Ecclesiastes
3:8 102

Isaiah
1:12 81
2:2–4 101
6:1–5 51
9 99
9:2 76
9:2–7 100
9:4 99
9:7 99
19:24–25 20
25:4 156
29:23 128, 168
30:19 87
30:22 11
30:27 49, 54–55, 55n134
30:33 49
33:2 87
33:11 49
42:6 79, 100
43:2 122
44:5 115
48:9–11 168
49:6 79, 100
49:14–16 115n151
49:16 116n151
50:6 91
52:7 100
53:3 91
54:10 100
55:12 100
56:6 55
59:1–8 102
60 99
60:1 77
60:9 55
60:9–11 99
60:14 99
60:19–20 79
63:9 82
63:19 108n122
65:5 49
65:8 162
65:15 165
66:12 100

Jeremiah
3:12 91
3:17 53n122
7:12–14 53
11:1–5 149
14:9 108
20:9 79
21:4 116
23:23–24 163
23:27 53n122
31:10 71
33:2 57
33:6 100
34:16 168
40:15 30

Lamentations
4:16 81, 90

Ezekiel
1:26–28 51
9 121
9:4 122, 132
20:35 85
34:26 162
36:20–23 168
36:23 168
37:26 100
39:7 168
41:14–21 80

Daniel
7:9 83
9:17 76
9:18–19 108n122

Hosea
2:8 56
12:12 71
12:13 72

Joel
2:32 58, 120n169

Amos
2:7 168
5:6 79
5:8 57
5:9 92n63, 93n66
9:1 51
9:6 57
9:11–12 133

Micah
2:3 96
4:1–4 101

Habakkuk
3:3 46
3:3–4 79

Zephaniah
3:5 76

Zechariah
2:10–12 100
7:2 86
8:23 57
9:10 99–100

Malachi
1:8–9 90
1:9 86
1:11 76, 168
2:2 149
2:9 90
4:1–2 76

New Testament

Matthew
2:1–12 37
5 126
5–7 67
5:1 67
5:3 67n183, 68
5:9 95n73
5:14–16 80
5:16 126
5:43–45 133
6:9 59, 128
6:9–13 127
6:25 123, 163
6:33 146
7:28–29 67
8:16 37
10:11–14 151
10:37 156
11:20–24 149n80
13:31–32 61
14:19 159
19:13–15 140
21:9 58
21:18–22 149n80
21:43 7
22:29–30 156
23:13–36 149n80
25:31–46 149n76
26:67 84
27:25 7
28:19 119, 119n167

Mark
1:32–34 37
6:9 123
6:41 159
9:25 38
10:13–16 140
11:12–14 149n80

Luke
1:5–23 132
1:49 128
1:68–79 143
4:31–37 38
6:17–19 67
6:17–49 67
6:20 68, 156
6:20b 67
6:20–22 141
6:20–31 67n182
6:24–26 149

6:27 133
6:27–28 xvi, 106
9:16 159
10:11 149n78
10:13–15 149n80
11:2–4 127
11:14–23 37
12:51–53 156
14:26 156
18:15–17 140
18:29–30 156
20:34–35 156
22:19 38
24 10n32
24:50–51 17
24:50–53 131,
  131n16, 132n17

John
1:7–9 77
1:12 121
1:18 83
4:22 4
5:43 121
8:12 77
8:58 121
10:10b 170
13:7 59
13:15–17 133
15:21 168
17:6 121, 128
17:11–12 121, 128
17:26 121, 128
20:31 170

Acts
2:21 120, 120n169
2:38 119
2:46 10
3:1 10
3:16 120
3:25 4
3:26 133
4:7 38, 58, 120
4:10 120
4:12 120

4:30 38, 58
5:17–26 10
5:41 168
5:42 10
8:16 119, 119n167
8:20–22 149
9:16 168
10:36 101
10:48 119
12:21 123
13:6–12 149
13:46 7
15:21 10
16:18 120
18:6 7
19:5 119, 119n167
19:11–12 37
19:13–16 38n65
19:13–17 120
20:35 133
21:13 168
21:17–26 10
23:3 149n78
24:2–3 97
28:28 7

Romans
1:7 101n99
2:1–11 148n75
4:11 122
6:1–14 123
8:29 124
9:6 4
10:13 58, 120,
  120n169
11:17 4
11:18 4
11:29 36n56
12:1–2 119
12:14 xvi, 106,
  133, 163
12:17–18 163
13:13–14 xxvii n2
13:14 xxvii n1,
  123

15:1–3 105
15:13 2
15:33 101n98
16:20 101n98

1 Corinthians
1:3 101n99
4:10–13 164
4:12 xvi, 133
5:4–5 149n78
6:11 119
6:18 156n98
7:2–7 156n98
10:16 162n121
11:17 151
11:27–32 138, 148
12:13 123
13:12 84–85
14:33 101n98
16:22 148n75

2 Corinthians
1:2 101n99
1:22 116
3:18 79, 126
4:6 82, 84
4:7–11 118–19
12:9 119
13:11 101n98
13:13 2

Galatians
1:3 101n99
1:8–9 149n78
3:10–14 148n75
3:27 123, 167
5:1 40
5:12 149n78
6:17 118n163

Ephesians
1:2 101
1:3–10 61
1:13 116
1:20–21 120
2:14 101

3:20 172
4:25–32 106
4:29 105

Philippians
1:2 101n99
1:20 119
2:5–11 120
2:6 120n172
2:9 120
2:9–11 58
2:10–11 12
4:9 101n98

Colossians
1:2 101n99
1:15 83
3:10 123
3:13–14 167
3:15a 101
3:17 128, 146, 170

1 Thessalonians
1:1 101n99
5:23 101n98

2 Thessalonians
1:2 101n98
1:12 124, 168
3:16 101n98

1 Timothy
1:2 101n99
1:20 149n78
2:8 159n108

2 Timothy
1:2 101n99

Titus
1:4 101n99

Philemon
3 101n99

Hebrews
1:1–4 120
2:11–12 120
12:14 101
12:14–17 148n75
13:4 156n98
13:20 101n98

James
2:5 156
2:7 124
3:6 105
3:9–10 149n78
3:10 105
4:11–12 106
5:14 124
5:14–16 140

1 Peter
1:2 101n99
3:8–9 20
3:9 xvi, 133, 150, 163
4:13–14 168
5:5 167

2 John
3 101n99

3 John
7 121

Revelation
1:4 101n99
3:12 121
7:3 132
7:3–4 121
9:4 132
14 121
14:1 121, 169
19:1–16 121
19:12 121
19:14 123
22:1–5 132
22:3a 133
22:3–4 61, 121

Apocryphal/Deuterocanonical Books

Sirach
45:6–22 54
50:13–21 13n52
50:20–21 131

Other Ancient Jewish Writings

Babylonian Talmud

Berakhot
20a 168
40b 16

Eruvin
96a 125n190

Hagigah
16a 111

Menahot
43b 14

Sanhedrin
74a 168

Sotah
10b 168
39a 111
40a 111
40b 112

Josephus

Jewish Antiquities
2.275–76 113n137
8.42–49 113n137

Midrash Psalms
36:8 116n152

Mishnah

Berakhot
9:5 55

Megillah
4:10 19n78

Tamid
3:8 14
5:1 13
7:2 13–14, 109

Yoma
6:2 14, 53

Numbers Rabbah
12:3 114

Testament of Levi
8:4–5 124

Other Ancient Christian Writings

Apostolic Constitutions
2.57 16
3.10 20

Augustine

Confessions
8.12.29 xxvii

1 Clement
60:3 16, 17n64

2 Clement
7:6 116

Clement of Alexandria

Stromata V
6.34.5 42

Epistle of Diognetus
5:1–2 164
5:5 164
5:11 164
5:15 164

Justin Martyr

Apologia
1.61 124
1.61.10–13 120

Letter of Barnabas
9:8 122

Odes of Solomon
39:7–8 122

Origen

On First Principles
2.3.2 xxvii

Shepherd of Hermas

Similitudes
8.2.4 124
8.6.4 120

Subject Index

Aaronic Blessing, 24–25, 112. *See also* Priestly Blessing
Aaronic priesthood, 24–26, 72
    high priest, 13–14, 53
    high priest's frontlet, 13–14, 54, 112, 114, 132
    instructions for, 25–26, 38, 93–94, 108–9
abundance, 170–72
Adams, Kevin, 135
Adonai (Lord), 42, 54–55, 173–74
Akkadian, 59, 78, 94, 115
Aletti, Jean-Noël, 132n17
Amidah, 14, 110
amulets, 11–12, 112–13
    Ketef Hinnom, 10–11, 112
antisemitism, 6–8, 98
apocalypticism, 123–24
Apostolic Benediction, 2
Arabic language, 47, 59, 92n63
archaeology, xii–xiii, xvii, 44–47
Assyria, Assyrian, 97, 115
Aster, Shawn Zelig, 78–79
Augsburg Confession, 167
Augustine, xxi, 104n108, 120n173

Baal/Baʿal, 44, 52, 56
Ballhorn, Egbert, 109–10
baptism, 164–66
    clothing, 123–25, 166–67
    cross, sign of, 121–23
    Jesus's name and, 119–20, 123–24, 164–65
    putting on Christ, 123–26
    sphragis, 116–18, 122
    YHWH, 124–25
Baptists, 165n130
Bar-Ilan, Meir, 115
Barth, Karl, xii, xvii n21, 3, 4n10, 18, 83–84, 170
"beam," 77–78
Beatitudes, the, 67–68, 95n73, 149
Benedict (pope), xvii n22
benedictions, 1–2, 137–44, 159
    Roman Catholic, 17–19, 137–38
Benedictus, 143–44
Biblical Theology Movement, 60
Birkat Kohanim (Priestly Blessing), 3, 13–14, 19–20
bless, blessings, 59–64, 106, 134
    abuse of, xv, 148–51
    actions, 131–32, 136–37, 151–52, 171
    biblical tradition, xvi, 36–37
    clergy, 19–20, 134–35, 139–40, 159
    as commendation, 150–51
    enemies, xvi, 106, 133, 151, 163
    God, 62–63, 131, 170
    God as agent, 26–27, 37, 60–61, 71
    God's name, 62, 133, 170
    Greek *eulogeō*, 63–64
    Hebrew *b-r-k* root, 59, 62–64

194 • Subject Index

home, children, 134–35, 140
hospitality, community, 140–41
human agency, 60–63
integrity of, 148–52
as magic, xv, 35–40, 112–13, 158
material, 156–58, 161–63
modern ideas of, xv, 36–37, 40, 158
morality and, 152–54
of objects and animals, 140–41, 161–62
as performative speech, 34–36, 40, 57–58, 139
physicality, 158–60, 163–64
power of, 36–40, 158
praise and, 62–63, 147–48
protection, 72–73
as transformative, 126, 140, 151, 153–54
truth-telling, 148–52
as volitive statements, 33–34
blessing publications, sample, 140–42
Blessings and Consecrations (United Methodist), 141
Book of Blessings (Roman Missal), 141
Book of Occasional Services (Episcopal), 142
branding. *See* tattooing and branding
Briggs, Richard, 18
Brocke, Edna, 19
Brunner, Emil, 56

Canaanite culture, 44–45
Caputo, John, 39–40
Celtic Christianity, 142
charity, interpretive, 105–6
Charry, Ellen, 167
Childs, Brevard S., 66n178
Christ. *See* Jesus Christ
Christians, 136
    blessing, 133–37, 169–70
    Celtic, 142
    clergy blessing, 19–20, 134–35, 139–40, 159
    conservative, xv, 103, 134, 148
    Coptic, 129
    Jews, Judaism and, 4–10, 19–20, 122

liberal, xv, 103–4, 148
as light, 79–80
name of God, 127–28, 168–69
prayer, 4, 16
putting on Christ, 123–26
singleness, 155–56
tattooing, 116–19, 121–22, 128–29
transformation, 79, 123n185, 126
vocational identity, 169–70
witness, 164–70
worship, 2, 96, 128, 145–46, 159–60
See also early Christians
church, the, 140–41
    nations, state and, 100–101, 103–4
    violence in, 104–5
Church of England, 153
Clement of Alexandria, 42
Clement of Rome, 116
clergy blessing, 19–20, 134–35, 139–40, 159
clothing, 123–25, 174
    and identity, 166–67
conservatism, xv, 103, 134, 148
Contemporary English Translation (CEV), 150
conversion, 153–54
Coptic Christians, 129
creation theology, 15–16
cross, sign of, 116, 123, 137
    baptism, 121–23
    name of Jesus, 118, 122
curses, 113n138, 148–49
Cyril of Jerusalem, 117–18

Daniélou, Jean, 116–18, 124
da Vinci, Leonardo, 92
Davison, Andrew, 61
Decalogue, 49, 66, 69–70, 114
Descartes, René, 129
Deuteronomic tradition, 49–52, 57
Deuteronomy, book of, 27–28
    name, presence of God, 48–53, 57
diversity, 98, 102–3, 166
Donghi, Antonio, 159
Douglas, Mary, 109
Dozeman, Thomas, 26–27, 30–31

early Christians, 116
    Jerusalem temple, 9–10, 132n17
    name of God, Jesus, 58–59, 168
Edom, 46–47
Egypt, Egyptian, 43–45, 52, 97n82, 115
    tattooing, 115, 129n6
'El, 44, 45n87, 53
Elder, Robert, 134–35
election, doctrine of, 5
'El Shaddai, 111
Emlet, Michael, 77–78
enemies, blessing of, xvi, 106, 133, 151, 163
Eucharist, 10, 38, 139. *See also* Lord's Supper
Evangelical Lutheran Worship, 142
exegesis, xii n4, xiv, xvi

face, 80–85
    countenance, 85, 90–91
    fallen, 91–92
    of God, 81–86, 91–93, 173–74
    of Jesus, 84–85
    lifting up, 89–93
    shining, 76–80, 92, 126
    smile, 91–93
favor, 86–91, 158
Fiddler on the Roof, 142
fire, 49, 51–52, 79
Ford, David, 82, 170–71
Fowl, Stephen, 105
Fox, George, 65n175
Freedman, David Noel, 85–86
freedom, 40, 43, 101, 104n108, 145
Fretheim, Terence, 89

Gafney, Wilda, 68–69
Gane, Roy, 92
gematria, 25, 57, 122
Gerleman, Gillis, 96
German Protestant churches, 18
    Israel Sunday, 6–7
Germany, 18, 42, 58, 65
Giddens, Anthony, 145
Gieschen, Charles, 120
give, giving (*ś-y-m*), 93–95, 171–72, 174

glory (*kābôd*), 52, 54, 78, 126
Glossa Ordinaria, 107
God, 58, 84–87
    abundance of, 170–72
    blessing, 62–63, 131, 170
    blessing agent, 26–27, 37, 60–61, 71
    covenant relationship, 148–49
    face of, 81–86, 91–93, 173–74
    favor, 86–91, 158
    glory (*kābôd*), 52, 54, 78, 126
    graciousness, 87–89
    guarding, 72–73
    hands, 83–84, 115n151
    heaven, 51–52
    knowledge of, bodily, 118–19, 129–31
    light, 77–80
    power of, 37–40, 59
    presence of, 48–53, 57–58, 87
    See also God, name of
God, name of, 13–14, 25, 37, 147–48
    Adonai as substitution, 42, 54–55, 173–74
    archaeology, 44–47
    as attribute, 52–53
    bearing, 113–14, 167–70, 174
    blessing, 62, 133, 170
    Canaanite culture, 44–45
    in curses, 113n138
    'El, 44, 45n87, 53
    'El Shaddai, 111
    ha-Shem, 42–43
    honor, sanctity of, 56–57, 59, 127–28, 168–69
    Jealous, 48
    liberation, 43–44
    New Testament, 58–59, 120–21
    origin, 44–47
    presence and, 48–53, 57–58
    Priestly Blessing, 40–41, 57–59, 107, 127, 167–68, 173
    proclamation, 57–58, 108–9, 147–48
    put on people, 70, 93–95, 108–9, 121–22, 126, 132, 174
    revelation of, 41–43, 128
    security, protection, 55–56, 118

Tetragram, 42–43, 55, 112
  in worship, 55–58
  See also YHWH
"God bless America," 150–51
gods, ancient, 48, 56, 83, 124n186
  Baal, 44, 52, 56
  Near Eastern, 52–53, 76, 115, 126n193
Good Friday liturgy, 8
"gracious" (ḥ-n-n), 85–89
gratitude, 146–48
Gregory of Nazianzus, 117–18
Gregory of Nyssa, 85n35
Gruber, Mayer, 76
Grüneberg, Keith, 162n123
Gudea (king), 115–16n151
Guelich, Robert, 68nn187–88
Guest, Matthew, 103n104

hands, 20, 116
  of God, 73, 83–84, 115n151
  opening, 158–59
  raising, 13–14, 111–12, 131–32
Hartman, Lars, 119n167
ha-Shem, 42–43
Hebrew poetry, 31, 56, 75, 85, 174
Hebrew verbs, 32–34
  jussive, imperative, 32–34, 36, 63, 76
Heckl, Raik, 70n192
Herodotus, 118
high priest, 13–14, 53
  frontlet, 13–14, 54, 112, 114, 132
historical context, 23–24
historical criticism, xii–xiv, xvi–xvii, 23–24
  name, presence of God, 48–49, 54–55
  Pentateuch, the, 28–29
Holmberg, Bengt, xiii
Holocaust, the, xviii, 4–6, 8–9
Holy Week, 7–8, 129
home, 134–35, 140
Hundley, Michael, 52–53
Huxley, Aldous, 145
hypostasis, divine, 51–54, 80–81, 120

Ibn Ezra, 27, 29n34
identity, 82, 125, 169–70
  baptism and, 164–66

  bearing God's name, 113–14, 167–70, 174
  clothing, 166–67
  religious, 114–16, 118, 129
  vocational, 116–17, 169–70
Imes, Carmen, 114–15
immigrants, 134–36
imperial peace, 96–99
Improperia, 8
Indiana Jones and the Last Crusade, 128
Israel, Israelites, 37, 81
  nations and, 99–101
  Sinai event, 27–30, 49–51, 126
  YHWH, God and, 58, 86, 115
  See also Jews; Judaism
Israel, State of, 5

Jacob, 119
Jagersma, H., 33n46
Jarvis, Cynthia, 39
Jerusalem, 115–16n151, 133
Jerusalem temple, 48
  early Christians, 9–10, 132n17
  God's name, presence in, 42–43, 48–53
  high priest, 13–14, 53
  Ketef Hinnom amulets, 10–11
  liturgy, 16–17, 109–10, 132
  Priestly Blessing, 2–3, 13–14, 30, 53, 108–10, 112
  Second Temple period, 54–55, 109, 124n186
  of Solomon, 2, 50, 52n116
Jesus Christ, 58–59, 168
  baptism, 119–20, 123–24, 164–65
  blessing, acts of, 131–32, 151–52, 171
  cross, 118, 122–23
  face, 84–85
  God's name, YHWH and, 120–21
  light, 77, 79–80, 126
  name, divine, 58–59, 120, 126, 164–65, 170
  peace, 101–2
Jethro, 46
"Jewish People and Their Sacred Scriptures in the Christian Bible, The," 9
Jewish Study Bible, The, 9

Jews, 115–16, 121–22
  antisemitism, 6–8, 98
  blessings, xviii, 14–16, 140, 142
  Christians and, 4–10, 19–20, 122
  tattooing, marking, 115–16, 121–22
Jordan, Mark, 154
Josiah, 48
Judaism, 4, 122, 155, 161
  bar mitzvah, 125
  Birkat Kohanim (Priestly Blessing), 3, 13–14, 19–20
  blessings, xviii, 14–16, 140, 142
  kiddush ha-Shem (sanctifying the Name), 168–69
  mezuzah, 113–14
  name of God, 42, 53, 111
  numerology/gematria, 25, 57, 122
  Priestly Blessing, 110–12
  Shekinah, 111
  Shema, 113
  tallit, 125
  tefillin, phylacteries, 113–14, 125
  worship, 9–10, 110–11
  See also YHWH
jussive verbs, 32–34, 36, 63, 76
justice, 76, 87
  blessing and, 150–52, 164
  Israel, 43–44, 101
  peace and, 96–97, 102–3

Kaczynski, Reiner, 133n21, 162, 163n126
Kapic, Kelly M., 131n16
"keep," 70
  Hebrew *šāmar*, 71–72
Kenite hypothesis, 46, 56n138
Ketef Hinnom amulets, 10–13, 112
kiddush ha-Shem (sanctifying the Name), 168–69
King, Martin Luther, Jr., 102
Kleinig, John, 144
Knight, Douglas, 79
Knohl, Israel, 24
knowledge, embodied, 118–19, 129–31, 167
Kugel, James, 14–15

lament, 144–46, 148
Langer, Ruth, 10n33
Lathrop, Gordon, 149, 154n93
Lent, 144–45, 164
"Letter from a Birmingham Jail" (King), 102
Levinas, Emmanuel, 82n26
Levine, Amy-Jill, 9
Lewis, C. S., xxi
Lewis, Theodore, 53
liberalism, xv, 98, 103–4, 148
light, 76–77
  Christians as, 79–80
  God and, 77–80
  Jesus and, 77, 79–80, 126
literary context, 23–24
LORD (*Adonai*), 42, 54–55, 173–74
Lorde, Audre, 98
Lord's Prayer, 1, 59, 65, 127
Lord's Supper, 10, 38, 152, 162n122
  blessing and, 138–39, 144, 152
  See also Eucharist
Lowth, Robert, 116n151
Lundbom, J. R., 85–86
Luther, Martin, 17–19, 37n58, 107, 167
  on marriage, 154–55
Lutkin, Peter C., 1

MacDonald, Nathan, 17–18
Macina, Robert, 108–9
magic, xv, 35–40, 112–13, 158
Manasseh, 50
Mariottini, Claude, 92–93
marking, 115–16, 121–22
  sphragis, 116, 118–19
  See also tattooing and branding
marriage, 153–56
material blessings, 156–58, 161–63
materialism, 170–72
medieval church, 7–8, 12, 17
  Glossa Ordinaria, 107
melammu tradition, 78–79, 126n193
melting pot, 98, 166
Mennonites, 104, 105n109
Mesopotamia, 78–79, 115

metaphors, biblical, 76–77, 99
　blessings, 28, 58, 157, 165
　clothing, 123–24, 166
　face of God, 81–84
　hands of God, 83–84
　Priestly Blessing, 76–77, 113
　voice of Scripture, 22–23
Midian, 45–46
Mignolo, Walter, 103
Milgrom, Jacob, 26–27
Miller, P., 73n200
ministry, subjunctive aspect of, 39–40
Mishnah, 13–14
Mishnaic rabbinic traditions, 12
Misunderstood Jew, The (Levine), 9
Moberly, R. W. L., 115–16n151
modernity, 103
　material blessings, 161–63
　materialism, 170–72
　mind and body, 129–30
　religion, 87–88, 104
　spirituality, 157–58
Moltmann, Jürgen, 170n147
moods, grammatical, 32–33
morality, blessings and, 152–54
Moses, 37, 72, 81, 126
　name of God, 42–43, 46, 55
　Priestly Blessing, 24–25, 29n33, 70
Mount Sinai, 27–30, 51, 54, 110. *See also* Sinai theophany
Müller, Cardinal Gerhard, 153

name theology, 127–28
naming, 119, 124–25
　gratitude and, 146–48
Nazarites, 26–27
Near East, ancient, 50, 78
　divine-fire, theophanies, 49, 54
　gods, 52–53, 76, 115, 126n193
　tattooing, marking, 115–16, 121n177
neoliberal order, 103–4
Newman, Carey, 124n186
New Testament
　name of God, 58–59, 120–21
　Priestly Blessing, 16, 18–19
Nietzsche, Friedrich, 169

Nimoy, Leornard, 111–12
Nostra Aetate, 7
numerology/gematria, 25, 57, 122

Old Testament, 4, 19
　blessings, 156–57, 162–63
　Christians and, 4, 19
Oppenheimer, Helen, 62n166, 138n35, 162n122
Origen, xxvii, 121–22

Paddison, Angus, 67n182, 67n185
parallelism, Hebrew poetry, 31, 56, 75, 85, 174
Paul (apostle), 10, 37, 84, 149, 163
　baptism, 123–24, 165–66
　blessing, 2, 4, 151, 162n121, 163
　face of Christ, 84
　Lord's Supper, 130
　marking, *sphragis*, 116, 118–19
　name of the Lord, 58, 119, 124, 168
　putting on Christ, 123–26
　transformation, 79, 126
pax Romana, 97
peace/*shalom*
　biblical, 96–97
　Christians and, 101–2
　definition, 95–97
　eschatological, 98–101
　imperial, 96–99
　justice and, 96–97, 102–3
　political dominance, 99–101
　prosperity and, 100–101
　speaking, 105–6
　violence, overcoming, 102–5
peacemakers, 95n73
Pedersen, Johannes, 96, 106n114
Pentecostal tradition, 134, 160
Pentateuch, the, 30, 70, 109–10
　blessings, 27–29
performative speech, 34–36, 40, 57–58, 139
Peter (apostle), 163
Peterman, Gerald W., 67n184
Peterson, Eugene, 91

phylacteries, 113–14, 125
physicality, 158–60, 163–64
    blessing actions, 131–32, 136–37
    worship, 158–60
pilgrimage, 128–29
political dominance, 99–101
praise, 146
    blessing and, 62–63, 147–48
Prayer of Jabez, The (Wilkinson), 157–58
Priestly Blessing
    amulets, 112–13
    Jerusalem temple, 2–3, 13–14, 30, 53, 108–10, 112
    Judaism, 3, 13–14, 19–20, 110–12
    as judicial metaphor, 76–77
    literary context, 26–27, 33–34, 109–10
    name of God, 40–41, 57–59, 107, 127, 167–68, 173
    purity and, 26–27
    structure, 24–27, 75, 173
    theophanies, 110–12
    as threefold, trinitarian, 106–8
    verbs, 30–34
    as witness, 167–69
    YHWH, 57–58, 75
    "you (singular)," 69–70
Priestly tradition, 49, 52, 54, 57, 72, 114
priests, Israel. *See* Aaronic priesthood
Procopius of Gaza, 118
prophecy, 36, 63, 68–69
prosperity gospel, 36, 156–58
Protestant churches, 161–62
    German, 18
    Holocaust commemoration, 6–7, 9
    Priestly Blessing, 18–20
Prudentius, 118
putting on, 94–95, 123–26
    name of God, 70, 93–95, 108–9, 121–22, 126, 132, 174

Rashi, 111
Razzouk, Wassim, 128–29
reading aloud, 22–23
Reformation, the, 7, 16–18, 20, 154
replacement theology, 7, 20

"reproaches," 8
Ricoeur, Paul, xii–xiv, 23n7
Rogation Days, 140–41
Roman Catholic Church, 9–10, 66n178, 151n84, 161
    benedictions, 17–19, 137–38
    Book of Blessings, 141, 149n81
    Holocaust commemoration, 6–8
    priesthood, 19–20
    same-sex couples, 153–54
    Vatican II, 7–8, 19–20
Roman Empire, 12, 116–17
Rossetti, Stephen J., 151n84
Rutter, John, 2

salad bowl metaphor, 98, 166
salvation, 76–77, 87–88
same-sex couples, 152–56
Sandy, Brent, 156–57
Schleiermacher, Friedrich, 161
Schwarz, Balduin, 146n67
seals, 116–18, 121–24
Second Temple period, 54–55, 109, 124n186
Septuagint, the (LXX), 63–64, 119n167, 123n182, 124n186
Sermon on the Mount, 67–68
Sermon on the Plain, 67, 133
Seybold, Klaus, 34–35, 58, 106n115, 109n125
shalom. *See* peace/*shalom*
Siddur/Daily Prayer Book, 142
Simon (high priest), 131–32
Sinai theophany, 10n33, 28–29, 49–51, 126. *See also* Mount Sinai
Siriwardena, Reggie, 64n174
smile, 91–93
Smith, James K. A., 160
Smoak, Jeremy, 110
solar worship, 76–77
Solomon, 2, 50, 52n116
Sonderegger, Katherine, 54
Soulen, Kendall, 57, 168
sphragis (seal), 116–18, 121–24
speaker-orientation, 30, 32, 34–35, 63
speech act theory, 35, 63

Spielberg, Steven, 128
Star Trek, 111–12
supersessionism, 7

tattooing and branding, 112, 114–18, 132–33
    Christian practice, 116–19, 121–22, 128–29
    Jewish, Israelite practice, 115–16, 121–22
    military identity, 116–17
    pilgrimage, 128–29
    religious identity, 114–16, 118, 129
Taylor, Barbara Brown, 84n32, 137
Taylor, David, 159
Te Deum, 144
tefillin/phylacteries, 113–14, 125
Ten Commandments, 49, 66, 69–70, 114
Tetragram, 42–43, 55, 112
Theodore of Mopsuestia, 117
theophanies, 110
    ancient Near Eastern, 49–50, 54
    fire, 49, 51–52
    name of God, 51, 53–54, 109
    Priestly Blessing, 110–12
    Sinai, 10n33, 29n33, 126
Thomas Aquinas, 120n173
Tomlin, Graham, 141
transformation, 79, 123n185, 126
    blessings, 126, 140, 151, 153–54
Trinity, the, 106–8, 120–22, 124–25
    trinitarian formulas, 2, 120, 137–38
truth-telling, 148–52
Tyndale, William, 85

Ugarit, Ugaritic, 45, 52–53, 56
understanding and apprehension, 21–22
United Methodist Church, 141
United Methodist Hymnal, 143–44
United States, 98, 103–4
    church, xv–xvi, 5–6
    "God bless America," 150–51
Urbach, Ephraim, 12

Van Slyke, Daniel G., 62n164
Vatican II, 7–8, 19–20

volitional verbs, 30–31
    jussive and imperative, 32–34, 36, 63, 76
volitive statements, 30–34
von Balthasar, Hans Urs, 81, 127–28
von Hildebrand, Dietrich, 146n67
von Rad, Gerhard, 49–51, 96

Westermann, Claus, 60, 131n16
Wilfand, Yael, 97
Wilhoit, James, 146–47
Wilkinson, Bruce, 157–58
Winner, Lauren, 166–68
Wittgenstein, Ludwig, 21–22
worship, 10
    contemporary Christian, 2, 96, 128, 145–46, 159–60
    early Christian, 9–10, 132n17
    Judaism, 9–10, 110–11
    name of God, 55–58
    physicality in, 158–60

"Yahweh," 11, 42–43, 46
YHWH, 14, 41–44, 48–50, 52, 72, 108
    Adonai (Lord), 42, 54–55, 173–74
    bearing the name, 108, 114–15
    high priest's frontlet, 13–14, 54, 112, 114, 132
    Jesus and, 120–21
    Midian, 45–46
    origins, use, 45–47
    Priestly Blessing, 57–58, 75
    radiance, 78–79
    speaking aloud, 14, 42–43, 124
    Tetragram, 42–43, 55, 112
YHWH-belief, 41, 44–51
"you (singular)"
    gender distinctions, 68–69
    in Greek, 67–68
    in Hebrew, 65–66, 68–69
    Priestly Blessing, 69–70
    "thee, thy," 64–65

Zangwill, Louis, 15
Zechariah (priest), 132, 143
Zenger, Erich, 4n11